ST JOHN'S GOSPEL

ST JOHN'S GOSPEL

an exposition

by

WALTER LÜTHI

Translated by

KURT SCHOENENBERGER

OLIVER AND BOYD
EDINBURGH AND LONDON
1960

OLIVER AND BOYD LTD
Tweeddale Court
Edinburgh 1

39A Welbeck Street
London W1

This is a translation of *Johannes: Das vierte Evangelium ausgelegt für die Gemeinde* by Walter Lüthi, published by Verlag Friedrich Reinhardt, Basle 1942.

ENGLISH EDITION
First published 1960

Printed in Great Britain
for Oliver and Boyd Ltd
by Robert Cunningham and Sons Ltd
Longbank Works
Alva

Preface

Until fairly recently the gospel of St John was purposely relegated to the fourth and last place in the teaching of the Church. Although John was 'the disciple whom Jesus loved,' his witness of Christ was too mystical for the spirit of the age. Of all the gospels the fourth was obviously exposed to the harshest criticism from the intellectual 'Age of Reason.' Consequently, for the most part the Evangelist John stood alone and neglected throughout the eighteenth and nineteenth centuries. Instead of embracing this divine unconformity, the Church on the whole did its utmost to accommodate itself to the spirit of the age. Time and time again the fear of being old-fashioned in the opinion of men outweighed the fear of thinking and speaking unbiblically in the judgment of God. That explains the strange fact that for decades the fourth gospel was almost completely banished from some pulpits. The Theosophists on the other hand espoused its cause eagerly, which served only to strengthen the feeling against John in theology and the Church. Meanwhile historians and students of the life of Jesus chose Mark as their 'favourite disciple,' while Matthew and Luke enjoyed particular popularity among the 'general run' of Christians. But John found asylum and shelter among the pious of the land. The fourth gospel seemed just good enough for the fostering and deepening of personal religious experience in a small circle.

Now that St John is being read in more and more pulpits again, it would not be unreasonable to talk of his return from exile. This unmistakable revival of interest in John can be ascribed in part to a new understanding of what was once rejected as being too mystical. So after the ages of reason and social awareness,

John might well have the not altogether enviable prospect in the near future of becoming the chief witness and 'favourite disciple' of a mystical or even occultistic age.

However, this satisfying awakening of sympathy for the essence and unique character of the fourth gospel can also be ascribed to the fact that the Church is once again beginning to appreciate the extraordinary and divinely uncompromising message of the Bible. Many eyes have lately come to see that the greatness of Heaven transcends the world and time. Many ears have become receptive to the 'great Voice' of Eternity. Countless knees bend before the false gods of these times. But, thank Heaven, there are also knees that bend before the majesty and splendour of the risen and exalted Lord. And John in particular has a special appeal for all hearts whose only comfort in life and in death is He who says, 'I am the way, I am the truth, I am the life, I am the bread of life, I am the light of the world, I am the good shepherd who giveth his life for the sheep.'

The interpretation of the fourth gospel contained in this book may be looked upon and explained as a sign of this newly-awakened knowledge of the divine and extraordinary message of the Bible, and of the estrangement between the Christian communities of the world. This book is made up of sermons which were given in the years immediately preceding the outbreak of the war and during the war here in the frontier town of Basle, 'on the edge of the crater,' and this circumstance has left definite traces in the sermons. They grew up out of daily association with the Word and out of the daily care of souls at a time when people were afraid, and yet often complacent and obstinate.

Even a superficial glance at the chapters will show that alternation of descriptive narrative and instructional explanation which is so peculiar to the fourth gospel. The first ten chapters in particular are so arranged that as a rule there is a concrete story to begin with, followed by an often very discursive interpretation. This peculiarity holds a certain danger for every reader of the Bible, and above all, for the preacher. There is a great temptation to dwell on the picture, and to leave the deeper implications and the conclusion untouched, just as you eat the soft tip of asparagus and lay the hard stalk aside. This is a great pity, because it is often precisely from the instructional part of the chapter that the true, comprehensive light is shed on the picture at the beginning. So, for example, we used to see in the fourth chapter only the idyllic picture of the woman at Jacob's well, but not the message of Christ as 'the Saviour of the world' (IV.42). In the ninth chapter we saw only the man who was born blind and how he was cured, but we did not see the great message of Him who in the instructional part of the chapter says of Himself, 'For judgment I am come into the world, that they which see not might see, and that they which see might be made blind' (IX.39). These two examples could easily be added to. The great panorama of the gospel only becomes visible when one reads the chapters as a consecutive whole, rather than making do with an arbitrary selection. Only by considering the gospel in its entirety does one realise that the message of the fourth Evangelist is not restricted to the edification of the individual, however much this may be provided for, but that here, no less than in Matthew, for instance, the universal message of the dominion of God is proclaimed to all creatures.

What finally persuaded me to publish these sermons was a paragraph which I read in November of last year, in a certain parish magazine, in which the minister appealed to his parishioners to take care of all written works on the subject of religion and the Church, and not to throw them away thoughtlessly. Today we are still able to make use of the printed word to spread the Gospel, a facility which is limited or even forbidden for many of our brothers in faith in this world. But we have no guarantee whatsoever that the time will not come for us too when the printed commentary must replace the minister in the community and the home. So I feel that we must make the most of our time.

WALTER LÜTHI

Basle, *Autumn 1942*

Preface to the fourth edition

Sixteen years ago, when I first published these sermons on the gospel of St John, I never dreamed that one day they would run to four editions, or that they would be translated into English. Then there was darkness over the earth and the heavens were darkened: it was so dark that men were beginning to search for light. It was no accident that it was the gospel of St John that opened its pages to us in those years 1939-42. We looked for Christ; and all at once we saw Christ alone: He became our only support in life and death. Thus to preach about this gospel was to bear witness to Christ. Our horizons have grown wider since then, but certainly not brighter. Whatever hitherto unexplored expanses of space may be opened up in the future, one thing is certain: they too will be dark and will need the Light. Why is it that these sermons, which were delivered with express reference to the events of that particular time, still apparently retain their appeal today? It is a cause for thankfulness when I am often told that they have helped people all over the world to find Christ – people who are lonely and troubled in the surrounding sea of unbelief – and thus have had an unforseen and ecumenical response. The Word of God is not bound by time or place; therefore His flock on earth is increasing and His Kingdom is being built. For all this, praise, honour and glory be to Him who sits upon the Throne.

WALTER LÜTHI

Berne, *Autumn* 1958

Contents

The Birth of Christ

In the beginning was the Word, and the Word was with God, and the Word was God. The same was in the beginning with God. All things were made by him; and without him was not anything made that was made. In him was life; and the life was the light of men. And the light shineth in the darkness; and the darkness comprehended it not. There was a man sent from God, whose name was John. The same came for a witness, to bear witness of the Light, that all men through him might believe. He was not that Light, but was sent to bear witness of that Light. That was the true Light, which lighteth every man that cometh into the world. He was in the world, and the world was made by him, and the world knew him not. He came unto his own, and his own received him not. But as many as received him, to them gave he power to become the sons of God, even to them that believe on his name: which were born, not of blood, nor of the will of the flesh, nor of the will of man, but of God. And the Word was made flesh, and dwelt among us, (and we beheld his glory, the glory as of the only begotten of the Father,) full of grace and truth. John bare witness of him, and cried, saying, This was he of whom I spake, He that cometh after me is preferred before me: for he was before me. And of his fulness have all received, and grace for grace. For the law was given by Moses, but grace and truth came by Jesus Christ. No man hath seen God at any time; the only begotten Son, which is in the bosom of the Father, he hath declared him.

[I. 1–18]

When we say that the first step is the hardest, we imply that it is at least humanly possible to take that step. There are times when people speak particularly carelessly and presumptuously of beginning again, thus reducing the new and unknown to an everyday phrase: it sounds at times as if we men had actually become capable of beginning and ending. But in the Bible we read differently. Here it is not man who thinks, says, and begins new things, because here all beginnings are God's affair. Unaffected by our proud talk of 'modern times' the Bible states that there is nothing new under the sun. The Bible takes very little interest in all that we, in our conceit, call beginning and breaking new ground. Indeed it knows and recognises only One who can begin and end, and that is Christ, because it was given to Him by God the Father to be the first and the last. On the first page of the Bible we read: 'In the beginning God created the heaven and the earth'; and in the passage we have just read John means that Christ was already there. Normally a man's age is reckoned from the day of his birth. In the case of Christ this is not so. Christ lived before that day on which His birth became an historical fact comprehensible to us men. He was active as creator and redeemer long before the world became aware of it, for Christ is older than the knowledge that we men have of Him.

It is of this eternal Christ that John speaks when he introduces his account of the birth of Christ with the mysterious words: 'In the beginning was the Word, and the Word was with God.' So Christ is, in accordance with the will of God, the beginner of all things. When, on the last page of the Bible, we are promised a new heaven and a new earth, this last new beginning once again means Christ, for Christ is not only the beginning but also the end. The birth of Christ, which the fourth gospel relates here, is consequently of greater import than the creation of the world, greater than what we call the end of the world. For Christ is not only the beginning and the end, but Lord of all beginning and Lord of the end; He alone has power from God to begin and to end; He was and is and eternally shall be.

This eternity of Christ's is confirmed here by John the Baptist when he 'bare witness of him and cried, saying, "This was he of whom I spake, He that cometh after me is preferred before me: for he was before me".' And it is this eternal Christ who, since the creation of the world, has never ceased to be active, right up to the present day. The fourth gospel affirms that, whether we know it or not, it is He to whom we owe our lives and our salvation – 'of his fulness have we all received, and grace for grace.' From the very beginning every living creature has lived by the fullness of His grace, which has up till now been concealed. But now the fullness of His grace can no longer remain hidden. Now it has been revealed in the mystery of Christmas. It is the eternal Christ who is born. If therefore John, in telling us here of the birth of Christ, goes so far back, we must not be surprised. He has his own good reason for differing from the rest of the Evangelists in beginning his Christmas gospel: 'In the beginning was the Word, and the Word was with God, and the Word was God. The same was in the beginning with God. All things were made by him; and without him was not anything made that was made.'

'In the beginning was the Word,' not the deed. It is characteristic of God that the word precedes the deed. When God acts, He is not in the habit of doing so precipitately; He first announces His deed through the word. Thus the whole Bible is to be regarded as God's word, which went forth as a declaration and a promise of deeds to come. Thus again it is the word and not the deed that is in the beginning, and when a real beginning takes place among human beings, God's word has gone before it. And so the Word of God went forth centuries before the event occurred of which John here says: 'And the Word was made flesh, and dwelt among us.' Thus when John reports the birth of Christ, he is taking us back over the years to the beginning of all things, indeed even farther back to where the ocean of eternity thunders on our shores: 'In the beginning was the Word, and the Word was with God, and the Word was God.' It is said in the Revelation: 'And I saw another angel fly in the midst of heaven, having the everlasting gospel to preach. . . .' When we hear the introduction to this first chapter which is so significant for the whole of the fourth gospel, it is as if we felt the wind of the beating wings of that angel who has 'the everlasting gospel to preach.'

But it is not only in terms of time that the Christmas gospel exceeds all limits but also in terms of place. It is not only an 'eternal gospel' but also, so to speak, an 'infinite gospel.' The other Evangelists also indicate the all-embracing breadth of this salvation; Matthew when he tells us of the Magi hastening from the darkness of the distant East to worship the Saviour of the world; and Luke when he speaks of the joy that is 'to all people.' To all people indeed. John, in his Christmas gospel, shows us God's universal control when we hear him say: 'All things were made by him; and without him was not anything made that was made,' and when he goes on to say of the Word that was in the beginning: 'In him was life; and the life was the light of men.' The Light of men indeed. And of John the Baptist he says that he came into the world to bear witness of the Light, 'that all men through him might believe.' All men indeed. And again: 'That was the true light, which lighteth every man that cometh into the world.' Every man and every thing indeed. In John's Christmas gospel we see, as it were, the Christ-child holding the world like a ball in His hands.

That is the eternal, infinite Gospel that neither time nor place can limit. In view of this, we are all the more amazed to hear John after all talk of a limit. This limit is a fact. John does not say whence it comes; it is simply there. A mysterious evil will stands in opposition to the eternal infinite will to save of our Father in Heaven – there is darkness. 'And the Light shineth in darkness; and the darkness comprehended it not' (R.S.V. 'has not overcome it'). 'He was in the world, and the world was made by him, and the world knew him not.' But the Evangelist goes on to elucidate: we human beings can become an obstacle to this Light. We are capable of accepting or rejecting the Gospel. What neither place nor time could do is possible for the heart of man: 'He came unto his own and his own received him not.'

'The darkness comprehended it not'; 'The world knew him not'; 'His own received him not.' Darkness, the world, His own. It is not only a dark spiritual power that secretly opposes Him; the forces and powers assume tangible and visible forms in secular and ecclesiastical conditions. The world is so very much shut off from the light that Caesar Augustus, engrossed in his own splendour, does not seem even to notice the light that came into the world with Christ. Herod however hears the news, is alarmed and immediately prepares to strike. And John sees no less worldliness in religious affairs. Together with Herod, the whole city of Jerusalem is alarmed, Jerusalem the city of the godly, the chosen, holy city. It is just where He should be most at home, among His own, in His church, that Christ is most consciously rejected: 'His own received him not.'

But Christ is determined not to halt before this threefold wall of resistance – darkness, the world and His own. The darkness may not comprehend it, nevertheless the Light shines. No darkness can overcome it. The world may not know Him, nevertheless He knows the world. His own may have no room for Him at the inn, nevertheless He is not prevented from coming unto them. No Herod, no landlord, no high priest can prevent Christ's being born in Bethlehem, in David's town, as Micah foretold. With this reference to the resistance which from the beginning faces our Redeemer, John shows us that opposition, which is already threatening here, and which rises throughout the fourth gospel, by way of a series of abrupt clashes and violent encounters, to the final struggle. It is God Himself whom we see fighting for a world which, from the very first, belongs to Him and which He has no intention of ever abandoning to any outsider. Thus it is God's constant love that we see at work here, for God is determined to retain the world He has created and, if necessary, to save it, whatever the cost. If necessary He will save it with His last resource. And so it has to be. God throws His last resource into the struggle against darkness, the world and His own; God sacrifices His dearest Son, who was with Him from the beginning: 'And the Word was made flesh, and dwelt among us.' 'The Word was made flesh.' He actually made it flesh. It is in the flesh that we men set up the greatest resistance to the Life and the Light, for even our soul belongs to the flesh, our innocent soul with all its misgivings and erring ways. The flesh is not only the root of our passions and that part of us which must most obviously suffer death; the flesh is also the abode of error and demons. And it is in this form where darkness has set up its strongest ramparts, where the world is most worldly and where even His own are of the world, that it pleases God to become part of the finite world of time. 'And the Word was made flesh and dwelt among us.' Heaven's invasion of the earth in that particular place where it is most earthly is good strategy. God is preparing here, so to speak, for the decisive blow. But, mark you, not in order to destroy, but to redeem. His incarnation strikes a powerful blow for love. The Word becomes flesh only that God may have mercy on the whole of mankind in its abysmal ignorance. In this 'holy war' God does not shrink from bloodshed; nor does He shrink from spilling the blood of His own Son.

God, who in the face of darkness, world, and 'religion,' caused the Christmas event to take place, is independent of all time and of the present day and its self-willed career. His Christmas is never dependent on favourable or unfavourable circumstances. I say this to all those of you who believe that they may not celebrate Christmas under the burden of peculiar circumstances: the Light that shines in the darkness stands in divine mercy above all time, above sad and happy times, above good and evil times. I say this for the sorrowing father who, four months ago, lost his only son and who, the other day, began a letter thus: 'Christmas, the day of very painful memories for us.' Christmas came nevertheless; the darkness was unable to overcome the Light. I say it also for the mother who, having newly decorated the Christmas tree, lost her first-born child yesterday, three hours after it was born. Even into such darkness does the Light shine. 'And the Word was made flesh, and dwelt among us, and we beheld his glory, the glory as of the only begotten of the Father, full of grace and truth.' These glad tidings apply even if we think of all the broken marriages and domestic discord, which are not exactly in keeping with this religious festival. And think of the discord in the relationships between nations! If Christmas were dependent on the state of the world, who, in these times, could pronounce and hear the word of the Light that shines in the darkness? But at this very moment we must ask ourselves: Is the Word that was in the beginning not valid now? Is the Redeemer any the less a Redeemer because the spirit of Christmas is lacking in the world today? Must He who was before the storm began to rage go with the wind that happens to be blowing? Even if we now see no sign of the eternal Light, why should we not believe in it? He who in the beginning had the Word, the first word, shall also have the last. Are we not to believe this? If not, why not? He who in the beginning not only had the Word, but who Himself was the Word, shall be and shall remain that Word to all eternity. That is what we believe. So John tells us here, on the very first page of his gospel, what he is to tell us repeatedly in the rest of the book, that the one thing that we need is faith: 'But as many as received him, to them gave he power to become the sons of God, even to them that believe on his name.'

John The Baptist

And this is the record of John, when the Jews sent priests and Levites from Jerusalem to ask him, Who art thou? And he confessed, and denied not; but confessed, I am not the Christ. And they asked him, What then? Art thou Elias? And he saith, I am not. Art thou that prophet? And he answered, No. Then they said unto him, Who art thou? that we may give an answer to them that sent us. What sayest thou of thyself? He said, I am the voice of one crying in the wilderness, Make straight the way of the Lord, as said the prophet Esaias. And they which were sent were of the Pharisees. And they asked him, and said unto him, Why baptizest thou then, if thou be not that Christ, nor Elias, neither that prophet? John answered them, saying, I baptize with water: but there standeth one among you, whom ye know not; he it is, who coming after me is preferred before me, whose shoe's latchet I am not worthy to unloose. These things were done in Bethabara beyond Jordan, where John was baptizing. [I. 19–28]

'I am not the Christ.' 'I am not Elias.' 'I am not the prophet.' 'I am the voice of one crying in the wilderness.' 'I baptize with water.' 'I am not worthy to unloose his shoe's latchet.' This sounds almost as if God wanted to give us the opportunity of admiring the great modesty of John the Baptist. Perhaps John really was a modest man, perhaps not. The Bible wastes no words over this. Perhaps the people who had to deal with this man found his manner rather arrogant and assuming. At any rate his enemies had no great opinion of his modesty. But that is neither here nor there. If any man wishes to derive from this a moral tale for the nursery, let him do so, but that would be to miss the point of what is going on here. John the Baptist has better things to do than parade his modesty. Christ has come. Christ is here. He has actually seen Him. He has come to baptise, and it so happens that he, John, recognised Him. 'He standeth among you, whom ye know not.' With the coming of Christ everything has changed. Now so many things that we thought essential to the existence of the world have become strangely unimportant. Now that Christ has come, and John knows that He has come, who can stay a moment longer with the Baptist?

Knowing that Christ has come, John utters his threefold denial: 'I am not the Christ,' 'I am not Elias,' 'I am not the prophet.' This is like withdrawing backwards in deference to a king. It is a strange testimony for Christ that the man who has come to be His witness should three times avow, 'Not I.' But this is the distinctive quality, the trade mark, so to speak, of all true Christian testimony. This threefold 'Not I' is matched by a threefold 'But he.' 'Make straight the way of the Lord.' 'There standeth one among you, whom ye know not.' 'He it is, who coming after me is preferred before me.' Because John has seen and recognised Christ, he can now say, 'Not I.' It is quite wrong for us to think that this withdrawal was a great sacrifice for him. He is delighted to make way for Him who is to come. Indeed, the Baptist is most anxious that the people should no longer flock to him, but that they should follow Him who is the greater. When summer comes, we gladly put out our fires; we are glad to be able to do without the little bit of warmth we can produce in our houses, and to be able to open our windows and let the great warmth that comes from outside and above flood in, that abundant warmth that Heaven itself wishes to bestow on us. Because John can assert three times, 'It is he,' he can also say three times, 'Not I.'

Thus there comes about the strange fact that our 'Yes' to Christ is always coupled with our 'No' to ourselves and the world. The world does not understand this, because it does not know God. The world always thinks that we who are Christians derive a sadistic pleasure from saying 'No' and from belittling everything great and beautiful and noble. The early Christians too were accused of despising and hating the world and men. There is, admittedly, such a negative, always exclusively privative Christianity, but this is a caricature. The true Christian community says 'No' because of its delight in God's greatness and splendour, rather than any pleasure in detracting from man's stature. When a man has once found the one pearl of great price, can he help it if he can no longer admire as genuine the other pearls which were, admittedly, good and which he regarded as genuine for many years? The man who has found the treasure hidden in the field cannot but question what he formerly considered as treasure; 'and for joy thereof goeth and selleth all that he hath, and buyeth that field.'

How did it come about that John was, so to speak, under suspicion of being Christ, Elijah or the prophet whose coming was prophesied? What exactly was the origin of this mistaken idea which we see John combating here? We must remember that all manner of things were going on around John. There occurred events that shattered the framework of the normal religious life. Thanks to the preaching of the Baptist, a kind of dread of God had seized hold of people's minds. In those days there was a new spirit abroad which the religious world was not used to. All kinds of evils were being exposed. People saw the true state of their hearts revealed. They saw themselves convicted and punished in their consciences. They thronged in sensational masses to the baptism of sinners. A movement, the extent of which was as yet unforeseen, rose up around this man on the banks of the Jordan. All manner of people were affected by it. It was still undefined, but people were beginning to sit up and take notice. No wonder that the thought of a religious revival forced itself on people's minds! No wonder that the greatest, last hopes of the people, which had for so long lain dormant in the writings of the old prophets, began to awaken! No wonder that we find cropping up here and there the name of Elijah, who was to come again before the Messiah in the last days! All that was not mere fancy.

But to all these vital questions John the Baptist can only say, 'This is not yet the real thing. When you hear me speak, even if the words differ from those of the Pharisees and the scribes, it is not yet Christ who speaks. It is merely the voice of one crying in the wilderness, calling to you, "Make straight the way of the Lord." And not even this do I call to you of my own accord; I learned it from another and am repeating it. The prophet Isaiah was the first to say it. And when I baptise with water, neither is that yet the real thing. And this great movement of baptism and repentance is merely heralding, merely proclaiming Him "whose shoe's latchet I am not worthy to unloose".' By this the Baptist means, 'Do not mistake the servant for the master, the herald for the king. Do not rest content with what you have seen and heard up till now. Do not set your expectations so low, and do not be so modest in your hopes. Do not rest content with this baptism with water. Do not feel satisfied with this popular movement, however imposing it may be, and however much it may occupy men's minds. When the other comes, then, then your eyes will be opened. I am not the Christ.'

And now a question. Is this testimony to Christ, uttered by John, perhaps superfluous for us Christians today? Is it out-dated and of no account for us because we know Christ? Why then do the Church authorities suggest these words as the text for a sermon in the course of the ecclesiastical year? It is important not to overlook the fact that the Christian community is instructed by our Lord to celebrate Advent. The Christian community finds itself in Advent again as soon as Christmas is over. It baptises with water but if it does this properly, it does so in expectation of Him who baptises with the Holy Ghost and with fire. It calls people to the Lord's Table, breaks bread and partakes of the cup. But if it celebrates Holy Communion properly, it does so in memory of that unique sacrifice on the Cross and at the same time in expectation of that great Holy Communion that in the end will be celebrated by a united community of all nations. And so we celebrate Holy Communion in Advent too: 'I will drink no more of the fruit of the vine, until that day that I drink it new in the kingdom of God.' In preaching the Christian community does not forget that some sermons still fall by the wayside, some upon stony places, some among thorns and only some on good ground. Even now, weeds grow among wheat. That is why the Church preaches with its eye on the new earth, and constantly looks ahead to the new Jerusalem, in which there will be no more temples or pulpits, because there man will no longer teach his brother. And so the Church, in its preaching and teaching, is the voice of one crying in the wilderness. We have not yet reached our goal even as Christians; we have not yet entered the promised land; we are guests and pilgrims here, going on our way. In this sense the Church is a Church in the wilderness.

I have of late been a little perturbed about our comfortable attitude to the Church of Christ. We feel it would be pleasant to settle down there and have jolly parties and forget that we are in Advent. It is a matter of concern to me to know that the poorest and the most wretched of our people often do not find their way to our church at all. And if now and again one of them does begin to come, he does so once or twice, only to be disappointed to see that he does not fit in with us because he is hungry and thirsty, languishing after the new earth. He must often get the impression here that we have already attained it. The most wretched of men should be able to see quite plainly in a church of Christ that 'This is not yet the real thing.' We are not contented and settled here, we are visitors. Admittedly the voice of a preacher is here proclaiming Christ, but in the wilderness.

And now one final point. Our report of the appearance and the preaching of John the Baptist closes with the words: 'These things were done in Bethabara beyond Jordan, where John was baptizing.' This sounds as if the Evangelist wished to mark a particularly important and memorable date. 'These things were done in Bethabara.' We feel like asking, 'What exactly did happen? Did something actually happen? What world-shaking things can happen when a man says three times, "I am not he," "I am the voice of one crying in the wilderness," "I baptize with water" '? Of course something happens. When a church seriously begins to be the voice of one crying in the wilderness, then this can happen:

'The Jews sent priests and Levites from Jerusalem to ask him, Who art thou?' The Jews, that is the authorities in Jerusalem, send priests and Levites. Nowadays we would say officials, experts who have to make inquiries about the Baptist, his character and his movements, in order to take legal proceedings against him if necessary. In other words a kind of official police visit. He is, to all intents and purposes, before a court of law here, a court of law that has the power to pronounce any sentence, even the death sentence. And it is a dogged and difficult cross-examination. The man in the hair shirt is being subjected to a veritable cross-fire of questions. This man who has come to prepare the way of the Lord is here standing before his interrogators from the capital, like a tramp who has been ordered by the police to prove his identity. The shadow of the Cross is already beginning to appear. And the Baptist answers. The Evangelist does not seem to take this as a matter of course. He seems to consider that under certain circumstances one can refuse to answer such questions. That is why he inserts: 'And he confessed, and denied not.'

This is what happens to a Church that wishes to be nothing but a Church and which will not let itself be misused for any so-called secondary purposes. Such a Church is taken seriously, so seriously in fact that it is considered important enough to be spied upon, supervised, and persecuted. This is what happens when the Church wishes to do no more than baptise with water and to be the voice of one crying in the wilderness, who believes in the Christ who has come and who will come again. This Church has ceased to be harmless. It is justifiably watched with great care because, wherever it may be, it is an alien Church. We can surmise now why the Evangelist ends his report so earnestly with the words: 'These things were done in Bethabara beyond Jordan, where John was baptizing.' He wants to put it on record that that was where the first clash with Jerusalem took place. In the fourth gospel we are from the very beginning in the midst of the Passion. We shall soon see this more clearly.

John The Baptist's Testimony to Christ

The next day John seeth Jesus coming unto him, and saith, Behold the Lamb of God, which taketh away the sin of the world. This is he of whom I said, After me cometh a man which is preferred before me: for he was before me. And I knew him not: but that he should be made manifest to Israel, therefore am I come baptizing with water. And John bare record, saying, I saw the Spirit descending from heaven like a dove, and it abode upon him. And I knew him not: but he that sent me to baptize with water, the same said unto me, Upon whom thou shalt see the Spirit descending, and remaining on him, the same is he that baptizeth with the Holy Ghost. And I saw, and bare record that this is the Son of God. Again the next day after John stood, and two of his disciples; and looking upon Jesus as he walked, he saith, Behold the Lamb of God! And the two disciples heard him speak, and they followed Jesus. Then Jesus turned, and saw them following, and saith unto them, What seek ye? They said unto him, Rabbi, (which is to say, being interpreted, Master,) where dwellest thou? He saith unto them, Come and see. They came and saw where he dwelt, and abode with him that day: for it was about the tenth hour. One of the two which heard John speak, and followed him, was Andrew, Simon Peter's brother. He first findeth his own brother Simon, and saith unto him, We have found the Messias, which is, being interpreted, the Christ. And he brought him to Jesus. And when Jesus beheld him, he said, Thou art Simon the son of Jona: thou shalt be called Cephas, which is, by interpretation, A stone. The day following Jesus would go forth into Galilee, and findeth Philip, and saith unto him, Follow me. Now Philip was of Bethsaida, the city of Andrew and Peter. Philip findeth Nathanael, and saith unto him, We have found him, of whom Moses in the law, and the prophets, did write, Jesus of Nazareth, the son of Joseph. And Nathanael said unto him, Can there any good thing come out of Nazareth? Philip saith unto him, Come and see. Jesus saw Nathanael coming to him, and saith of him, Behold an Israelite indeed, in whom is no guile! Nathanael saith unto him, Whence knowest thou me? Jesus answered and said unto him, Before that Philip called thee, when thou wast under the fig tree, I saw thee. Nathanael answered and saith unto him, Rabbi, thou art the Son of God; thou art the King of Israel. Jesus answered and said unto him, Because I said unto thee, I saw thee under the fig tree, believest thou? thou shalt see greater things than these. And he saith unto him, Verily, verily, I say unto you, Hereafter ye shall see heaven open, and the angels of God ascending and descending upon the Son of man.

[I. 29–51]

If it is true that God bears the sin of the world, as we have just heard in the testimony of John the Baptist, then we can be happier about life. There was once a generation which was very full of the joy of living and took a simple delight in life; it was full of admiration for the Architect and Creator of this beautiful, rich, practical, orderly world. We today cannot raise this same enthusiasm for the Creation. The world is no longer beautiful, it has become poor; so poor in fact that it now seems to have missed its original purpose. Disorder has taken the place of order. And consider particularly the most beautiful, rich, practical and orderly of all creatures, man; how has he fallen! We might well despair if we were dependent only on this belief in the Creation. This direct, simple, cheerful trust in the Creator is now shattered. Any man who began his journey with this belief alone was bound to be ship-wrecked. There is a great deal of this ship-wrecked belief today.

But now here is this word which is so arresting if we take the trouble to consider it; the word of a God who bears the world and mark you, not the beautiful world but the devastated world; not the rich world, but the world that has forgotten, forsaken and mistaken its original purpose. This God is prepared to bear not the orderly world but the world that has been thrown into utter chaos. This is the amazing God in whom we can believe, the God who actually bears even the sin of the world. So if it is true that God bears the ruined, dissolute world, then surely all is not lost. Indeed, we can be a little more hopeful and have a little more confidence in the world. We can even to some extent be glad that we have been given life in this world. In fact we can even dare to believe in the future, now that it no longer lies so doubtful and obscure before us. God bears the world: everybody knows that. But that God bears the sinful world is written neither in the stars nor in the hearts of men; no, we can learn that from one source only and that is the Bible, which we have gathered together to hear today. It is written in the Bible: that is the glad tidings of the Gospel. God bears the world which has become unbearable. God bears the very sin of the world.

So far John the Baptist has proclaimed in no uncertain terms that God conquers sin. 'He that cometh after me,' he has said, 'is mightier than I.' He will purge the threshing-floor, He will sweep clean with a mighty broom. John can see the winnowing-fan in His hand. He will separate the wheat from the chaff. He will come and make a clean sweep among men. 'And now also the axe is laid unto the root of the trees.' God conquers the sin of the world. We can now to some extent understand the Baptist who is horrified by the sin of the world. Does not this horror touch us nowadays? Do we not feel that the forbearance of God must be exhausted, and that the boulder standing on the brink of the precipice must surely be ready to overbalance? In the face of God's holiness, do we not often feel a shiver down our spines as we wait for a thunderbolt from Heaven to flash down at any moment and strike where it is most needed? Do we not often find ourselves thinking that as surely as two and two make four there is Divine justice; and as surely as there is Divine justice it will not permit those things which now seem to be allowed to happen so freely? The reason why we go about with bowed shoulders is that we fear a holy and righteous God, and have every reason to fear Him; and so our hearts are full of anxiety and we are so quickly and easily a prey to terror. But now the

Baptist has become aware of another fact, a fact that greatly surprises even him, namely: God bears the sin of the world. He takes it unto Himself: He does not merely conquer sin, He also bears it. Even the heathen know that God conquers sin. That there is a God who punishes and avenges is universal knowledge. Even devils know that God conquers sin, and they tremble. But that God bears the sin of the world is written here in the Bible, and nowhere else. It has been worth while to come to church only to hear this. Hearing this news makes our lives worth living. If one day we could no longer hear it we would have lived our last happy hour and be consumed with fear. But now it is established that God bears the sin of the world. God bears the sin of continents and of countries; of this country, this city and this house. God bears the sin of the world, as John here testifies, and so we can go on living. Now we may straighten our bowed shoulders which at any moment expected a thunderbolt from above, and we can rejoice that God is prepared to bear the sin of the world.

But how does this come about? The whole world knows how God conquers sin: its wounds prove that He does. But how does God bear sin? And how does He both conquer and bear sin at the same time? That is something we cannot see in this world and its wounds. Quite different wounds would have to begin to bleed before that became obvious. Nobody can understand that, not even John the Baptist himself. But he says it; he says it because he has to and just as it is laid on his spirit and his lips. 'Behold,' he says, 'Behold the Lamb of God, which beareth the sin of the world.'

John the Baptist now sees a lamb, an animal that above all is used for a sacrifice. And he has to point to that man called Jesus, the son of Mary, who comes from Nazareth, and who, the day before, came to be baptised. John himself does not yet know what he means when he calls Jesus of Nazareth the Lamb that bears the sin of the world. But he says it. He declares it in obedience to the call that was laid upon him. Even the Baptist is overcome with amazement that God claims both to conquer and to bear sin, and that He evidently intends to do it through the unusual man who came to be baptised the day before, above whom the heavens opened, and of whom the voice said, 'This is my beloved Son in whom I am well pleased.' We tend to think of John as a strong man. But have you noticed how remarkably bewildered and helpless he seems here? Twice he says, almost apologetically, 'I knew him not,' as if he wanted to say, 'I didn't know yesterday that I would say such a thing today; I should never have dreamed of it. But now I am declaring it because I must. Make of it what you will, this is He. Behold the Lamb of God, which bears the sin of the world.'

In conquering and bearing the sin of the world, God goes so far as to send into the world His Son whom He loves, and whom He bids conquer and bear, even to the extent of suffering on the Cross. Who can comprehend that? Who can confess Christ in any other way than John who here says, ' "I knew him not," but now I know Him because He has been shown to me by the Spirit from above'? None of us knew Him at first. To each one of us there had to come that happy day when we were able to say, 'Now I know Him, because He has been shown to me by the Spirit.'

Each one of us? No. There are among us some people who sit there sad and hungry, as if they were fasting, and who are thinking, 'If only I too could confess that I knew Him not, and that I know Him now.' And there are others among us who must in all honesty admit, 'I once knew Him better than I know Him now, and then I estranged myself from the Man who bears the world. And when I lost sight of Him, everything grew dark again and once again I saw only the Man who conquers and punishes.' It is unutterably sad when one can no longer see the Lamb that bears the sin of the world. Peace and happiness then seem to be in the grip of a frost. But we have come here today to hear the tidings of the God who conquers and bears. To those among you who do not know Him yet, we can say, 'God bears sin.' And to those among you who have forgotten this we can say again, 'God bears sin by letting Himself be conquered.' And to fortify for the struggles of the coming week those among you who are fotunate enough to know Him, we will confirm anew, 'Behold the Lamb of God which beareth the sin of the world.' And if there is one man among you who can leave this church this morning and say, 'Now I know Him,' then the Holy Ghost has intervened, and has wrought a miracle that far surpasses our comprehension.

If God bears the sin of the world, that means that you, and I, and every other poor sinner will no longer have to bear it. God takes sin upon Himself. John the Baptist's testimony can equally well be translated: 'Behold the Lamb of God which taketh away the sin of the world.' We can lay our sins on Him, we can cast them upon Him. When something has made you justifiably angry you need not vent your dark rage on your wife and children, or on your colleagues; you can lay it on the Lamb. You need not nurse your fury at some injustice you have suffered, which is smouldering and growing inside you, nagging at you and preventing your sleeping; you can discard it. He will bear for you the sin that burdens your life as a dark secret, and which in moments of dejection seems like a curse to you. There is also a place on the shoulders of the Lamb for those sins of sensuality, covetousness and ambition which dim our eyes, and make us falter on the path of life, for the Lamb takes away the sin of the world.

A short while ago we had a heavy fall of snow, and the filthy slush was cleared up and taken away outside the town by gangs of men. If only they had taken away that other filth that does not lie in front of our houses! But they could not shovel that away. That filth is waiting for another Man, for one particular Man who will bear it away outside the town on His back. This Man will take away that other snow that lies old and dirty, cold and hard, on our hearts, and there kills in the bud all life and love, all green shoots and all fruit. He wants to take it away 'outside the town'; He wants to take away on His back this dirty snow of last year, and the year before, that is still lying on our souls, our marriages and families, our country, our work and leisure. He can and will take away 'outside the town' the snow, which for so long has made your life desolate and wintry, and has prevented spring from coming, birds from singing and flowers from blooming. Yes, He can take away all these things that shroud your existence in perpetual winter, in the midst of a world where love grows cold, and where injustice covers the streets knee-deep; He can and will take them away 'outside the town.' And He wants to bless your life anew so that your tree may bear fruit and ripen. 'Behold the Lamb of God, which taketh away the sin of the world.'

Make a start now! Make a start before your own door! Do not think that because your neighbour has not begun yet you will not be so foolish as to do so. No, someone must begin, someone must be first. And even if the whole world around us is still covered with its icy burden, someone must begin to shovel away the snow and throw it on Him who will bear it away 'outside the town'; someone must clear a path to his neighbour's door, from house to house, from street to street. So long as a path is continually kept open between neighbours, and sin is thrown on to the Saviour, this world cannot freeze up altogether, however cold and dreary it may be. And there are paths not only from house to house, but from country to country and race to race. Do not stop shovelling, for it has been worth carrying on ever since the Baptist said, 'Behold the Lamb of God, which taketh away the sin of the world.' God does not want to lead the world into an all-destroying Ice Age, or He would not have let the Redeemer be born into it. Do you not see that there is hope for the world because there is a Lamb of God which takes away sin? We may see men or whole nations as if buried by an avalanche. Did you not read the other day about some men who dug out their friends from an avalanche that had overtaken them? You probably read it, and you probably admired their action. How easy it is to admire! Perhaps you handed the newspaper to your wife and said, 'Look at this, that's what I call friendship,' and yet at the same time you did not notice a neighbour groaning under the avalanche of his sin and longing for you to dig your way through to him. He who bears the sin of the world does not want us to let one another freeze to death. The lamb of God which takes away the sin of the world is a reality. He is the path through the deep snow; He is the bridge over the deepest waters; He is the breach in the thickest wall; He is the way through the grave; He is the path through Hell. Do you not see that this is the meaning of salvation? This is the Lamb of God which takes away the sin of the world.

On the day when John the Baptist makes his testimony to Christ and points out Jesus of Nazareth, two men are standing beside him. One is called Andrew; the other, whose name is not mentioned, is the Apostle John, who later becomes the favourite disciple of Christ. And now these two begin to walk along behind Jesus. Does this surprise us? Jesus sees them and asks, 'What seek ye?' They answer, 'Rabbi, where dwellest thou?' They do not want to lose sight of the place where this man lives; and 'He saith unto them, Come and see. They came and saw where he dwelt, and abode with him that day.' Now does this surprise us?

But let us go on. The two men have brothers. John has a brother, James; Andrew has a brother, Simon Peter, and both of them tell their brothers the news. When a man has discovered the Lamb which takes away the sin of the world, is it surprising that he goes and tells his brother so that he may know it too? Who could be silent about it? Andrew first finds his brother Simon and says, 'We have found the Messias,' and he brings him to Jesus. When a man has found the Messiah, can he wait even a single hour before taking his brother to Him?

And that is not all. These men are deeply attracted to Jesus. 'The day following Jesus . . . findeth Philip and saith unto him, Follow me.' Philip is a neighbour of Peter and Andrew. They come from Bethsaida, the small fishing town at the upper end of the lake. Why is this so carefully mentioned here?

Finally, two small points. The smallest details are of importance when the hour of God strikes. We notice that the Evangelist remarks, 'It was about the tenth hour.' John remembers the exact time that he first saw Jesus. It was two hours before sunset.

This detail has imprinted itself unforgettably on his memory. Does this surprise us? Surely a man is more likely to forget his own birthday than the day when he was able to say, 'I knew Him not, but now I know Him'?

And the second point, especially for these who will go home sad because they have not yet experienced such a 'tenth hour.' Has it not happened to you? It happened to Simon Peter and Nathanael. Neither of them recognised Jesus at first, but He recognised them. There you have it. Jesus knows you before you know Him. Jesus walks behind you and watches you before you walk behind Him and watch Him. 'Before that Philip called thee, when thou wast under the fig tree, I saw thee.'

The Marriage Feast at Cana

And the third day there was a marriage in Cana of Galilee; and the mother of Jesus was there: and both Jesus was called, and his disciples, to the marriage. And when they wanted wine, the mother of Jesus saith unto him, They have no wine. Jesus saith unto her, Woman, what have I to do with thee? mine hour is not yet come. His mother saith unto the servants, Whatsoever he saith unto you, do it. And there were set there six waterpots of stone, after the manner of the purifying of the Jews, containing two or three firkins apiece. Jesus saith unto them, Fill the waterpots with water. And they filled them up to the brim. And he saith unto them, Draw out now, and bear unto the governor of the feast. And they bare it. When the ruler of the feast had tasted the water that was made wine, and knew not whence it was: (but the servants which drew the water knew;) the governor of the feast called the bridegroom, and saith unto him, Every man at the beginning doth set forth good wine; and when men have well drunk, then that which is worse: but thou hast kept the good wine until now. This beginning of miracles did Jesus in Cana of Galilee, and manifested forth his glory; and his disciples believed on him. [II. 1–11]

'This beginning of miracles did Jesus in Cana of Galilee.' Christ, like us, is at the beginning of a year, the 'acceptable year of the Lord,' that begins with the miracle at Cana. In his Christmas gospel, the Evangelist John takes us to the beginning of all things, where nothing exists but He who always was and ever shall be: 'In the beginning was the Word, and the Word was with God, and the Word was God.' And with His word God created the light and the sea. 'And,' we read, 'the Spirit of God moved upon the face of the waters.' This God that moves over the waters, and stands over the waters, and rules over the waters, speaks to us now in the account of this event at Cana. We may be sure that it is not merely by chance that the first miracle that Jesus performs is concerned with water. Water is an unruly element; it is a law unto itself; it seeks out and finds its own course even if it has to eat away rocks and move mountains. Our forefathers were afraid of fire, but water was a source of even greater fear to them, as it is to us. Fire can be controlled more easily; we are helpless in the face of water when it pours down from the sky, rushes down slopes, destroys dams, washes away bridges and swallows up fields, gardens, and peaceful cottages. This is the element on which Jesus performs His first miracle. There are six jars standing full of water, and on this water He exercises His authority. He is at work here as the Lord who was in the beginning with God, and who moved over the waters with God, and who 'was made flesh, and dwelt among us, and we beheld his glory.' He begins to manifest this glory at the marriage feast at Cana. The water in the six jars has to obey in the name of Him who set up His throne over the raging sea (Daniel VII), in the name of Him who once brought His people dry-footed through the Red Sea. Jesus changes water into wine. How? That passes our comprehension as does the mystery of His presence on the first day of the Creation, when He moved over the waters with the Father and the Spirit.

But this man who changes water to wine at the marriage feast at Cana can change other things too. It is good for us to be told this so clearly at the beginning of this year. The year is new, it is true, but no doubt we have found to our cost during the past week that we are still our same old selves. For that very reason the year is not new, for only new men can make new years. Does this have to be? Do we have to put up with it? Is there really never going to be a truly new year? God gives us His answer to this anxious question in the incident at Cana. There really will be a new year. Things will not always remain as they are, for He who changes water to wine can also change men. The blood of man is of a most curious nature. It is the most unruly element, wilder than fire, more powerful than water. True, but should not He who rules the waters also rule blood? That is a bold question, but is faith ever anything but bold? Christian faith does not consist merely in believing that Christ, on the occasion of a wedding feast at Cana, changed the water in six pots to wine. It costs us nothing to believe that past events really happened. But, a Christian must believe that Christ brings about changes at all times, and therefore even today. We do not cling to permanence; on the contrary we believe that everything that exists undergoes change, because we believe in the almighty Changer whose Spirit, at the beginning of all things, moved above the waters.

These words about the marriage feast at Cana, which for generations have been set for a text at the beginning of the year (and surely not without reason?), are a tonic for our faith, and a comfort more precious than the wine of which the governor of the feast speaks. In the year that has just begun we shall need such provision on our way. For from the very beginning our faith will constantly be sapped, so to speak, by many battles, temptations and disappointments. We will often be in danger of growing tired and letting the torch sink low. But the gospel of the marriage feast at Cana will give us support, and exhort us to new faith and new courage. Christ is saying to us here, 'It is not necessary for a single one of us to remain as he was before: we are not condemned to be always the same miserable creatures.' One thing or another can, and may, change in this new year; it may become a 'year of the Lord.' We may be able to control our anger better; we may become less of a prey to despondency; we may become more able to resist the temptations that come our way, more grateful for the happiness that has fallen to our lot. There is a chance of our becoming more charitable to our neighbour, generally more understanding and willing to devote more time to the needs of others. And however many times we may stumble and fall, even today we can remember the six jars, which are not mentioned without reason at the beginning of the gospel of St John. They are a sign that we shall rise again, not because we are so strong or good or noble, but because Christ lives, Christ who has the power to change water into wine.

When once water is turned into wine for one of us, perhaps not six jars, but at least a glass-full or perhaps just a few drops, he acquires new courage. He is so joyful and so inspired that it is not only he who is affected; he also has renewed hope for others, for his own family, for his children, even for those who cause him particular difficulty, and who give him the frustrating impression that they will be unaffected by any amount of warnings, indulgence, or severity because the threads of control are slowly slipping out of his hands. How many parents have been driven to despair by their children? That should not happen as long as the six jars are standing there, saying to us that Christ is powerful. There is good reason in daily prayer for your children to the One who changes water into wine when His hour has come.

Here we also get renewed faith in marriage. Many married people, even some who believe in Christ, live despondent and discouraged side by side; people who have long ago lost their confidence in each other and are now reluctantly resigned to these conditions, having ceased to think that this state of affairs may still change. We feel like encouraging them continually: 'Stick to it! Don't let go! Don't give up! Don't resort to arbitration! Don't go to the divorce court, where you will only be separated on worldly counts. Divorce is so easy, but Jesus will not have it. Go to the true Judge, for it is not a coincidence that it is at a wedding that Christ changes water to wine, thereby giving us courage. He raises us up again and again after the heaviest of falls and gives us confidence in one another.'

'This beginning of miracles did Jesus in Cana of Galilee, and manifested forth his glory.' Here Jesus manifests His glory with six jars of water. Should He not manifest it all the more with man, who is more than water, man who is the crown of Creation? His glory is revealed every time a human being begins to change for the better. When the warm wind of God begins to blow and the ice in our hearts begins to melt, all Heaven rejoices and exults at this, the greatest and most mysterious change in a human being. God's glory shines through the whole of Heaven, which rejoices over a sinner who repents.

But if Christ has the power to still the raging waters in our personal lives, marriages and families, how should He falter in the face of so-called circumstances? May not the six water-jars of Cana hold meaning in business life and politics? Can we even for a moment believe in what happened at Cana without taking our belief with us to work tomorrow, so that those over and under us may feel something of our conviction? Armed with this belief, are we not bound to go to our place of work convinced that we must not be satisfied nor relax until a ray of Christ's glory begins to shine there? Beginning with ourselves, should we not try to redress obvious wrongs or, failing that, should we not pray, and call continually for help to Him who changed water into wine at the marriage feast at Cana?

Yes, far-reaching hope derives from this miracle performed at Cana. Believing in this, we cannot but have faith in a new Switzerland. That same Christ who changed water to wine also has power to direct the hearts of nations like streams, or, more explicitly, the hearts and thoughts of statesmen and members of parliament, the hearts of party leaders inside or out of the Church, the hearts of writers and teachers both in pulpits and in schools up and down the land, the hearts of ordinary men, directors, editors and financiers, right down to the errand boy and the apprentice. If a man goes back on this belief, a man, shall we say, who has ceased to believe that Christ is Lord, with power of life and death even over the managing director of a chemical plant, or the chief shareholder of a brewery, or over an armaments manufacturer, that man has ceased to believe in the miracle at Cana. At least our forefathers knew what it meant to believe in the miracle at Cana: Huldrych Zwingli believed in a new Zürich, Jean Calvin suffered and fought for a new Geneva, the young Luther risked his life for a renewal of the Church, both in its leadership and its membership, and clearly believed in a new Europe. Look for a moment at the circumstances in which this miracle occurs! At a gay and lively wedding feast where one would least expect to see the glory of God revealed, in the midst of wine and music, where since the days of the Flood there has been feasting and drinking and courting; the last place to expect that anything could be changed by God. Where the world is most worldly, at a wedding feast, to the annoyance of every Catholic and Protestant Kill-joy, there occurs this miracle of which we read, 'This beginning of miracles did Jesus in Cana of Galilee, and manifested forth his glory.'

But now there is a problem in the report of the event at Cana. Those who have understood and accepted what I have said so far may follow what is to come: on the other hand they may not. We can get sadly caught up in this difficulty. It consists in this, that Christ changed the contents of six water-jars. They were big jars (a commentator has amused himself by calculating that this wine would have been sufficient for a thousand men) but even so, what are jars; what significance have they in comparison with streams, rivers and oceans? In view of this, what happened in Cana is justifiably called a miracle, a sign of His glory, but only a sign. It is not His full glory but, so to speak, only a slender ray. Apart from these six jars there is still so much raging water where the waves surge dangerously high. There are still so many things that simply have not changed and remain as they always will. It is not the finish, the conclusion, not the whole that occurs in Cana, it is only a sign, an indication. I might say that only a man whose eyes have been opened to the brightness of this sign can really begin to see how thick is the darkness that still broods over this world. Even Christ's greatest deeds of this day and of all time are merely signs of His ultimate glory.

That is a source of regret to His followers and it can become a vexation. There is a vexation in the gospel of Cana. The mother of Jesus embodies this regret or vexation. This mother has already seen other signs and she has not forgotten the signs she saw at the birth of this Child. She remembered them and treasured them in her heart. But now for once she would like to see more than mere signs; she would like to see the great hour and the great day. And Mary urges Him on. Who can blame her? If we do not understand this mother we have not yet grasped the importance of what is happening here. Is there not a certain amount of this importunity of Mary's in all of us? But Christ gives His mother this memorable answer: 'Woman, what have I to do with thee? mine hour is not yet come.' Jesus always speaks like this when He repulses the Tempter, and He gives this same answer to His followers when they approach Him demanding a sign and even try to dictate to Him what He should or should not do. Much as He loves them, they too receive the answer, 'Woman, what have I to do with thee? mine hour is not yet come.'

'Not yet.' There is a 'not yet' hanging over even the most fulfilled of religious lives. The man who forgets or disregards this 'not yet' lapses into this kind of insistence; his intentions are human rather than godly; he renounces obedience and humility in the fervour of his zeal, plunges into fanaticism, furthers the work of the Devil and consequently receives the Saviour's answer: 'Mine hour is not yet come' – 'not yet'.

The Christian stands between two extremes. On the one side the six jars of water and all the signs of Christ that point to the end; on the other this 'not yet' that makes us impatient. On the one hand faith through seeing; on the other, faith without seeing. We stand between the two, waiting impatiently with the whole of creation. These signs of which God never deprives us are a source of encouragement. Without them we could never bear to wait. With them God wishes, so to speak, to encourage His children not to be satisfied with the signs alone, but to await the final glory, the end, when not only a few people will change, but when there will be a new Heaven and a new earth in which justice will abide; when not only the water in a few jars, but all water will be transformed; when God 'shall wipe away all tears from their eyes' and it can be said, 'There is no more sea.' Thus the Christian stands, between hope and humility, comforted and dashed, exalted and cast down at the same time. That is what believing implies. That is what John means when he remarks at the end of his account of the incident at Cana, 'and his disciples believed on him.'

The change has certainly begun, although perfection has not yet been reached. Things in us and around us certainly can and must change, though, even in the new year, the earth is still the same as before, and we still have the same old Adam in us. But now Christ has raised up one very special sign in contrast to all the others, a sign not of His glory but of His lowliness and humiliation; His sinner's Cross. On the one hand the six jars of water, on the other the Communion cup to which the poor sinner is called with the words, 'Drink ye all of this,' the cup from which we shall have to drink until one day we may drink it anew with Him in His Father's Kingdom.

The Cleansing of the Temple

After this he went down to Capernaum, he, and his mother, and his brethren, and his disciples: and they continued there not many days.

And the Jews' passover was at hand, and Jesus went up to Jerusalem, and found in the temple those that sold oxen and sheep and doves, and the changers of money sitting: and when he had made a scourge of small cords, he drove them all out of the temple, and the sheep, and the oxen; and poured out the changers' money, and overthrew the tables; and said unto them that sold doves, Take these things hence; make not my Father's house an house of merchandise. And his disciples remembered that it was written, The zeal of thine house hath eaten me up.

Then answered the Jews and said unto him, What sign shewest thou unto us, seeing that thou doest these things? Jesus answered and said unto them, Destroy this temple, and in three days I will raise it up. Then said the Jews, Forty and six years was this temple in building, and wilt thou rear it up in three days? But he spake of the temple of his body. When therefore he was risen from the dead, his disciples remembered that he had said this unto them; and they believed the scripture, and the word which Jesus had said.

Now when he was in Jerusalem at the passover, in the feast day, many believed in his name, when they saw the miracles which he did. But Jesus did not commit himself unto them, because he knew all men, and needed not that any should testify of man: for he knew what was in man.

[II. 12–25]

We read here that when Christ 'had made a scourge of small cords, he drove them all out of the temple.' Our generation is again beginning to suspect that God can, in fact, make a scourge of cords and strike out with it. We can hear it cracking and whistling above our heads. We see it descend now here, now there, on the backs of individuals and of whole nations. For years now we have gone on our way bowed down, and with our shoulders bent, constantly expecting that some day it will strike us too. Indeed, every morning we wake up amazed that it has not happened already, for there is no earthly reason why we should not also be ripe for this scourge of God which a whole generation is now experiencing.

And then we hear something that can be found in no newspaper, because it is written only in the Bible. Usually, when one man raises a whip against another, his intention is to insult and humiliate. Here we are told, however, that when God takes up the whip against men it has a different meaning and purpose; in God's hand the whip is a purifier. However much men may misuse this instrument of punishment, here we read in black and white that God does not use it in order to insult the dignity of man; God uses it for cleansing. However inexplicable it may seem at times, now that things have once again reached the stage where God makes a scourge of cords, do not forget, but keep the thought beside you in every new day, in every new week, in this year that has just begun, whatever blows it may have in store for you, that in the second chapter of St John's gospel we read that God uses the scourge to cleanse.

Christ's scourge, however, is not used just anywhere, but in one definite, particular place, in the forecourt of the Temple, in the House of God. So we must be more precise and say that in God's hand the scourge is an instrument for cleansing the Temple. The Temple is the first place to be cleansed. The judgment begins in the House of God. This mainly because it is a very great offence to desecrate the place where God's glory dwells, where He is praised in song and music and, it is to be hoped, also worshipped. But there is another reason why God begins with the Temple; God cleanses the Temple because He acknowledges it. Christ does not merely pass by on the other side the church that

He comes upon in His days on earth; on the contrary, He goes into this church and cleanses it. If we repair a tool we intend to use it again, and if one cleanses a church one does not intend to do away with it. Christ wants to see the Church used in the service of God. He sees in it the tongue on which His Father has laid the Word, the channel through which the Father intends to let the 'living water' flow. So if this channel is choked it has to be cleared. It is not hate that wields the scourge of God in the Temple, it is love. 'Whom the Lord loveth he chasteneth.' The scourging here is not to condemn but to attract, and call and receive. The words of the cleansing of the Temple are good news: God 'scourgeth every son whom he receiveth.'

So we must not be at all surprised that God's scourge, that is whistling over the heads of nations, is also directed at the Church. We must not let it trouble us, for example, that modern warfare strikes particularly at churches, which are visible from afar. When we hear that a distinguished archbishop or prelate has been turned out of his palace and is now living in a two-roomed flat, must we not regard this and similar news in the light of the story of the cleansing of the Temple? The five-hundred-year-old church at Saanen in the Bernese Oberland, which was built on rock, and which was magnificently restored between 1927 and 1930, was set on fire by lightning on the night of 11 June 1940. This was justifiably regarded throughout the churches of Berne as a sign that concerned the whole of the Christian Church. The local minister writes about it as follows: 'This disaster gave rise not only to great sadness at the loss of this sacred House of God, but also to self-examination and repentance.' A soldier who read the news of the burning down of his home church wrote to his family as follows: 'The burning down of the church at Saanen gives us food for thought. Is it a sign from above? Our conscience pricks us and we cannot help but search our souls. Whichever way we look at it, this tragedy gives reason for contemplation and self-examination.' Wherever lightning may strike the Christian Church in the West, whatever churches may go up in flames, let us regard it in the light of the story of the cleansing of the Temple. If every church and synagogue in the world were to be set alight, the flames would not outshine this light.

In the Christian West where we have our origin, there were various advantages in the old days, in confessing oneself a Christian. The Church was not only widely tolerated but welcomed, respected and privileged. The Church was rich. Admittedly these advantages were not so crudely obvious as in the Temple of Jerusalem. We had no stalls for oxen, sheep-pens and dovecots in the forecourts of our town halls and under the eaves of our churches. But the spirit that is intent on gain was deep-rooted in the Church. Admittedly we went to church for the most part for spiritual gain, but nevertheless for gain; for spiritual pleasure, but nevertheless for pleasure, and in order to reap what benefit we could. This spirit that in all circumstances is intent on profit before anything else was to be found not only in the forecourts, but also inside the church, in the pews and pulpits. And now Christ is engaged in purging the Western Church of this spirit of pleasure. We are now asked in all seriousness, 'What do you seek in the Church? God or yourself? Why do you go to church? To find yourself or God?' Christ wants to make His Church poor again now. The saying, 'as poor as a church mouse,' is to mean something again. In this large-scale cleansing which has begun, He wants to take from the Church everything except that which the Church is, everything but the Word. He will leave her that; and He will leave her the water of Baptism and the bread of Holy Communion. He will put His Church on a diet of 'bread and water.' Anyone who still wishes to make a profit there will not be happy for long in this Church. There will be a great exodus (in fact it has already begun), an exodus of money-changers and profiteers. Happy the Church in which this happens! It will emerge purified from these days of judgment, for the scourge is an instrument of cleansing.

And now let us look more closely at this cleansing of the Temple by the scourge of God. For what happens here is not so easy to understand as one might think at first glance. On closer inspection a number of questions crop up. How is it that these dealers and money-changers let themselves be driven out by Jesus? And what about those who are evidently in league with them, the rulers of the Temple, the secret participants in this good business? Does a man abandon his interests without resisting (and here is a case of considerable financial interest) as evidently is the case here? Would it not be perfectly easy for the rulers of the Temple to prevent this poor man from Nazareth from disrupting their profitable business? And, what is even more remarkable, Jesus made a scourge of cords, but it does not say that He struck anyone with it. They withdrew of their own accord before He struck them.

When we picture to ourselves what this means, all these people who, after all, have control of the Temple, making off without a struggle, we must be convinced that there is no human or natural explanation of this behaviour of Jesus's opponents. What happens here in the forecourt of the Temple is a miracle. At the beginning of this chapter we are told about the miracle at Cana. At the end we have a reference to 'the miracles which he did' in Jerusalem. What is said here, in the middle of the chapter, about the cleansing of the Temple is no less a sign and a miracle. No doubt it was included among those which, as we are told at the end of the fourth chapter, were seen in Jerusalem by Galilean pilgrims, who were highly impressed by them. Just as Christ on the sea rebukes the storm, 'Peace, be still,' just as elsewhere He commands the unclean spirit to depart, so here that same Christ calls to the dealers and changers to be gone. And they have to go, whether they want to or not. As Christ drives the unclean spirit out of men, as He cleanses others of leprosy, here, in cleansing the Temple, He performs a similar miracle. Now we are beginning to see the cleansing of the Temple in a slightly clearer light. For this sign has something in common with all the signs and miracles. All the miracles of Christ point beyond themselves to something greater and more far-reaching. This is true of the cleansing of the Temple. It is a sign of the future. What happens here in the courts of the Temple is typical of the Messiah. The same is true here as of everything that the Lord does. When He calms a storm, it does not mean that there will be no more storms, but that He wants to assert His dominion over the whole of creation. And when He cleanses a leper there will still be other lepers, but with this one cleansing Christ has raised His sceptre over a world where leprosy will no longer be able to carry on its destructive work. And Christ knows full well that with this one cleansing of the Temple it is not cleansed once and for all. As soon as He has turned His back, the money-changers and dealers will return, under the protection of the Temple guards, with their cattle-stalls, sheep-pens and dovecots, with their exchanges and banks, and the forecourt of the Temple, which according to God's will is a forecourt of the Gentiles, a forecourt for all peoples, will once again be occupied in this improper way. But with this one purge of the Temple forecourt Christ has indicated that day when the forecourt of the Gentiles will embrace the fullness of all peoples.

As yet the Church is still the net with the good and the bad fish, the field in which both wheat and weeds grow. But after this one cleansing of the Temple, who does not long for the future day of thorough, complete cleansing? Who would not like to be purified now of the spirit of the money-changer and the dealer? Who does not hunger and thirst to be purified of ambition and avarice, to be pure in heart, and thought and feeling, pure in mind and motive?

And who would not like to belong now to a purified nation, a nation that is innocent, transparent, open in every aspect, a nation that has nothing to hide at home or abroad, a nation without secret diplomacy? And who would not like to be a purified member of a purified Church, a Church that is free from the evil bonds which hamper its work, a Church whose members are prepared for the end, happy and free, without fear of death or the Devil?

But is there a Church like this? Will there ever be one? Will there ever be complete, universal purification before the Day of Judgment? Not everyone will be able to understand the necessary answer. Only those who know something of that longing, that hunger and thirst, will be able to hear it. Yes, there is such a thing as perfect purification. It does exist before the Day of Judgment. It is to be found in one place only. The One who cleanses the forecourt of the Temple clearly has in mind not only the Day of Judgment but another day as well. He knows, as is written at the end of this chapter, what is in the hearts of men; He cannot be deceived. He knows what is needed to bring about perfect purification. He knows that only one thing will help this race of men and this Church, and that is purification in His blood. This is total purification, when Christ no longer makes a scourge but bares His own back to it. Christ knows that He will not purify the Church by whipping the money-changers. But by letting Himself be whipped He is bringing about purification in this one place. The scourge that strikes God Himself is the true and effective instrument of the cleansing of the Temple. But not only does He let Himself be whipped; even more than that is needed for complete purification. He allows Himself to be put to death. In this connexion He alludes to the day when the temple will be destroyed and 'in three days I will raise it up.' He is speaking allegorically of His body. Only where the Cross of Christ stands is purification to be found, and it is here in this world for everyone who hungers and thirsts after a pure heart.

That is why Christ knocked over all the tables in His Church. But He has set one table, one single table in the centre of it. That is the Communion table, which reminds us that Christ has brought about once and for all a cleansing, a complete purification of the Church. This Communion table points to the day of which it is written, 'there shall in no wise enter into it anything that defileth.'

Jesus and Nicodemus

There was a man of the Pharisees, named Nicodemus, a ruler of the Jews: the same came to Jesus by night, and said unto him, Rabbi, we know that thou art a teacher come from God: for no man can do these miracles that thou doest, except God be with him. Jesus answered and said unto him, Verily, verily, I say unto thee, Except a man be born again, he cannot see the kingdom of God. Nicodemus saith unto him, How can a man be born when he is old? can he enter the second time into his mother's womb, and be born? Jesus answered, Verily, verily, I say unto thee, Except a man be born of water and of the Spirit, he cannot enter into the kingdom of God. That which is born of the flesh is flesh; and that which is born of the Spirit is spirit. Marvel not that I said unto thee, Ye must be born again. The wind bloweth where it listeth, and thou hearest the sound thereof, but canst not tell whence it cometh, and whither it goeth: so is every one that is born of the Spirit. Nicodemus answered and said unto him, How can these things be? Jesus answered and said unto him, Art thou a master of Israel, and knowest not these things? Verily, verily, I say unto thee, We speak that we do know, and testify that we have seen; and ye receive not our witness. If I have told you earthly things, and ye believe not, how shall ye believe, if I tell you of heavenly things? And no man hath ascended up to heaven, but he that came down from heaven, even the Son of man which is in heaven. And as Moses lifted up the serpent in the wilderness, even so must the Son of man be lifted up: that whosoever believeth in him should not perish, but have eternal life. For God so loved the world, that he gave his only begotten Son, that whosoever believeth in him should not perish, but have everlasting life.

[III. 1–16]

'He gave his only begotten Son, that whosoever believeth in him should not perish.' 'Should not perish'! Today these words come straight from our hearts. We all have this in common; those of us who have remained here in this town, on the edge of a volcano, and those who for reasons of safety have moved into the country: we do not want to perish. This one thought possesses us day and night; it haunts us and we cry out in our distress, 'God in heaven, we do not want to perish!'

And now this gospel, which from time immemorial has been read and heard in the church on the Sunday after Whitsun, this good tidings comes like an answer from God to our supplication: 'Thou shalt not perish, for "whosoever believeth in him should not perish, but have eternal life".' In the last fifteen years I can remember shouting this in the ears of deaf people, and today I should like to shout this word in the ears of all of us who seem to be so hard of hearing: 'You will not perish.' I have often spoken this word to people on their death-bed as a last message, putting the comfort of our faith in a nutshell. And so I should like to shout to you who are living on the edge of this volcano, and looking death in the face, you who are beginning to reckon with the possibility of dying, 'You will not perish, for "God so loved the world, that he gave his only begotten Son, that whosoever believeth in him should not perish, but have everlasting life".'

'Whosoever believeth in him.' 'Whosoever'! 'God so loved the world.' 'The world'! We are given this glad tidings of the salvation of those who are lost, not for ourselves alone but for everyone, for the world, including those tens of thousands who now lie buried beneath the ruins of burning cities. The words 'God so loved the world' apply also to our country, this small suffering region. He did not create the world in order that it might perish. Never under any circumstances will it be God's final intention that this world should perish, for 'God so loved the world, that he gave his only begotten Son, that whosoever believeth in him. . . .' He would not have sent Him, He would not have let Him bleed to death on the Cross for a world which was then to perish after all. Not for nothing does God make such a sacrifice, not in vain does He give 'his only begotten Son.'

'Whosoever believeth in him.' With these words God bids us look at the crucified Christ. If from the bottom of your hearts, you really want not to perish, then look at Him. In Him every man who can now believe (and how fortunate are those who believe) can find visible and tangible proof that we are not condemned to perish. From the Cross the words fall into our despairing hearts, ' "Thou shalt not perish," for this is God's will.' In order to impress on our minds that the Cross is the place of salvation, Jesus recalls in this context a remarkable event in the history of God and Israel, from the time when God's people had to dwell for forty years in the wilderness as a punishment for their sin. One day God sent down a terrible plague of serpents on His people, because of their continual ingratitude. At the same time, however, God set up that strange token of salvation to which Christ alludes with the words, 'as Moses lifted up the serpent in the wilderness, even so must the Son of man be lifted up.' Admittedly God chastises; He may chastise an ungrateful people with serpents and scorpions; nevertheless He does not want us to perish, but to be saved. That is why He set up that serpent of brass on a pole in the middle of that unfortunate people in the wilderness. And if a man was so terrified by a snakebite that he could not speak, he only had to look up at this sign to be saved. Look up now, all of you! If your thoughts are like serpents, particularly if thoughts of remorse and self-accusation come creeping along like snakes and threaten to strangle you, then look up now to the sign of salvation that God has set up in Jesus Christ, high above our heads and visible from afar over this stricken world. Look up now to the sign of the Cross! If such thoughts still occur to you, then take them at once and commit them to the Cross, for 'God so loved the world, that he gave his only begotten Son, that whosoever believeth in him should not perish, but have everlasting life.'

But we are not only not to perish. There is more in this glorious threefold Gospel, infinitely more: we are to live, not to perish but to 'have everlasting life'. We are to live. By that is meant a great deal more than our brief stay on this earth and in what we call time. We are to live eternally. That makes us realise all the more fully what it would mean to perish. It is conceivable that a man should live a long life on earth and yet perish; and conversely it is conceivable that a man should die an early death and yet be one of those who do not perish. In other words, dying is not the worst thing that could happen either to us or our children, our aged or infirm, our fathers or brothers on active service; but it is a very serious matter if we have not attained everlasting life, be it in life or in death. It is only when we 'have everlasting life' that we do not perish.

Thus we are immediately faced with the question, 'How can we have everlasting life? How can we attain it if we have not yet got it?' Our text for today gives us the surprising answer, 'We cannot give it to ourselves.' Just as we were unable to give ourselves our earthly life, so we cannot give ourselves eternal life. Just as we had to be given our mortal life at God's hand by our parents, so we can receive eternal life only as a gift. Eternal life, too, is attained only by being born, and because in this case it is not the first, involuntary birth but a second, voluntary birth that is offered to us, it is called being born again. God wants to give a life to those who believe in Him, a life that no bomb can smash to pieces, eternal life, which we can receive by being born again: 'Verily, verily, I say unto thee, Except a man be born again, he cannot see the kingdom of God.'

'What is all this about being born again?' we ask with Nicodemus, and with equal urgency. 'How can these things be?' And Christ answers in His turn, 'Look up, beyond the Cross, even higher, to the Lord risen and lifted up in splendour.' There, in the mystery of Easter and in the mystery of Christ's Ascension, must we seek to be born again into eternal life. From thence we are reborn. Peter says so in his first Epistle; God 'hath begotten us again unto a lively hope, by the resurrection of Jesus Christ from the dead.' And Jesus says it here too: 'No man hath ascended up to heaven but he that came down from heaven, even the Son of man.' Christ points upwards here; the whole of the

Bible points upwards when it is dealing with the second birth and the second life. Do not look at yourself now. If you look at yourself you will always despair of attaining eternal life, because in yourself you see nothing but your old mortal body. But even if you were to see nothing in yourself you should look up, for there you are born again because Christ rose from the dead. There, in Him, your eternal life is as it were deposited and in safe keeping as an imperishable, immaculate and immortal inheritance. And no one can wrest this eternal inheritance from your hands or tear it from your heart, once you have made it yours by faith.

But, of course, old Nicodemus does not understand this. 'How can a man be born when he is old? can he enter the second time into his mother's womb, and be born?' You see, Nicodemus is looking down instead of up. Nicodemus is looking at himself, at his old age, instead of at Jesus. Jesus tries to help him in his helplessness, and adds by way of explanation, 'Verily, verily, I say unto thee, Except a man be born of water and of the Spirit, he cannot enter into the kingdom of God.' Be born of water. Jesus offers old Nicodemus water, not for drinking but for washing. That is the water that flowed in Jordan when John the Baptist called a generation to repentance, and conversion, and forgiveness of sins. It is the water in which sinners are baptised. Does this mean that Nicodemus is a child who has got dirty and must be washed? Yes, Nicodemus is a child who needs water, water to wash in. In fact he will be a child of death if he does not let himself be washed by this water. He will die if he is not born again through the forgiveness of his sins. 'Verily, verily, I say unto thee, Except a man be born of water. . . .' And Jesus offers the Spirit to Nicodemus who bears the title of a 'master of Israel.' He is urgently in need of the Spirit through which he can be born again. Does this mean that Nicodemus is forsaken by all good spirits, that he has to be born again through the Spirit? Yes, for no spirit can give us birth again, no spirit can awaken us to everlasting life, except it be that other Spirit, the eternal, holy Spirit that comes from above. 'Except a man be born of water and of the Spirit, he cannot enter into the kingdom of God.'

'Except a man be born again.' That does happen nowadays and has always happened. But it is especially comforting that it can happen at this particular time. Or is it perhaps not something to make us sit up and take notice when Christ shouts into a world of death the message of being born again? Even now, though it may be our time for dying, it is God's time for giving birth. Up till now there has been no lack of children of faith. It is one of the rays of hope for us that clearly there is no sign yet of a drop in the birthrate in the Kingdom of God; every day people are attaining everlasting life, life through 'water and the Spirit.' In the past week not a few of us have had cause to meditate on our sins and examine ourselves, people who have accepted water, not like Pilate, who washed his hands in innocence, but in the sense in which Jesus urges it on Nicodemus. Eternal life is now becoming visible. The God who is able to raise up children from stones for Abraham, can also raise up children of faith from green or dry wood, from iron and steel, from this hellish world. It calls forth increasing amazement and gratitude that so much everlasting life is apparent around us: self-pitying invalids become sympathetic towards the suffering of others; selfish people are shaken out of indifference; faint-hearted people gain courage to resist and persevere. Of course, we also meet people who drink themselves senseless, so that they do not have to think any more, and people who just as senselessly complain or curse; but still children are born to God; something of the 'visibleness' of God's Kingdom is appearing: 'Verily, verily, I say unto thee, Except a man be born again, he cannot see the kingdom of God.'

He cannot *see* the Kingdom of God. It is simply not true that complete darkness has fallen on the world, however dark the ways of the nations may seem to us. The man who has been born again, of water, and of the Spirit, can now really see. Even in these dark nights the man who believes can make out the suspicion of a Milky Way in the otherwise starless sky above the world, something like a white thread running through the midst of the nations. Of course, it is primarily judgment that is becoming visible, but it is God's judgment, judgment that is relative to God's dominion and power. The aspect of God's dominion that is becoming visible is simply the fact that God will not be mocked, not even in the politics of any nation, large or small. It is wrong to presume that God has nothing to do with politics. His hand prevails and holds the threads of government too. And though we are often troubled by our inability to see His ultimate aim, we can at least recognise what He is beginning, and conclude that God's justice reigns and that He will not abandon His fight. How He puts to shame that unworthy selfishness which spread abroad among neutrals even in the last war, and which culminated in our helping, not so long ago, to send a negro emperor begging from court to court. The spirit of that rejected negro emperor has haunted us in the past weeks and months. God is just. Then if God takes the selfish politics in the past decades of us lesser transgressors so seriously, how great will be the fall of the mightier transgressors! Do not worry about God's justice. The first thing we notice about it is that it is in good hands. God does not hang the petty thieves and let the big ones go, a criticism often justly levelled at our human justice. God's scales of justice are true. And the greatest fall will be reserved for those who rise to the greatest heights of transgression. I heard this week of a woman whose simple faith was able to comprehend this white thread and who spends her afternoons visiting her relatives and friends, giving them light and support through her faith by reference to God's word. If you have become convinced that you will not perish but live, pass on this convinction. There is the work of a good Samaritan to be done among those who despair and curse. 'For God so loved the world, that he gave his only begotten Son, that whosoever believeth in him should not perish, but have everlasting life.'

Our whole continent is now undergoing a process of birth. Last week I heard a little old woman say something about Europe that could not be put more simply and aptly: 'Europe has become proud; it must fall.' Yes, Europe must fall, but not into Hell, not into a common grave; it must fall in accordance with God's will down to where Christ wants to lead proud old

Nicodemus from his pulpit: down to being born again of water and the Spirit. When a woman gives birth to a child we say that she is 'confined.' Europe is now 'confined'; we know that it is a confinement for a new birth. For the man who can believe, these days are a period of birth, a period of birth from above. We feel exactly like a mother who said that in these anxious days she felt just as she did when her confinement was due, 'Now there is no going back, no other way out, I must go through with it.' Yes, Europe must go through with it now. But listen, you people, by the crater of the volcano; it is not a case of going through with it to death, but to life itself. That is God's will and resolve. And, who knows, perhaps these are the labour pains of that last, great, all-embracing 'confinement' which we are waiting for: 'For God so loved the world, that he gave his only begotten Son, that whosoever believeth in him should not perish, but have everlasting life.' You shall not perish!

The Parable of the Bridegroom

For God sent not his Son into the world to condemn the world; but that the world through him might be saved. He that believeth on him is not condemned: but he that believeth not is condemned already, because he hath not believed in the name of the only begotten Son of God. And this is the condemnation, that light is come into the world, and men loved darkness rather than light, because their deeds were evil. For every one that doeth evil hateth the light, neither cometh to the light, lest his deeds should be reproved. But he that doeth truth cometh to the light, that his deeds may be made manifest, that they are wrought in God.

After these things came Jesus and his disciples into the land of Judæa; and there he tarried with them, and baptized. And John also was baptizing in Ænon near to Salim, because there was much water there: and they came, and were baptized. For John was not yet cast into prison.

Then there arose a question between some of John's disciples and the Jews about purifying. And they came unto John, and said unto him, Rabbi, he that was with thee beyond Jordan, to whom thou barest witness, behold, the same baptizeth, and all men come to him. John answered and said, A man can receive nothing, except it be given him from heaven. Ye yourselves bear me witness, that I said, I am not the Christ, but I am sent before him. He that hath the bride is the bridegroom: but the friend of the bridegroom, which standeth and heareth him, rejoiceth greatly because of the bridegroom's voice: this my joy therefore is fulfilled. He must increase, but I must decrease. He that cometh from above is above all: he that is of the earth is earthly, and speaketh of the earth: he that cometh from heaven is above all. And what he hath seen and heard, that he testifieth; and no man receiveth his testimony. He that hath received his testimony hath set to his seal that God is true. For he whom God hath sent speaketh the words of God: for God giveth not the Spirit by measure unto him. The Father loveth the Son, and hath given all things into his hand. He that believeth on the Son hath everlasting life: and he that believeth not the Son shall not see life; but the wrath of God abideth on him.

[III. 17–36]

'He that hath the bride is the bridegroom: but the friend of the bridegroom, which standeth and heareth him, rejoiceth greatly because of the bridegroom's voice. This my joy therefore is fulfilled.' These words of John the Baptist are noteworthy in more than one respect. Firstly because, taking them in the light of the usual conception of the Baptist, they seem strangely uncharacteristic. Can we see this man, who lives on locusts and wild honey, who wears a garment of camel's hair, and who preaches in the wilderness, can we really see this man as a 'friend of the bridegroom,' as best man? That sounds almost ludicrous. It is a real surprise to us to hear from the hard lips of John the Baptist, who, in the length and breadth of the country, is represented to us as a preacher of wrath, the allegory of the bride and bridegroom, the allegory from the Song of Solomon, the most tender and sincere allegory there is of the relationship between God and His people.

But surprising though that may be to us, it was not so surprising to the Baptist. He had always known that the coming of the Messiah would be not only the Last Judgment, but at the same time a royal wedding feast. From the very first, when he started crying out his message on the banks of the Jordan, that is what he meant. His call to repentance was from the beginning also a call to salvation, an invitation to the marriage feast. His invitation to the baptism of sinners was always match-making, and He that was to come, who would be mightier than he, would be the bridegroom. Do not think that the Baptist pilloried everyone indiscriminately as a generation of vipers. This match-maker knew perfectly well that there would be not only stubborn people among his audience, but also those who would hear in humility and fear that the axe was laid unto the root of the trees. He knew what large numbers of people would let themselves be wooed and saved for the bridegroom. He knew what a large crowd would flock to meet Him who was coming, as if to a marriage feast. Otherwise he could not have said, 'He that believeth on the Son hath everlasting life.' or, even more explicitly, 'He that believeth on him is not condemned.' 'For God sent not his Son into the world to condemn the world, but that the world through him might be saved.'

This is what we must hear this morning and also, please God, take to heart: on the Day of Judgment there is salvation. The Day of Judgment will be a wedding day for the man with faith. The community of God can be joyful on the Day of Judgment. In his famous painting of the Last Judgment, Michelangelo represents Christ as an angry athlete with raised hand ready to strike down any who come too near Him. The Baptist sees a different picture. The Lord of the Last Judgment will be a bridegroom for the true believer. 'He that believeth on him is not condemned.' Do not be surprised by the boldness of these words, nor put off by the misuse to which they have lent themselves. In certain sects particularly there is an unlawful practice of usurping this splendid promise by declaring something like this: 'Those who belong to us, whose names appear on our list of members and who pay their subscription to us, will not be condemned.' Do not let this manifest misuse deter you from accepting these words of salvation with confidence, trust and gratitude. The man who believes in Him need fear condemnation no longer. He can belong to the bridal community, stand behind the Baptist, and listen and rejoice greatly with him at the sound of the bridegroom's voice.

Believing in Him is the only condition. Which of us would not like to fulfil that one condition? Who would not like to belong to those who believe and are saved? That is why it is important for us to know what it means to believe in Him. I shall try to explain it comprehensively, but succinctly. Luther says in his first thesis that, in order to believe in Christ and have eternal life, we must submit to the rule of Christ; let Christ reveal to us the state of our own hearts; repent anew each day and then let Him admit us into His grace, which is new every morning; at the same time be mindful of the price that Christ paid for this gift of grace; and begin each day thankful for this grace, knowing that we can thank God the whole day long by our good works.

Eternal life! All of us cling to life and are concerned about it, and we have very good reason to do so today. Some time ago someone asked in a newspaper why modern man no longer fears death as much as his counterpart in the Middle Ages. The answer he got was that modern man is no less afraid, but that it is life that frightens him and for which he fears. That is quite true. The fear of death has become a fear for life. When this fear for life comes upon us (and it happens to us all), how fortunate are those who can sustain themselves with the certainty that they have a life that no one can take away; not a short, earthly life, but an eternal life. This eternal, indestructible life is not dependent on the grace and favour of any man or time, but solely on the grace of Him who is alluded to in the words: 'He that believeth on the Son hath everlasting life.'

And he who believes in Him is also spared at the Judgment. We have a presentiment of what judgment means. The earth is shaking under the judgments that are now being passed, and humanity is trembling under their weight. The history of the world is its judgment. And now we hear the call, 'He that believeth on him is not condemned.' He whose faith can comprehend that even the most dreadful judgment that the future will bring, the Last Judgment, can no longer do him any harm, has support and assurance in all temporal judgments. How can any sword, or need, or cold, or fire, or disgrace, or prison do him any harm now that he has escaped that very worst punishment? We heard in the last sermon that we 'should not perish,' and now we comprehend entirely what that means: not to be condemned, never, never to perish! There is the root of all comfort. The knowledge of being spared at the Last Judgment comforted our fathers, and made them so patient and brave and steadfast in all the trials of life and the fear of death. The man who believes in Him can hear the voice of the judge as the voice of the bridegroom for he will not be judged.

But what about the man who does not believe in Him? What about the man who tries to manage without Him in his fear of death and fear for life, and who tries to bear the burden of sin alone? Of that man we read here: 'He . . . shall not see life; but the wrath of God abideth on him.' 'He that believeth not is condemned already. . . .' 'And this is the condemnation, that light is come into the world, and men loved darkness rather than light, because their deeds were evil.' For the unbeliever the Last Judgment has already begun: the wrath of God will abide on him until the end comes, but for him there will be no end, because God's wrath will abide on him to all eternity. Only the man who believes in Him has eternal love around him, and no longer eternal wrath. This, of course, is not intended to mean that the man who believes is 'well out of it', that he is 'sitting pretty,' and can 'have a good time' in the worldly meaning of the phrase, while others fare miserably. No, the man who shelters under eternal love must still share the blows incurred by these times; he is still very much a part of this poor, condemned and stricken world. But he differs from the rest in one respect. To the man with faith such blows are fatherly, God's disciplinary blows. For the man who enjoys eternal love all things are for the best, even blows. But for the man who does not believe in Him, they are blows dealt in anger, blows of destruction and blows of fate, which drive their victims to animal stupidity or to deeds of despair.

Looked at in this light, it is puzzling that there are people (and who is not repeatedly one of them?) who prefer the blows of anger to the blows of love, puzzling that we again and again prefer darkness to light, that we want to abide under wrath when we could abide under love. I said it is puzzling, but this puzzle is not a question of fate, it is a question of will. I do not assert this on my own account. In this passage here, 'He that believeth not,' the original Greek text clearly indicates human volition and speaks of arrogant disobedience. The man who refuses to believe in Him, who refuses to obey Him, abides under His wrath.

And so, this morning, we are quite suddenly and inevitably faced with the decision: 'Shall I, or shall I not? Shall I believe or not? Shall I abide under wrath or under the protection of eternal love?' Of course this question is not levelled at us like a revolver. In this particular place it is put to us in a friendly manner, temptingly, appealingly and winningly; and the friendly wooer is John the Baptist. He stands and rejoices greatly because of the bridegroom's voice. The man who does not hear this cry of joy from the mouth of the Baptist has in fact become incapable of hearing, and is rapidly becoming incapable of feeling.

Now we see a second reason why this joyful cry of John the Baptist is so remarkable. Someone said to me after a service in Advent that he could never understand why Christ calls the Baptist the greatest of all men born of woman, saying that he is greater than a prophet and then adds that he that is least in the Kingdom of Heaven is greater than he. What are we to make of that? We find the answer here. The Baptist himself gives it to us when he says, 'A man can receive nothing, except it be given him from heaven.' The Baptist sees that he is limited by Heaven. He sees a mysterious barrier set up by Heaven between Jesus and himself, the bridegroom and the best man, which he may not cross. Of course he may listen to the voice of the bridegroom, he knows that the door to the royal wedding has been thrown open, and rejoices greatly because of the bridegroom's voice; but he rejoices for the others, for all those who follow the bridegroom and may 'enter into the joy' of the Lord. To him, however, it is not yet given to enter. He must still stay outside, *ex officio*, so to speak. However he will eventually enter the Kingdom of Heaven for eternity and there sit at table as one of the very great. Here and now he has to remain less than the least in the Kingdom of Heaven, for 'a man can receive nothing, except it be given him from heaven.'

Why is this? Why this incomprehensible staying outside? Why this fast imposed on the Baptist? The answer lets us see deep into the heart of the redeeming love of the Father. Israel is unwilling. In Jerusalem the door closed after that purge of the Temple. Only one man sought Him out that night, Nicodemus; and even that one man went away from Him timid and uncertain. That is why Jesus has left Jerusalem and is now tarrying in Judaea. The Baptist has to fast for Israel's sake. Because Israel hesitates and wants to stay outside, it is the duty and office of the Baptist to remain outside too. Believe me, the Baptist would gladly have joined Jesus; he would have been only too pleased to give up his own activities to follow Jesus as one of His disciples. But for Israel's sake he has to stay behind. He cannot follow his commander-in-chief, as he has to stay behind to take care of the reinforcements. He has to continue his match-making in Israel until his dying breath. This is the measure of God's faithfulness to the Jews; this is how He keeps the promise that He once made to Moses and their forefather Abraham. For the sake of the salvation of Israel He makes His most faithful servant fast and wait. So the Baptist becomes a shining example of how God keeps His covenant. Today the Baptist is still pointing out the bridegroom to Israel and, like an untiring best man, recruiting guests for the wedding feast; and he will go on recruiting as long as we are in Advent and until the Day of Judgment. Seeing the patience of God with Israel in John the Baptist, should not we too be patient? Shall we strike and destroy Israel while God is still waiting and recruiting? After all, do not we too live by His forbearance and patience? Which of us does not again and again need the voice of the Baptist who is working and recruiting through the ages?

And then there is a final reason why the words of the Baptist are so remarkable. Let us note the time when they are spoken. He has not yet been cast into prison, but his influence has already begun to wane: 'Rabbi, he that was with thee beyond Jordan, to whom thou barest witness, behold, the same baptizeth, and all men come to him.' His followers can hardly bear to see their master in decline, and they become anxious and uneasy. Surely we can all understand that? We all become nervous when we begin to fail. Nothing in the world is so unacceptable to our nature as decline. But in his decline the Baptist remains a joyful messenger: 'He must increase, but I must decrease.' Though these words are understandably human, it would be wrong to read regret or even jealousy into them. He does not state this fact reluctantly, nor even with resignation, but joyfully. The Baptist is extremely pleased to see the bridegroom increase in stature. It is his very joy that the One of whom he bore witness from the beginning must now increase. But the joy of the Baptist does not originate in himself; after all, he is, and remains, a fasting and self-denying messenger. His joy has its beginning and origin in the bridegroom. Just as a dark mountain peak is lit up by the rays of the morning sun, so the joy of the Baptist comes from the bridegroom. The Baptist stands outside and listens; he stands outside, but he rejoices greatly because of the bridegroom's voice, and now his joy is complete: in other words, his allotted measure of joy is now full.

'He must increase, but I must decrease.' We must consciously resist drawing from these words a little moral for ourselves on the lines that we too should rejoice when we have to decrease. Admittedly we all have good reason for such considerations at the present time, for we must begin to learn in no uncertain manner what decreasing implies. All nations and churches are very much on the wane at present. How restricted the Church's freedom of activity has become! But now that is not of importance to us. Even if midnight draws near, if the night comes in which no man can work, we still have this one assurance: the bridegroom is coming. Never will man's wane prevent His waxing. He will increase until the mustard seed has grown into a great tree that fills the whole world, for three times we read here: 'The Father . . . hath given all things into his hand,' so that He can bestow Grace, or condemn.

Jesus and the Woman of Samaria

When therefore the Lord knew how the Pharisees had heard that Jesus made and baptized more disciples than John, (though Jesus himself baptized not, but his disciples,) he left Judæa, and departed again into Galilee. And he must needs go through Samaria. Then cometh he to a city of Samaria, which is called Sychar, near to the parcel of ground that Jacob gave to his son Joseph. Now Jacob's well was there. Jesus therefore, being wearied with his journey, sat thus on the well: and it was about the sixth hour. There cometh a woman of Samaria to draw water: Jesus saith unto her, Give me to drink. (For his disciples were gone away unto the city to buy meat.) Then saith the woman of Samaria unto him, How is it that thou, being a Jew, askest drink of me, which am a woman of Samaria? for the Jews have no dealings with the Samaritans. Jesus answered and said unto her, If thou knewest the gift of God, and who it is that saith to thee, Give me to drink; thou wouldest have asked of him, and he would have given thee living water. The woman saith unto him, Sir, thou hast nothing to draw with, and the well is deep: from whence then hast thou that living water? Art thou greater than our father Jacob, which gave us the well, and drank thereof himself, and his children, and his cattle? Jesus answered and said unto her, Whosoever drinketh of this water shall thirst again: but whosoever drinketh of the water that I shall give him shall never thirst; but the water that I shall give him shall be in him a well of water springing up into everlasting life. The woman saith unto him, Sir, give me this water, that I thirst not, neither come hither to draw. Jesus saith unto her, Go, call thy husband, and come hither. The woman answered and said, I have no husband. Jesus said unto her, Thou hast well said, I have no husband: for thou hast had five husbands; and he whom thou now hast is not thy husband: in that saidst thou truly. The woman saith unto him, Sir, I perceive that thou art a prophet. Our fathers worshipped in this mountain; and ye say, that in Jerusalem is the place where men ought to worship. Jesus saith unto her, Woman, believe me, the hour cometh, when ye shall neither in this mountain, nor yet at Jerusalem, worship the Father. Ye worship ye know not what: we know what we worship: for salvation is of the Jews. But the hour cometh, and now is, when the true worshippers shall worship the Father in spirit and in truth: for the Father seeketh such to worship him. God is a Spirit: and they that worship him must worship him in spirit and in truth. The woman saith unto him, I know that Messias cometh, which is called Christ: when he is come, he will tell us all things. Jesus saith unto her, I that speak unto thee am he.

And upon this came his disciples, and marvelled that he talked with the woman: yet no man said, What seekest thou? or, Why talkest thou with her? The woman then left her waterpot, and went her way into the city, and saith unto the men, Come, see a man, which told me all things that ever I did: is not this the Christ? Then they went out of the city, and came unto him.

In the mean while his disciples prayed him, saying, Master, eat. But he said unto them, I have meat to eat that ye know not of. Therefore said the disciples one to another, Hath any man brought him ought to eat? Jesus saith unto them, My meat is to do the will of him that sent me, and to finish his work. Say not ye, There are yet four months, and then cometh harvest? behold, I say unto you, Lift up your eyes, and look on the fields; for they are white already to harvest. And he that reapeth receiveth wages, and gathereth fruit unto life eternal: that both he that soweth and he that reapeth may rejoice together. And herein is that saying true, One soweth, and another reapeth. I sent you to reap that whereon ye bestowed no labour: other men laboured, and ye are entered into their labours.

And many of the Samaritans of that city believed on him for the saying of the woman, which testified, He told me all that ever I did. So when the Samaritans were come unto him, they besought him that he would tarry with them: and he abode there two days. And many more believed because of his own word; and said unto the woman, Now we believe, not because of thy saying: for we have heard him ourselves, and know that this is indeed the Christ, the Saviour of the world.

[IV. I–42]

'We have heard him ourselves, and know that this is indeed the Christ, the Saviour of the world.' These words spoken by the Samaritans show most clearly that the salient point in this chapter is that people here acknowledge that Jesus really is the Christ, the Saviour of the world. It is not a foregone conclusion that men will acknowledge it. When it happens we see the miracle of all miracles, the miracle of faith. And that is what happens in this chapter. When we are allowed, as it were, to witness this miracle of the birth of faith, we are bound to sigh, 'If only that could happen to each one of us and to me personally, so that I too might own that Christ is the Saviour of the world.' And if we have already experienced this, then our longing becomes a prayer that we may be confirmed anew and strengthened in the knowledge of Christ as the Saviour of the world. For in this world of today our faith needs refreshing, not only every Sunday but every day. We all need this faith in a Saviour of the world in order to be able to live and enjoy life. In this connexion we think of our nearest and dearest who live under the same roof and sit at table with us. Ineeed our prayer and longing go even further. We think of people far away, people whom we have come across somewhere or another, people who now live quite near us or perhaps at the other end of the world. Our prayers that Christ may become known to everyone as the Saviour of the world, just as He becomes known to these people here in this fourth chapter, embraces the farthest ends of the earth. We can only be happy again if this world has a Saviour, It seems to me that without this knowledge we should not be able to laugh again for the rest of our lives, in view of the condition in which we see the world at present. However the world does have a Saviour, and through Him everything that now troubles us takes on a different aspect. It is not that we are relieved without further ado of the troubles which it is our lot to bear; they take on a different aspect from the moment we can grasp that Christ is the Saviour. From now on we can no longer consider our troubles apart from the Saviour. If a Saviour exists (and thank God He does), then troubles have no individual existence in their own right beside Him. So we can know that our very personal cares, the worries of the past week, are taken up and borne by this hand of compassion that is held out to us this morning in this chapter. Happy are those who can now join in and say, 'We have heard him ourselves, and know that this is indeed the Christ, the Saviour of the world.'

That the Samaritans recognise in Jesus the Saviour of the world is a miracle for two reasons. Firstly in view of Jesus Himself, and secondly in view of the people to whom the miracle happens.

It is a fact that you cannot tell who He is 'a mile off.' To the Samaritans He is a stranger resting on His way through their country. To them He is a man, tired, hungry, and thirsty. No mortal eye can see in Him at this moment the slightest trace of His true identity. So you cannot blame a man if, being unable to recognise Jesus, he takes Him for anything but the Christ and the Saviour of the world. If you saw someone looking for shelter from the scorching sun, would you take him for the Saviour of the world? Can we see a man who has to send his companions to buy food because he is hungry as the Saviour of the world? If a man has to ask, 'Give me to drink,' because he is thirsty, is he our idea of the Saviour of the world? Indeed Jesus's appearance here is anything but that of the Saviour of the world. But that is what we are up against if we try to judge by appearances. In His disguise and lowliness He appears to us as one who became a man, grew up in a small town, got into conflict with the leaders of his Church, and in the end wretchedly breathed his last on the cross, Anyone who has never been troubled by the scandal of His Cross and His shameful humiliation is completely ignorant of the meaning of belief in Christ. That is the difficulty these people are faced with and that is our difficulty too. The man who comes to believe in Him arrives there only through a miracle. When we reach the point of being able to acknowledge, 'This is indeed the

Christ, the Saviour of the world,' a miracle has opened our eyes and filled our hearts with light.

This recognition however is a miracle not only in view of Jesus, but even more so in view of the circumstances of the people who are here given the gift of faith. In the forefront of them all stands this woman of Samaria. We have all heard many edifying things about this woman at Jacob's well, which we need not repeat here. A few things however we must mention. This creature is completely reserved towards Jesus. On this hot afternoon she is not seeking the Saviour of the world at Jacob's well; her needs are much more simple, more commonplace. The hot summer weather has made her thirsty and she merely wants to refresh herself at the well, nothing more. One glance at the state of her religion also reveals a very primitive state of affairs. Admittedly she has some faith, but only the faith of the Samaritans, and that faith is centred on the well of Jacob and Mount Gerizim. Here at Jacob's well lies salvation for her, and here on Mount Gerizim, and nowhere else, is the place for true worship. Thus her faith is bound up with the traditions of this place. But her morals also show that she is enslaved. A commentator has observed that she fetches water in the afternoon, in the heat of the day, and not in the cool of the evening, like the other women and girls of her city, and points out that this going alone shows that she has had a depraved past; because of her wicked conduct she is an outcast, shunned by everyone.

Her behaviour towards Jesus reveals the extent of her inhibitions. She unexpectedly meets a man at Jacob's well. This in itself is reason enough to arouse her deepest distrust. She knows what men are, and she has had enough unhappy experience of them. Many a one has cast her off like a worn-out shoe. Besides He is a Jew. That shuts the door for her completely. She refuses the stranger the drink that He asks for, and in doing so inquires how on earth He can even think of demanding a service of her, a woman of Samaria. No Jew would put his lips to a cup from which a Samaritan had drunk. It is obvious that there can be no dealings between these two. This woman has shut herself up like a clam towards Jesus, and indeed towards people in general. And yet Jesus seeks the completely buried path to this down-trodden woman and finds it. He patiently loosens all her bonds as one would untie tight knots. He frees her belief in the water that flows in the well, and then offers her different water, 'living water.' He frees her conception of faith from the well of Jacob and Mount Gerizim, and finally offers her the Kingdom of Heaven by saying to her, 'I am he,' the One whom we, and the whole world, need, and long for and for whom we are waiting, the Saviour of the world. That is how this woman found the Saviour. That is what happens when someone finds the Saviour. It is He who seeks the way to us, and not the other way round. It is He who finds us, not we who find Him. He is our Saviour because He seeks the impossible, that which is lost beyond hope. It is He Himself who opens the door of faith which, we could not open ourselves with the help of a squadron of cavalry. That is why faith is a miracle.

And now let us consider the way in which Christ makes Himself known, and how He works the miracle of faith in this lost woman. He offers her the gift of faith by bringing up the question of her guilt, rather as He did with Nicodemus in the last chapter. By bidding her, 'Go, call thy husband,' He gently touches on the sore point of her life. She defends herself and tries to evade the issue by giving Him an answer which is a half-truth and therefore a half-lie: 'I have no husband.' He does not condemn her for this, and does not punish her unnecessarily, but He insists on revealing the full extent of her sinful life: 'Thou hast well said, I have no husband. For thou hast had five husbands; and he whom thou now hast is not thy husband.' So Jesus uncovers a well of sin and misery. Jesus uncovers completely in order to cover up completely.

When Jesus wants to free us of our sin He usually says to us, 'Go, call thy husband.' Jesus wants to have beside us those who have offended against us, and those who have sinned with us. He does not want to save us individually; He knows that we live as a community and that a human community is a community of sin. And because He understands our community of sin, He wants to give us a community of salvation. That is why, when Jesus holds out His saving hand and performs the wonder of faith in the Saviour, we usually have to go through the narrow place where we are first of all told, 'Go, call thy husband,' wife, neighbour, servant, employer, colleagues. Jesus shows us that He is the Saviour of the world by showing us first of all that He is our personal Saviour, and then immediately calling our husband or wife or neighbour or colleague. He starts by revealing Himself to us as the Saviour of our small, personal world, and then immediately shows Himself as the Saviour of the whole world around us. In His dealing with this woman of Samaria we see again how Christ works from the part to the whole. She, who was before cast out and shunned by the whole community, is now allowed to pass on to them and her city the news of the Saviour of the world. A short time ago she was a black sheep, and now she is allowed to be a shepherdess to the others. She, who until a short time ago was a rotten apple, spreading corruption, is now allowed to go back into her city with the news, 'I have found the Messiah.' She is allowed to become a messenger and lead her fellow citizens in the cry, 'We have heard him ourselves, and know that this is indeed the Christ, the Saviour of the world.'

And now we must take a look at the disciples, who are the second group in this chapter. There is also a third group as we shall see next time. In their own way the disciples are just as slow as this woman to grasp the purpose of the Saviour. Let this be a comfort to us. The disciples too went away to satisfy their physical need. They went into the city to buy food. And now when they come back, they are astonished to see Jesus talking to this woman. But soon their astonishment is to be even greater, for when they place the food in front of Him He does not touch it. And when they invite Him, 'Master, eat,' He gives them the answer, 'I have meat to eat that ye know not of.' Jesus really does not feel like eating. There has entered into Him the same thing as before, when for forty days and forty nights He needed no food, and did not starve, after the baptism by the Jordan. But what is it that has taken away His need to eat?

Let us picture to ourselves for a moment what has happened here. Jesus has had to leave Jerusalem, Jordan and the Temple for northern Galilee, which is safer for Him, because He is already aware that hearts are hardened against Him in Jerusalem. And now, on His way to the north, He passes through Samaria, a seat and fortress of darkness, and a very stony field in God's vineyard. Samaria is considered completely unfruitful. And yet Jesus finds fruit in this stony field. Indeed He has been able to soften the hardest of all these stones, this woman, the most despised of all these despised people. In this unexpected fruit Jesus sees a sign that the disciples do not yet recognise. In this moment He sees before Him the whole of the field of God, from the very beginning to the end of the earth. He sees how in ancient times a grain of seed was sown here, perhaps by Moses or one of the prophets, in the soil of Samaria. It was ignored. But now, after many centuries, the time has come when He has been able to reap what was once sown by others. A door has opened in this place which has hitherto been securely locked. And with this one door Jesus sees all the locked doors of the future open up. In Jerusalem, in pious Judæa, the door refuses to open but it opens here, among these people who are half heathen. Why should it not also open among the completely heathen? He can see an immense harvest. No wonder that His appetite fades as a result. He can see the end, perfection. 'My meat is to do the will of him that sent me, and to finish his work.' He has been able to see a shoot, and then an ear, and now He can already visualise the whole harvest, the whole waving field of ripe corn: 'Say not ye, there are yet four months and then cometh the harvest? Behold I say unto you, Lift up your eyes, and look on the fields; for they are white already to harvest.'

As yet the disciples see practically nothing of the harvest. For them the corn is still very far from ripe. It will be four months yet before the harvest wagon and the reapers go out to the fields. Jesus sees the field white and ready for cutting, whereas they do not. When a woman of Samaria comes to the Kingdom, and when men of Samaria begin to ask him to stay with them, how immense the harvest must be that is ripening on the earth for the Father!

With this glance into the future the Saviour of the world looks at our own times too and says, 'God's field is sown.' His field is not frost-bound and infertile, however much it may look like it these days. His harvest is ripening. Even if the field now seems so hopelessly hard, it will nevertheless produce fruit in time. It cannot fail to do so if even that poor little field in Samaria can. God's harvest is ripening today in every nation of the world. Unfavourable though the weather may seem for God's green crops, though hailstorms and torrential rain may come, and blight devastate them, God's harvest is ripening. Even if we can now see only isolated, meagre stalks, we may be sure that much, in fact the whole, will come from little. 'Lift up your eyes, and look.' We can now let Christ, the Saviour of the world, give us a view of the Kingdom, a view of the whole, and with the eyes of the Kingdom of Heaven look out into the world. We shall then acknowledge in faith with happiness and confidence, 'There are still four months to the harvest, but our Father in Heaven can see His wheat grow yellow and ripen. He can see the field already ripe for harvesting.'

We should all like to be part of the wheat, when the angel harvesters come and bundle up the weeds and burn them, but take the sheaves of corn into the eternal granaries. Until then let us patiently wait, and believe and work while it is day.

Jesus Heals the Son of a Nobleman at Capernaum

Now after two days he departed thence, and went into Galilee. For Jesus himself testified, that a prophet hath no honour in his own country. Then, when he was come into Galilee, the Galilaeans received him, having seen all the things that he did at Jerusalem at the feast: for they also went unto the feast. So Jesus came again into Cana of Galilee, where he made the water wine. And there was a certain nobleman, whose son was sick at Capernaum. When he heard that Jesus was come out of Judæa into Galilee, he went unto him, and besought him that he would come down, and heal his son: for he was at the point of death. Then said Jesus unto him, Except ye see signs and wonders, ye will not believe. The nobleman saith unto him, Sir, come down ere my child die. Jesus saith unto him, Go thy way; thy son liveth. And the man believed the word that Jesus had spoken unto him, and he went his way. And as he was now going down, his servants met him, and told him, saying, Thy son liveth. Then enquired he of them the hour when he began to amend. And they said unto him, Yesterday at the seventh hour the fever left him. So the father knew that it was at the same hour, in the which Jesus said unto him, Thy son liveth: and himself believed, and his whole house. This is again the second miracle that Jesus did, when he was come out of Judæa into Galilee.

[IV. 43–54]

Because Jesus lives, what we have just read is not only a story. In other words, the event related to us here that happened in, shall we say, the year 30 of our chronology, between Cana and Capernaum, could quite easily happen in the year 1941, here in Basle. Indeed, this story was recorded and handed down to us so that we might gain new courage and hope, hope in Jesus, who lives and works today no less than in His days on earth.

What exactly does happen here between Cana and Capernaum? What is this thing that, because Christ lives, can also happen here in Basle, if God wishes? Let us look carefully at the account.

On his way from Jerusalem Jesus has stayed in Samaria for two days, and is now about to enter Galilee, that part of the country which could, strictly speaking, be called His native land, where He grew up and in which He feels at home. He is well known there as a man and as a member of the community. But Jesus knows that for that very reason He will meet particular resistance in this district: 'For Jesus himself testified, that a prophet hath no honour in his own country.' Nevertheless, and perhaps because of that, He now goes to Galilee. Of course, people in His native Galilee have heard something of His extraordinary fame. Galilean pilgrims who had been to the feast at Jerusalem brought back the astonishing news that this Jesus of Nazareth, this countryman of theirs, can, so to speak, do more than other men. There are Galileans who can testify that, in Jerusalem, they saw with their own eyes how sick people were healed by the word and hand of this Jesus. His reputation as a healer of the sick and a performer of miracles has preceded Jesus to Galilee.

Jesus enjoys this reputation, not only in Galilee, but also among us, today. The fame of His healing and helping, because He lives, has followed Him through all the subsequent history of the Church down the centuries, even to the present day. Here in Basle there is still a distinguished group of people who saw the healing and helping Christ at work in the person of Johann Christoph Blumhardt, whom they knew personally. And just now there is a book being read, written by a Geneva doctor, which states that Jesus heals and helps today because He is alive today. Even if only a quarter of the cases cited in this book are really cures by Jesus, then that in itself is a mighty testimony to the fact that Jesus can heal and help in all kinds of need.

Two statements are made here about the Galileans. Firstly: 'Then, when he was come into Galilee, the Galileans received him, having seen all the things that he did in Jerusalem at the feast.' Yet at the same time Jesus says of the Galileans, 'A prophet hath no honour in his own country.' These two statements seem to contradict each other. The Galileans receive Him and yet do not receive Him. They receive with open arms this man who performs miracles, heals the sick and helps in every kind of need. But as Prophet, as the Messiah, as the Saviour and Redeemer of the world He has no honour in His own country. So we come up against the disturbing fact that, even if we have received Jesus as a help in trouble, we are nevertheless far from accepting Him as the Redeemer. We can receive Jesus in Galilean fashion, as it were, for in the towns of Capernaum, Chorazin and Bethsaida, where He performed such great deeds, He was very readily accepted but only because and so long as He answered people's needs. However gratefully we recognise and acknowledge that Jesus lives today, and therefore heals and helps, we must take care not to seek His cures rather than His salvation, otherwise the words, 'A prophet hath no honour in his own country,' will apply to us. For because Jesus lives He not only heals and helps, He forgives sin and saves us from eternal death. Does Jesus on the Cross have any significance for you? Is Christ still Christ to you when He covers your sin with His blood, and when He delivers you into eternal life? Does the Holy Communion mean anything to you? Or is it sufficient for you that He works miracles?

At any rate Jesus's reputation as healer and helper has penetrated into a quiet sick-room, filled with anxiety. In Capernaum in Galilee there lives one of King Herod's high officials. His only son is at death's door. This father has heard of Jesus; he has learned that He is on His way to Galilee and is at present staying in Cana. He makes the twenty-mile journey to find Jesus, and ask Him to come down, and heal his son. At first Jesus sees in this man a typical Galilean who wants a cure but not salvation. That is why He retorts, 'Except ye see signs and wonders, ye will not believe' – a criticism that applies not only to this supplicant, but to all 'Galileans,' right down to the present day.

But in his anxiety for his child, this man is neither hurt nor deterred; on the contrary, he humbly repeats his request, this time with the words, 'Sir, come down ere my child die.' We could translate this as 'my beloved child,' for in the original text a word of great tenderness is used in which you can, as it were, feel the anxious beating of this troubled father's heart. 'Sir, come down ere my beloved child die.' Is it this father's grief that touches and moves Jesus? Perhaps; Jesus has always let Himself be touched and moved, for He is absolutely human after all. Nevertheless we wonder if there is not something more here to touch and move Him? He has heard a word spoken by this man that does not have a very Galilean ring about it. This is probably the first Galilean to address Him with this word. He can hardly believe His ears. This word is 'Sir,' 'Lord,' 'Master': 'Master, come down ere my child die.'

This man has cried out, 'Master.' This does not sound merely like a toadying and selfish request: it really sounds like faith; and Jesus puts the man to the test to find out what he means by this 'Master.' It is a hard test. This man's one burning wish is that Jesus should come to the sick-bed of his son. Jesus denies him this wish and sends him away with the words, 'Go thy way; thy son liveth.' With these few words He sends him away. With these few words He puts him off. He might at least have given him a bottle of medicine or some ointment, but He does not even give him that, and He has only a few words for him. Will the father let himself be put off? Will he really go with only these few words? That will decide whether it was faith that made him address Jesus as 'Master.' For a second the decision hangs in the balance, then it is made. The man is prepared to obey. He has believed. With boundless astonishment the narrator confirms, 'And the man believed the word that Jesus had spoken unto him, and he went his way.' And this man who believes Christ's words implicitly and without seeing, is a Galilean, one of the people of whom Jesus complained, 'Except ye see signs and wonders, ye will not believe.'

And now we would expect this man to hurry home that very day to his beloved child. He could still reach Capernaum because it is only the seventh hour, that is, the first hour of the afternoon. But he does not hurry home. Surprisingly enough he takes his time about it. He does not start on his return journey until the next day, and it is then that he meets his servants who come to meet him and say, 'Yesterday at the seventh hour the fever left him.' How strange! From the moment when we hear that this man believes in Jesus the Lord and in Jesus's words, his sick child obviously recedes into the background, as if another had moved forward as the centre of interest.

A great miracle has been performed on the son of this official of Herod. He can get better and live. But an even greater miracle has been performed on the father. He can now believe in Jesus. When this man left home he was small and pitiable, just as we are when we are in the same position. But Jesus has replaced his pitiful state by faith. When this man started out, his whole world was a small sick-room, and in it a death-bed and on that death-bed his beloved son. We can understand that only too easily. But now this man turns back and sees the world again, the wide world of God and the broad sky above it. In the Old Testament we read that King Saul went to seek his father's asses and found a kingdom. This man set out to find a doctor for his son, and found the Lord, the Lord of all lords and the King of all kingdoms, the King of time and eternity. He set out to find a cure for the small patient in his house, and he found eternal salvation for the whole household; the father, the mother, the child, and the servants: and into the bargain he found earthly healing for the child. The climax of this story is not the healing of the son but the shout of joy in which the angels in the eternal heavens join. 'And himself believed, and his whole house.' 'Bless the Lord, O my soul, and forget not all his benefits: who forgiveth all thine iniquities; who healeth all thy diseases; who redeemeth thy life from destruction; who crowneth thee with loving-kindness and tender mercies' (Ps. CIII).

What happens here is beyond the comprehension of this Galilean ruler in another respect too. He has come to Jesus 'purely on a private matter' as he would say in his official language, as the head of a family and as the father of a sick boy. He has sought help for this boy, and has received unexpectedly greater help. As a result this man takes on an importance greater than he has ever dreamed of or sought, an importance far above his own person and his own house. Did you not notice how significant it was from the very beginning that Jesus goes to Galilee, and that this official is a Galilean? It probably struck not a few of us as almost superfluous that this was related in such detail. But in the Word of God nothing is superfluous. In fact it is of decisive importance. Jesus immediately sees in this man a representative of Galilee. And just as He sees in the Samaritan at Jacob's well a first shoot of Samaria, so He sees here in this official a first fruit, apart from His disciples, from the fields of Galilee. Jesus sees the Galilean in this man, not only in his initial request for a miracle but also in his subsequent belief. Something unheard-of in Galilee has happened here, in that this official and his whole house now believe in Christ. With the faith of this one family a grain of wheat has been sown in the soil of Galilee that can bear fruit thirty, sixty or a hundred-fold. When Jesus takes into His flock a man from among His own people, a great decision has been made for them. When a Hindu comes to believe, that signifies something for India; when an African believes in Christ, something important has happened for that continent; and when a Frenchman, or a German, or a Swiss comes to believe, it is by no means only a private affair. On the contrary, it is a matter of great moment for his country. Jesus does not redeem individuals as such: if He does, they are the first shoots from their own people. When Jesus chooses a man from among His people, like this Galilean here, it is like pulling up a stalk of corn out of the earth, as children do. A clod of earth always comes up with it. And so it is with the redeemed of the Lord. They are never redeemed for themselves alone: they are redeemed for their roots, their family and their people.

And now we can understand why the Evangelical Church has from its earliest days set this text on the healing of the ruler's son to be read on the day when we celebrate the Reformation. It throws new light on what reformation was, is and will be. The Reformers were men who lived at a time when there was a very great deal of sickness, and a particularly high deathrate. They themselves and their countries and their times were ill. The whole world was one sick-room and death-chamber. Like this ruler, these men ran to Jesus in their distress. They saw beyond doubt that no other doctor, no ointment nor plaster was of any avail, and that only the one Healer could help now. Again and again they went to Jesus with their own troubles and those of their times. The same thing happened to them as happened to the Galilean ruler, for they found in Jesus not only a help in need and a worker of miracles; they found in Him the Redeemer of body and soul. And so they began to believe in the Word of Jesus. They received from Him the promise of help, and they proclaimed among their generation the message that Jesus can and will help. But like the ruler, they saw that Jesus's help embraces much more than that which they had at first sought. So they became messengers and heralds of the far-reaching, comprehensive help of God. And people were healed just as in the story of the ruler. The Reformation healed many who had been sick, and called many who had been dying to a new life. But the message of the Reformation reached far beyond these little, transitory cures. It proclaimed eternal health and eternal salvation. But do not imagine that this faith in the Word came to the Reformers without a struggle. In our worldly folly we always imagine the Reformation as a victorious and splendid movement which met with nothing but success. That is not the case at all. These men had to believe in the Word, and go their way before they were able to see its fulfilment, just like the Galilean ruler. The twelfth Psalm was not one of Luther's favourites for nothing: 'Help, Lord; for the godly man ceaseth; for the faithful fail from among the children of men.' Not for nothing was Calvin once driven from office into exile, and not for nothing did Zwingli die on the field of a battle already lost. These men did not achieve success easily. Indeed, if we judge their lives by their success, we become less inclined to speak of success in connexion with them.

But they believed in the Word, and in that belief they went their way. They did not foresee that their faith was to assume an importance over and above themselves, and to affect the whole world for many centuries to come. At first they too went their way as individuals, but quite unexpectedly and unintentionally they took on significance for whole nations; Luther for Germany; Calvin for what was, at that time, the world-wide sphere of French influence; Zwingli for Switzerland. So the Reformation came about because a few men believed in the Word, and went their way in their faith without seeing, or, as Luther once said, 'Like a blind nag.'

That casts a brighter light on our present situation. Everywhere people are ill and dying. Many of us have left the bedside of a sick or dying person to come here. One is anxious about his only child, another about several children; one is worried about his small children, the other about his grown-up ones; or perhaps someone's marriage is going wrong, or his business, or perhaps he is ill himself. It is impossible to conceive how much distress there is in front of one pulpit at one service. And we can all bring our personal sorrow in confidence to Jesus, because He lives, and will heal and help if it is His will. So if you who are gloomy and despondent open your ears now to these words, 'Go thy way; thy son liveth,' you will be able to take new hope in this Jesus who heals and helps. But that father had to wait twenty-four hours before he was able to see the fulfilment and confirmation of this holy promise. It may be that we shall have to wait twenty-four days, or that God will make us wait twenty-four months, or even twenty-four years. That is why in our case too the important thing is faith, that faith without seeing; what matters is that it should be said of us too, 'And the man believed the word that Jesus had spoken unto him, and he went his way.'

Yes, the whole era in which we live is desperately sick. Death is everywhere around us. We feel that our whole generation is like this boy lying on his death-bed, and Europe at least has become a single death-chamber. Even in spite of this general distress we can take heart and be wakened to faith by the Lord of all nations. We can believe and hope not only as individuals, but as a nation. And believing and hoping as a nation means believing in the victory and reconstruction of all that is now being ruined. For us as Swiss, believing in Christ means now being and remaining Europeans with faith, for Christ's sake, in the restoration of the violated dignity of man, and of the downtrodden rights of the people, even if it takes another twenty-four months or even twenty-four years.

But of course the Word of God with its promises reaches far beyond earthly distress and present troubles. The promises given to us in God's Word embrace the whole, they include the body and the soul of man, they pledge a new Heaven and a new earth in which justice dwells. And if we had to wait another twenty-four centuries, for in God's sight a thousand years are like one day, yet Christ lives. And because Christ lives He can heal and help. But He can do more than that; He can save and redeem. He can save us from eternal Hell and redeem us from death into everlasting life. 'And the man believed the word that Jesus had spoken unto him, and he went his way.' Yes, believe in His Word and go on your way! That is how reformation comes about.

Jesus Cures an Impotent Man at the Pool of Bethesda on the Sabbath Day

After this there was a feast of the Jews; and Jesus went up to Jerusalem. Now there is at Jerusalem by the sheep market a pool, which is called in the Hebrew tongue Bethesda, having five porches. In these lay a great multitude of impotent folk, of blind, halt, withered, waiting for the moving of the water. For an angel went down at a certain season into the pool, and troubled the water: whosoever then first after the troubling of the water stepped in was made whole of whatsoever disease he had. And a certain man was there, which had an infirmity thirty and eight years. When Jesus saw him lie, and knew that he had been now a long time in that case, he saith unto him, Wilt thou be made whole? The impotent man answered him, Sir, I have no man, when the water is troubled, to put me into the pool: but while I am coming, another steppeth down before me. Jesus saith unto him, Rise, take up thy bed, and walk. And immediately the man was made whole, and took up his bed, and walked: and on the same day was the sabbath.

The Jews therefore said unto him that was cured, It is the sabbath day: it is not lawful for thee to carry thy bed. He answered them, He that made me whole, the same said unto me, Take up thy bed, and walk. Then asked they him, What man is that which said unto thee, Take up thy bed, and walk? And he that was healed wist not who it was: for Jesus had conveyed himself away, a multitude being in that place. Afterward Jesus findeth him in the temple, and said unto him, Behold, thou art made whole: sin no more, lest a worse thing come unto thee. The man departed, and told the Jews that it was Jesus which had made him whole. And therefore did the Jews persecute Jesus, and sought to slay him, because he had done these things on the sabbath day.

But Jesus answered them, My Father worked hitherto, and I work.

Therefore the Jews sought the more to kill him, because he not only had broken the sabbath, but said also that God was his Father, making himself equal with God.

Then answered Jesus and said unto them, Verily, verily, I say unto you, The Son can do nothing of himself, but what he seeth the Father do: for what things soever he doeth, these also doeth the Son likewise. For the Father loveth the Son, and sheweth him all things that himself doeth: and he will shew him greater works than these, that ye may marvel. For the Father raiseth up the dead, and quickeneth them; even so the Son quickeneth whom he will. For the Father judgeth no man, but hath committed all judgment unto the Son: that all men should honour the Son, even as they honour the Father. He that honoureth not the Son honoureth not the Father which hath sent him. Verily, verily, I say unto you, He that heareth my word, and believeth on him that sent me, hath everlasting life, and shall not come into condemnation; but is passed from death unto life. Verily, verily, I say unto you, the hour is coming, and now is, when the dead shall hear the voice of the Son of God: and they that hear shall live. For as the Father hath life in himself; so hath he given to the Son to have life in himself; and hath given him authority to execute judgment also, because he is the Son of man. Marvel not at this: for the hour is coming, in the which all that are in the graves shall hear his voice, and shall come forth; they that have done good, unto the resurrection of life; and they that have done evil, unto the resurrection of damnation. I can of mine own self do nothing: as I hear, I judge: and my judgment is just; because I seek not mine own will, but the will of the Father which hath sent me. If I bear witness of myself, my witness is not true. There is another that beareth witness of me; and I know that the witness which he witnesseth of me is true. Ye sent unto John, and he bare witness unto the truth. But I receive not testimony from man: but these things I say, that ye might be saved. He was a burning and a shining light: and ye were willing for a season to rejoice in his light. But I have greater witness than that of John: for the works that the Father hath given me to finish, the same works that I do, bear witness of me, that the Father hath sent me. And the Father himself, which hath sent me, hath borne witness of me. Ye have neither heard his voice at any time, nor seen his shape. And ye have not his word abiding

in you: for whom he hath sent, him ye believe not. Search the scriptures; for in them ye think ye have eternal life: and they are they which testify of me. And ye will not come to me, that ye might have life. I receive not honour from men. But I know you, that ye have not the love of God in you. I am come in my Father's name, and ye receive me not: if another shall come in his own name, him ye will receive. How can ye believe, which receive honour one of another, and seek not the honour that cometh from God only? Do not think that I will accuse you to the Father: there is one that accuseth you, even Moses, in whom ye trust. For had ye believed Moses, ye would have believed me: for he wrote of me. But if ye believe not his writings, how shall ye believe my words?
[v]

The disguise worn by God incarnate is transparently thin here. In this chapter we can hardly disregard any longer the majesty of the Lord which, according to the will of God, is normally hidden from human eyes. This shining forth of God's splendour is apparent in other parts of the Apostle John's testimony to Christ, but in this chapter the majesty of Christ strikes us very forcibly. We must be blind not to see it, we must be deaf not to hear it. Let us note both what happens and what is said. As a rule we tend merely to nibble, as it were, at these early chapters of the fourth gospel, rather as one bites off the tender tip of asparagus, laying aside the tougher stalk. We must guard against indulging in this kind of nibbling, for very often the narrative introduction reflects a bright light on the more obscure substance of a chapter.

But as well as the majesty of the Lord, we see revealed in this fifth chapter our own mean condition and human misery. Right at the outset we are taken to a wretched place: a pool outside the town. A bathing-pool at the foot of the town wall! Not a healthy spot considered in the light of the demands of modern hygiene. Some sick people who bathed in it had been cured by God's help. But this could happen only when from time to time, according to popular belief, an angel troubled the water and the mud was stirred up. This, however, was very rare. Who knows how long all these sick people had been waiting? Consequently a great deal of misery accumulated at the edge of this pool of the sick. Then the public authorities took a hand in the matter and built a waiting room, and, when that became crowded out, they built a second, and a third, and a fourth and a fifth; and they were all filled. We are told that there are many impotent folk there; lame, blind and paralysed; a sign that rarely did anyone go away cured. And that slight chance is even lessened by the fact that each time the pool is at last troubled only one of that crowd can step in, either because the pool is stirred up for only a short time, or because the people are so weak. In short, a picture of boundless misery. How slender are the straws that we men clutch at in our distress! That was not the case only in those days. In times of famine people live on roots and the bark of trees, and similarly there are spiritual famines when we are glad of the slightest chance of help. And yet Jesus is so near, Jesus who, as we were told in the last chapter, is the Saviour of the world!

When we think of the small chance that these miserable people had, are we not reminded of a similar state of need today? I refer to the scandalous system of lotteries. Things have come to a sorry pass when the greater part of a generation, with official sanction, even with government support, places its faith anxiously in a lottery ticket and waits for weeks in the hope of being lucky next time or the time after. This total lack of hope is characteristic of our generation too.

Such is the pitiable condition of spiritual poverty to be found at the pool of Bethesda, before the walls of Jerusalem. And now the Saviour of the world comes to this place, we do not know how or why, the Saviour, pointed out by the Baptist as the one great future. It is as if the Apostle John wished to say to us, 'There is no place, however devoid of hope, that is inaccessible to Him, or which He has forgotten. Moses and the Prophets did not hope in vain. There stands the man to whom the writings of the Old Testament point with a hundred fingers; there stands the hope of our fathers, clothed in flesh and blood. "Had ye believed Moses, ye would have believed me: for he wrote of me." "Search the

Scriptures; for in them ye think ye have eternal life: and they are they which testify of me." But look! Now that He is here and the great hope has been fulfilled, the priests, with their Scriptures in their hands, do not recognise Him.' That is what John has to say again and again, what we met in the very first chapter: 'He came unto his own, and his own received him not.' A generation, whose Church has nothing but paper hopes left, has sunk to the lowest depths of wretchedness. The lack of hope is the real wretchedness of men.

Jesus enters into conversation with one of the sufferers at the pool of Bethesda. We are not told why He addresses this particular man, and why only this one. What He learns from him reveals an abyss of misery. This man has experienced despair. He has been lying here for thirty-eight years. He stands, or rather lies, alone: 'Sir, I have no man. . . .' One might presume that these unhappy creatures would at least have a spirit of comradeship, not to mention a community of purpose. One might hope that distress would bring human beings closer to one another and bridge differences between them. But we forget how easily personal distress can make us callous towards others. Among the infirm at the pool of Bethesda there is a kind of club law; the right of the strongest prevails among these weak people. There is a struggle for existence among the healthy people inside the town, and a similar struggle outside the gates in the porches of the incurable. Can you imagine the heart-rending scene when the pool is once again troubled and the things of which this man complains happen? 'Sir, I have no man, when the water is troubled, to put me into the pool: but while I am coming, another steppeth down before me.'

Christ reveals His majesty and power through this one man. But how? The Son reveals His majesty by subordinating Himself completely to the Father. The Son reveals His power by declaring that the Father alone is almighty and powerful. The assertion, 'Not I, but the Father,' runs like a red thread throughout the chapter. The Father is mentioned fourteen times here: 'My Father worketh hitherto, and I work'; 'Verily, verily, I say unto you, the Son can do nothing of himself, but what he seeth the Father do: for what things soever he doeth, these also doeth the Son likewise.' Jesus is here the completely dependent and obedient Son. His majesty lies in His complete acceptance of His lowliness. And that is the only reason why Jesus does not clear away that whole heap of misery at the pool of the infirm. Christ knows that in the plan and decree of the Father, the time when sickness and death and misery will cease has not yet come. That is why He has to content Himself with filial obedience. That is why He limits Himself to certain examples, and certain signs which He sets up, and to healing individuals. In order to remain obedient to the Father, He withdraws from this place after healing one man, almost as if He were fleeing from it. He wants to avoid the panic of hope that will break out in the five porches. Besides, it is a feast day in Jerusalem. The Saviour of the world chooses this one man, who is certainly one of the most wretched, just like a prince who, walking through his father's kingdom, comes into a slum quarter, and is so seized by pity that he throws into the lap of the most miserable man he sees everything he has on him, given him by his father. This man is, so to speak, the embodiment of wretchedness. The spirit of misery that prevails in this place has overcome his soul. Hopelessness has become second nature to him.

But now hope has come in the person of Jesus. Here stands the Man who, as we saw in the case of the woman of Samaria at Jacob's well, can penetrate any accumulation of refuse. Jesus addresses the man with the violently startling words, 'Wilt thou be made whole?' So obviously unexpected is this question to the poor man, that he simply cannot agree and quite forgets to say, 'Yes.' Instead he begins to tell the story of his illness, just as he has told it a hundred times over. It has become like a gramophone record, which he can put on at will. But here for a change is a man who does not enter into the spirit of the story; on the contrary, He says abruptly to him, 'Rise, take up thy bed, and walk. And immediately the man was made whole, and took up his bed, and walked.' And just look at that bed! For thirty-eight years it has been the symbol of his misery, and now he is to take it on his back, and carry it in triumph through the streets, as a symbol of his cure. There is almost something of divine humour in this command of the Lord, as if He wished to say something like, 'Change places now. It has carried you long enough: now you carry it for a change.' More or less as a dentist gives a child its extracted tooth in a little box, so that it can take it home and triumphantly show everyone the scoundrel that caused it so much pain, so here the Lord says to the man, 'Rise, take up thy bed, and walk.' But besides showing the man's joy, this command indicates the joy shown by the Saviour of the world. A cry of rejoicing is heard in this command, which finds its echo in the very halls of eternity, where the angels serve night and day. 'Rise, take up thy bed, and walk.' This is the sort of inconceivable thing that happens when the Father works and, through Him, the Son.

But today happens to be the Sabbath, and on the Sabbath in Jerusalem no one walks around, even with a brief-case under his arm, far less with a bed on his back. Consequently the man does not get far with his triumphal burden; he is soon stopped and arrested by the police. There are sanctimonious people here who dictate to God when He is allowed to heal a sick man and when not; who prescribe to the angels when they will rejoice and when not. These scribes soon find out who is the perpetrator of this 'misdemeanour,' and Jesus is threatened with death, because the penalty for gross violation of the Sabbath is death. Indeed a kind of blindness and deafness are often closely linked with piety. Let us watch our piety. When Christ bids us watch and pray, He means by that not only watchfulness in regard to the world, but, first and foremost, watchfulness in regard to ourselves. So let us take care that our piety does not become a guarantee, and lead to pride and self-righteousness. Sanctimony can make us incapable of recognising the deeds worked by the Father and, through the Father, by the Son. If that happens, Father and Son pass over piety in their work instead of working with it and through it. By paying too much attention to other people's failings we may completely miss the moment when the angels rejoice that the Father and, through Him, the Son, is at work. Piety that forgets that we confess a God, and have an active Redeemer, becomes an obstacle in the Kingdom of God.

But this very obstacle which impedes Christ is to reveal His majesty and the splendour of His work. Christ comes into conflict with sanctimony here, and what He explains to the scribes and Pharisees of Jerusalem is one of the most splendid parts of the whole gospel. In these noble words we can see the royal mantle of Christ gleam through His lowliness. What has happened to this man here, says Christ, is small and insignificant compared with what is yet to come. It is only a sign of something much greater. The little bit of earthly life that has been given to this man is only a small allusion to the eternal life which the Saviour of the world has to offer and bestow. His voice will be heard by the dead. I tell you sanctimonious people of Jerusalem, who neither hear nor see, that His voice will penetrate graves, and the works of the Father and the Son will be revealed in the dead. 'For the Father loveth the Son, and showeth him all things that himself doeth: and he will show him greater works than these, that ye may marvel. For as the Father raiseth up the dead, and quickeneth them: even so the Son quickeneth whom he will.' 'Verily, verily, I say unto you, He that heareth my word, and believeth on him that sent me, hath everlasting life, and shall not come into condemnation; but is passed from death unto life. Verily, verily, I say unto you, The hour is coming, and now is, when the dead shall hear the voice of the Son of God: and they that hear shall live. For as the Father hath life in himself, so hath he given to the Son to have life in himself.'

And then there are words in this chapter which make us look even higher. But before we can look up to these hills from which our help comes, we have to look back for a moment into the valley, and return to the man who has been healed. A little while later Christ meets him again in the Temple and accosts him with the strange words, 'Behold, thou art made whole: sin no more, lest a worse thing come unto thee.' What could this worse thing be? Was the illness that had befallen him not bad enough? It was certainly bad; in fact, speaking from a human point of view, this is the worst of all the cases mentioned in the gospels. The woman with an issue of blood has suffered for twelve years, this man for thirty-eight. The blind man has borne his burden from birth, but he has the loving care of a father and mother round about him. The man sick with the palsy at Capernaum also lies in misery on his couch, but he is brought to Jesus by four men. This fellow had no one to carry him; his was the very worst case of all, which makes us all the more astonished at Christ's words, 'Behold thou art made whole: sin no more, lest a worse thing come unto thee.'

Sickness and death are serious, but it is far more serious to persist in sin, unreconciled. Lying lame for thirty-eight years is a serious case of long duration, but there are not only cases of protracted sickness, but also cases of protracted sinning and these are far more serious. What is so bad is that healthy people continue to sin without gratitude. Here we have a hardened case of alcoholism, there of fornication, adultery, blackmail, covetousness, lying, or brutality. The Father wants to work on these hardened cases of sin, as well as on sickness and death, and through the Father also the Son. In them the Father, through the Son, wants to reveal His greatest glory. Through the Son He wants to bestow on men not only health on earth and eternal life, but reconciliation for the poor sinner. To draw a parallel from everyday life: the King has committed to the charge of his son not only the Ministry of Health, but also the dispensation of justice in the office of judge and mediator. The Father has 'committed all judgment unto the Son,' 'And hath given him authority to execute judgment also, because he is the Son of man. Marvel not at this: for the hour is coming, in the which all that are in the graves shall hear his voice, and shall come forth; they that have done good, unto the resurrection of life; and they that have done evil, unto the resurrection of damnation.'

Here the redeeming heart of Christ is revealed to us. The most splendid thing is not that the man at the pool of Bethesda can walk after lying ill for thirty-eight years, although that is splendid enough, but that for the sake of Christ there will be resurrection for the poor sinner. Conversely, however, the worst thing is not that a man has to lie for thirty-eight years on a sick-bed, but that there is a possibility that body and soul may perish into Hell. And the most splendid thing that we have heard so far is that for Christ's sake there is salvation from this second death.

'My Father worketh hitherto, and I work.' Only now can we realise the full extent and splendour of this work. And we remember that the Father, through the Son, has worked on us. He has rescued us from eternal death, and from that sick-bed which lasts not only for thirty-eight years but for eternity. Because Christ, the Saviour of the world, has so glorified His mercy through us, there is at this time a community in every nation which has learned by experience that God in His mercy is greater than our chronic cases. This community has gone out into the world in gratitude for the salvation it has experienced. Its task, is to declare the glory of Christ to all 'hardened cases.' What the 'incurables' lack is someone to put them into the pool when the water is troubled. They need people who will help them, and who, for the sake of Christ, will be Good Samaritans to them and be patient with them. If only you knew how desperately few people are prepared, for the sake of Christ, to give their time for 'hardened sinners' and to be at their disposal! If only you knew how astonishingly small is the number of people a hardworking clergyman can attend to! If only you knew how many people will continue to be in need and persist in the state of sin into which they have fallen, if an active community does not soon arise, urged on by gratitude for the salvation they have experienced. Every 'chronic case' left lying in this way will rise up and reproach us on the Day. How many poor sinners will then have cause to accuse us with the words, 'I had no man who, when the water was troubled, reached out his hand to me and led me into the Word of the Lord.'

If we think of our negligence in connexion with the Last Judgment, we shall discover to our surprise that even as redeemed sinners we have remained 'habitual sinners,' and that every morning we grieve the Redeemer anew. Our case will be just as old as we ourselves are. But it is the glory of Christ that He is greater than your case or mine, that before Him none of us remains hopeless, for He is greater than the oldest case, even than that of Adam. His glory shines forth once more in this story, and once more the angels rejoice.

The Feeding of the Five Thousand

After these things Jesus went over the sea of Galilee, which is the sea of Tiberias. And a great multitude followed him, because they saw his miracles which he did on them that were diseased. And Jesus went up into a mountain, and there he sat with his disciples. And the passover, a feast of the Jews, was nigh. When Jesus then lifted up his eyes, and saw a great company come unto him, he saith unto Philip, Whence shall we buy bread, that these may eat? And this he said to prove him: for he himself knew what he would do. Philip answered him, Two hundred pennyworth of bread is not sufficient for them, that every one of them may take a little. One of his disciples, Andrew, Simon Peter's brother, saith unto him, there is a lad here, which hath five barley loaves, and two small fishes: but what are they among so many? And Jesus said, Make the men sit down. Now there was much grass in the place. So the men sat down, in number about five thousand. And Jesus took the loaves; and when he had given thanks, he distributed to the disciples, and the disciples to them that were set down; and likewise of the fishes as much as they would. When they were filled, he said unto his disciples, Gather up the fragments that remain, that nothing be lost. Therefore they gathered them together, and filled twelve baskets with the fragments of the five barley loaves, which remained over and above unto them that had eaten.

Then those men, when they had seen the miracle that Jesus did, said, This is of a truth that prophet that should come into the world. When Jesus therefore perceived that they would come and take him by force, to make him a king, he departed again into a mountain himself alone.

And when even was now come, his disciples went down unto the sea, and entered into a ship, and went over the sea toward Capernaum. And it was now dark, and Jesus was not come to them. And the sea arose by reason of a great wind that blew. So when they had rowed about five and twenty or thirty furlongs, they see Jesus walking on the sea, and drawing nigh unto the ship: and they were afraid. But he saith unto them, It is I; be not afraid. Then they willingly received him into the ship: and immediately the ship was at the land whither they went.

The day following, when the people which stood on the other side of the sea saw that there was none other boat there, save that one whereinto his disciples were entered, and that Jesus went not with his disciples into the boat, but that his disciples were gone away alone; (howbeit there came other boats from Tiberias nigh unto the place where they did eat bread, after that the Lord had given thanks:) when the people therefore saw that Jesus was not there, neither his disciples, they also took shipping, and came to Capernaum, seeking for Jesus. And when they had found him on the other side of the sea, they said unto him, Rabbi, when camest thou hither? Jesus answered them and said, Verily, verily, I say unto you, Ye seek me, not because ye saw the miracles, but because ye did eat of the loaves, and were filled. Labour not for the meat which perisheth, but for that meat which endureth unto everlasting life, which the Son of man shall give unto you: for him hath God the Father sealed. Then said they unto him, What shall we do, that we might work the works of God? Jesus answered and said unto them, This is the work of God, that ye believe on him whom he hath sent. They said therefore unto him, What sign shewest thou then, that we may see, and believe thee? what dost thou work? Our fathers did eat manna in the desert; as it is written, He gave them bread from heaven to eat. Then Jesus said unto them, Verily, verily, I say unto you, Moses gave you not that bread from heaven; but my Father giveth you the true bread from heaven. For the bread of God is he which cometh down from heaven, and giveth life unto the world. Then said they unto him, Lord, evermore give us this bread. And Jesus said unto them, I am the bread of life: he that cometh to me shall never hunger; and he that believeth on me shall never thirst. But I said unto you, That ye also have seen me, and believe not. All that the Father giveth me shall come to me: and him that cometh to me I will in no wise cast out. For I came down from heaven, not to do mine own will, but the will of him that sent me. And this is the Father's will which hath sent me, that of all which he hath given me I should lose nothing, but should raise it up again at the last day. And this is the will of him that sent me, that everyone which seeth the Son, and believeth on him, may have everlasting life: and I will raise him up at the last day. The Jews then murmured at him, because he said, I am the bread which came down from heaven. And they said, Is not this Jesus, the son of Joseph, whose father and mother we know? how is it then that he saith, I came down from heaven? Jesus therefore answered and said unto them, Murmur not among yourselves. No man can come to me, except the Father which hath sent me draw him: and I will raise him up at the last day. It is written in the prophets, And they shall be all taught of God. Every man therefore that hath heard, and hath learned of the Father, cometh unto me. Not that any man hath seen the Father, save he which is of God, he hath seen the Father. Verily, verily, I say unto you, He that believeth on me hath everlasting life. I am that bread of life. Your fathers did eat manna in the wilderness, and are dead. This is the bread which cometh down from heaven, that a man may eat thereof, and not die. I am the living bread which came down from heaven: if any man eat of this bread, he shall live for ever: and the bread that I will give is my flesh, which I will give for the life of the world. The Jews therefore strove among themselves, saying, How can this man give us his flesh to eat? Then Jesus said unto them, Verily, verily, I say unto you, Except ye eat the flesh of the Son of man, and drink his blood, ye have no life in you. Whoso eateth my flesh, and drinketh my blood, hath eternal life; and I will raise him up at the last day. For my flesh is meat indeed, and my blood is drink indeed. He that eateth my flesh, and drinketh my blood, dwelleth in me, and I in him. As the living Father hath sent me, and I live by the Father: so he that eateth me, even he shall live by me. This is that bread which came down from heaven: not as your fathers did eat manna, and are dead: he that eateth of this bread shall live for ever. These things said he in the synagogue, as he taught in Capernaum. Many therefore of his disciples, when they had heard this, said, This is an hard saying; who can hear it? When Jesus knew in himself that his disciples murmured at it, he said unto them, Doth this offend you? What and if ye shall see the Son of man ascend up where he was before? It is the spirit that quickeneth; the flesh profiteth nothing: the words that I speak unto you, they are spirit, and they are life. But there are some of you that believe not. For Jesus knew from the beginning who they were that believed not, and who should betray him. And he said, Therefore said I unto you, that no man can come unto me, except it were given unto him of my Father.

From that time many of his disciples went back, and walked no more with him. Then said Jesus unto the twelve, Will ye also go away? Then Simon Peter answered him, Lord, to whom shall we go? thou hast the words of eternal life. And we believe and are sure that thou art that Christ, the Son of the living God. Jesus answered them, Have not I chosen you twelve, and one of you is a devil? He spake of Judas Iscariot the son of Simon: for he it was that should betray him, being one of the twelve.

[VI]

Not one of the five thousand doubts that Jesus, by His command, has created enough food for them all out of the five loaves and two fishes. No one can deny that they are all satisfied. If the meal had not appeared so naturally and smoothly, almost as if they had been sitting at table, they would have been reminded of the Old Testament miracle, when God sent down manna from Heaven. How then can we doubt an event that those taking part accept as a fact? Is our opinion of Him to be less than the Devil's, who knows that this man standing before the five thousand can make food not only out of five loaves of bread and two fishes, but out of stones?

But this miracle performed by the Saviour of the world, who was with God from the beginning as the Word, and by whom all things are made; this sign of His power to create and redeem, goes further than to satisfy those who witness it. Jesus's act of creation immediately produces a natural after-effect, and it is to this that we have to devote our attention. The participants in this great meal see that here is a man who really can do more than eat bread, He can create it. That is why He is the man for them. At one stroke the five thousand are welded together, so to speak, into a single will. They rise up as one man and, like the eruption of a volcano, the demand surges out, 'This man and no other. This man who creates bread must be our king.' That almost uncanny spirit of unity which we might call mass hysteria stretches out its ghostly hand towards Jesus. They want to make Him king, by force if necessary. That is what happens when a nation rises up in revolt and elects a leader if a suitable one can be found. It is no accident that the gospels stress that these five thousand were men. A movement of men has broken out here and all they need is a leader. They seek Him; they will not let Him go, and pursue Him round the lake. A swarm of bees crowds round its queen and lifts her up and bears her away, and the queen for her part unites these thousands of bees: similarly these five thousand men swarm round Jesus; they want to embrace Him and carry Him off, and in return want to be upheld and led by Him wherever He wants to take them. And they are certain that soon there will be not only five thousand, but fifty thousand or five hundred thousand: the whole nation will bear, shoulder-high, this man who creates bread.

And we ask, 'Is that not understandable? Is that not the most natural and obvious thing to happen?' Do we by any chance think differently from these five thousand men? Do we not support a government that can ensure work and food for everyone, and the end of unemployment? We are all worried that unemployment will follow this dreadful war. Have we not constantly tried to find, in these days of great economic hardship, men, or even one man, who can create bread? And not only our own people, but all the nations of the world, would gladly pay homage to the man who could, once and for all, solve the problem of food and employment. And again we ask, 'Is that not understandable?' Or even, 'Is that wrong?' What is wrong in expecting the Saviour of the world to help us where we need it most, for example asking Him to help us to get on in our jobs, or to be able to make more use of each day, or to be able to work with more concentration and thoughtfulness, or to take less offence at our superiors, or to get less annoyed with our subordinates? Is it wrong to make the happy discovery that Jesus can strengthen our weak nerves? Why should we not make Christ the king and ruler of each day, if we can thereby become more patient mothers and more understanding fathers to our children? Why should we not choose Christ for our leader because He has managed to save a ship-wrecked marriage? He Himself allows and encourages us to take Him whole-heartedly into our everyday lives; He Himself taught us to pray, 'Give us this day our daily bread,' and by that is meant everything that a man needs to live: health, bread, domestic happiness, and peace and order in the land. And He also heals the sick and those who are suffering in body and mind. By providing bread for these five thousand men in the wilderness He shows once again that He knows what a man needs to live.

But now, in spite of everything, the Lord withdraws from the eager hands of the five thousand. He knows that man lives by bread, yet not by bread alone, but by every word that comes from the mouth of God. These men want only bread from Him, not His living Word, and so He escapes from them. Matthew says at this point that that evening, after the five thousand were fed, 'Jesus constrained his disciples to get into a ship,' although night was approaching and the wind was against them. And He Himself withdraws to where they cannot find Him, and that night takes a path where no man will follow Him. It is not easy for Him to flee like this, because He knows that men need bread to live. They do not find Him again until the next day and then in a place which for Him is a kind of refuge from their enthusiastic demands, the synagogue at Capernaum. They will scarcely try to make Him king there!

And there in the synagogue the discussion between Jesus and the spokesman of the five thousand begins. This discussion with the five thousand – and they stand for us, of course – shows how charitable, patient and kind He is to people who want bread, and would like to live. What trouble He takes with them! No amount of time is too much for Him and He does not lose patience. Again and again He goes into their questions and answers their doubts and needs. That is how we should be able to deal with a man who wants bread because he must live.

He begins the discussion by saying, 'You have sought me out

because you got bread from me in the desert and had your fill of it.' Their silence indicates agreement. Then He goes on to say, 'I have other, more precious food than what you had last night.' Whereupon they ask Him, 'How can we get this more precious food?' And He answers, 'You do not have to find it. The Father in Heaven will provide this eternal food for you: all you have to do is to accept it and believe in Him whom God has sent – just believe!' But now the complete helplessness of the five thousand appears again. 'How are we to believe if we cannot see? We should like to see, not just believe. Our forefathers were lucky, for they saw manna falling from Heaven, "Our fathers did eat manna in the desert; as it is written. He gave them bread from heaven." ' Jesus would like to give them bread from Heaven, and they, half distrustful, half curious, say, 'Lord, evermore give us this bread.' And now He speaks quite plainly, ' "I am the bread of life: he that cometh to me shall never hunger; and he that believeth on me shall never thirst." I do not want to give you less than my Father gave to your fathers when He sent down bread from Heaven in the desert. I want to give you more. "Your fathers did eat manna in the wilderness and are dead." Many, many nations have eaten bread and yet have gone the way of all flesh. But I am the living bread. "He that believeth on me hath everlasting life. I am that bread of life." '

They wanted to make Him king: they wanted to make Him what other men can be: they wanted to make Him merely the provider of bread. But Pharaoh in Joseph's time, Nebuchadnezzar in Daniel's day, and Caesar Augustus, could also provide bread. Jesus wants to provide something that no other man, neither emperor nor king, can offer; he wants to give them eternal life. He does not want to be classed with the great men of the world or put on a level with benevolent temporal rulers. He can give them more than any earthly ruler, and for their own sake has evaded their attempts to crown Him king. To give in to their insistent demands would have been to betray them. For a mere scrap of bread, they would have thrown their eternal inheritance to the winds.

Besides, He does not need five thousand men to make Him king. He is King already, not by the grace of man but by the grace of God. He does not need to be chosen as leader by men, for He is already the Leader, supported by His Father's angels: 'All that the Father giveth me shall come to me: and him that cometh to me I will in no wise cast out. For I came down from heaven, not to do mine own will, but the will of him that sent me . . . that of all which he hath given me I should lose nothing, but should raise it up again at the last day.' That is the King who reigns by the grace of Heaven alone. And in case anyone is still not quite sure that this is the only true King, Jesus puts it even more clearly. He Himself, who has come from the Father, will die according to the will of the Father. His death will provide the meat and drink that gives eternal life to all those who believe. His body will be broken, His blood will be spilled, and by these the nations will live. They will eat His body in faith, and drink His blood in faith, and that will be their life. What an unusual king! He offers eternal life, saying at the same time, 'I shall die'; quite the opposite to earthly kings. The kings of this world demand the flesh and blood of their subjects. But this One, on the shores of the lake of Gennesaret, offers His own flesh and blood to His people, ' "And the bread that I will give is my flesh, which I will give for the life of the world." Whoever eats of me in faith shall live for my sake.'

This discussion has quite another effect on its hearers than that produced earlier by the miracle in the desert. After Jesus has told them so clearly, 'I am the eternal life and whoever eats of me and accepts me in faith shall live'; after He has offered Himself to them, we read that they 'murmured' and 'strove among themselves.' These very men who wished to make Him king after He had fed them will help to crucify Him, because He is indeed a provider of bread, but more than that, He is the Saviour of the world.

And even His disciples say, 'This is an hard saying; who can hear it?' 'From that time many of his disciples went back and walked no more with him.' Once again we ask, 'Are we surprised?' Does it not trouble us all that Christ offers us life by dying and that, although He can provide bread, those who want merely bread from Him do not receive Him? Surely if we do not feel deeply troubled by this we have missed the real import of this chapter? It is significant that Johann Albrecht Bengel, a deeply religious interpreter of this gospel, suddenly interrupts his commentary towards the end of this chapter, and prays, 'Lord Jesus, uphold me in my faith, so that I shall not chafe at any of Thy words, even if I cannot reconcile myself to them all.' That is honestly spoken. This chapter does in fact ask us if we will say 'Yes' to Jesus, even when He does not help us and our nation in the way that we think He should, but in His own way. We are asked if we will still be prepared to hear and follow Him, when we have nothing left at all but the belief that He is the Bread of Life. During the coming festival perhaps someone will come, poor and empty, to the Lord's Table, to drink the cup and eat the bread and, though he may be able to feel nothing, will yet have faith.

From that time many turned away and walked no more with Him. In the end twelve disciples were left, and we know how long these stayed with Him. The day came when they were all troubled, and even the twelve were on the side of the five thousand, and no longer understood their master. At the beginning of the chapter there were five thousand: at the end there are twelve, and one of these is a traitor. To these twelve we hear Him address the kingly words, ' "Will ye also go away?" Even if you go too, I am still King.' Our will and support cannot make Him this sort of King: He is ordained King by God.

By refusing the demands of the five thousand Jesus remains true to the tradition that God has laid down from the beginning of time for His Kingdom on earth. In Sunday school just now we are reading those informative chapters in the first book of Samuel (chs. VI–X), where suddenly the people come to the prophet-judge and say, 'We will have a king over us; that we also may be like all the nations.' Samuel is dismayed and prays to God. Up till now God's people have not had a king: only the heathen nations have kings. Now God's cause is to be, as it were, nationalised. God warns His people, by making the prophet tell them that to demand a king is to renounce God. If they want a king they will have to give him their best vineyards, olive-groves and cornfields, their sons and their daughters. In spite of this warning, however, they persist in their demand and God says, 'Hearken unto their voice, and make them a king,' a king with all the accompanying disadvantages.

So these five thousand want a king: they want to drag God's Kingship down to an earthly level. But the King of kings remains free and, instead of ascending their throne, ascends the Cross which the Father has prepared for Him. Christ stays free. Thank God that Christ remains free even when five million or five hundred million people want to make Him king. And He will extend His freedom to all who believe.

Jesus in Jerusalem at the Feast of Tabernacles

After these things Jesus walked in Galilee: for he would not walk in Jewry, because the Jews sought to kill him. Now the Jews' feast of tabernacles was at hand. His brethren therefore said unto him, Depart hence, and go into Judæa, that thy disciples also may see the works that thou doest. For there is no man that doeth any thing in secret, and he himself seeketh to be known openly. If thou do these things, shew thyself to the world. For neither did his brethren believe in him. Then Jesus said unto them, My time is not yet come: but your time is always ready. The world cannot hate you; but me it hateth, because I testify of it, that the works thereof are evil. Go ye up unto this feast: I go not up yet unto this feast; for my time is not yet full come. When he had said these words unto them, he abode still in Galilee.

But when his brethren were gone up, then went he also up unto the feast, not openly, but as it were in secret. Then the Jews sought him at the feast, and said, Where is he? And there was much murmuring among the people concerning him: for some said, He is a good man: others said, Nay; but he deceiveth the people. Howbeit no man spake openly of him for fear of the Jews.

Now about the midst of the feast Jesus went up into the temple, and taught. And the Jews marvelled, saying, How knoweth this man letters, having never learned? Jesus answered them, and said, My doctrine is not mine, but his that sent me. If any man will do his will, he shall know of the doctrine, whether it be of God, or whether I speak of myself. He that speaketh of himself seeketh his own glory: but he that seeketh his glory that sent him, the same is true, and no unrighteousness is in him. Did not Moses give you the law, and yet none of you keepeth the law? Why go ye about to kill me? The people answered and said,

Thou hast a devil: who goeth about to kill thee? Jesus answered and said unto them, I have done one work, and ye all marvel. Moses therefore gave unto you circumcision; (not because it is of Moses, but of the fathers;) and ye on the sabbath day circumcise a man. If a man on the sabbath day receive circumcision, that the law of Moses should not be broken; are ye angry at me, because I have made a man every whit whole on the sabbath day? Judge not according to the appearance, but judge righteous judgment. Then said some of them of Jerusalem, Is not this he, whom they seek to kill? But, lo, he speaketh boldly, and they say nothing unto him. Do the rulers know indeed that this is the very Christ? Howbeit we know this man whence he is: but when Christ cometh, no man knoweth whence he is. Then cried Jesus in the temple as he taught, saying, Ye both know me, and ye know whence I am: and I am not come of myself, but he that sent me is true, whom ye know not. But I know him: for I am from him, and he hath sent me. Then they sought to take him: but no man laid hands on him, because his hour was not yet come. And many of the people believed on him, and said, When Christ cometh, will he do more miracles than these which this man hath done?

The Pharisees heard that the people murmured such things concerning him; and the Pharisees and the chief priests sent officers to take him. Then said Jesus unto them, Yet a little while am I with you, and then I go unto him that sent me. Ye shall seek me, and shall not find me: and where I am, thither ye cannot come. Then said the Jews among themselves, Whither will he go, that we shall not find him? will he go unto the dispersed among the Gentiles, and teach the Gentiles? What manner of saying is this that he said, Ye shall seek me, and shall not find me: and where I am, thither ye cannot come?

In the last day, that great day of the feast, Jesus stood and cried, saying, If any man thirst, let him come unto me, and drink. He that believeth on me, as the scripture hath said, out of his belly shall flow rivers of living water. (But this spake he of the Spirit, which they that believe on him should receive: for the Holy Ghost was not yet given; because that Jesus was not yet glorified.) Many of the people therefore, when they heard this saying, said, Of a truth this is the Prophet. Others said, This is the Christ. But some said, Shall Christ come out of Galilee?

Hath not the scripture said, That Christ cometh of the seed of David, and out of the town of Bethlehem, where David was? So there was a division among the people because of him. And some of them would have taken him; but no man laid hands on him.

Then came the officers to the chief priests and Pharisees; and they said unto them, Why have ye not brought him? The officers answered, Never man spake like this man. Then answered them the Pharisees, Are ye also deceived? Have any of the rulers or of the Pharisees believed on him? But this people who knoweth not the law are cursed. Nicodemus saith unto them, (he that came to Jesus by night, being one of them,) Doth our law judge any man before it hear him, and know what he doeth? They answered and said unto him, Art thou also of Galilee? Search, and look: for out of Galilee ariseth no prophet. And every man went unto his own house.

[VII]

We must not let the seeming disorder of this chapter confuse us. There is always disorder at a feast, but if we take the trouble to sort out our impressions, we shall see three quite distinct groups of people. First of all there are those nearest to Jesus, His brothers; then the ordinary people 'who knoweth not the law'; and the third group consists of the chief priests and Pharisees, and their officers. It is characteristic of the language of the fourth gospel that this thin, but influential, upper crust of Israel is simply and briefly called 'the Jews.' If we look more closely at these three groups, we shall see that we are not the audience but in fact actors in the drama. We are reminded of the old soldier, sitting in a cinema, watching a film about army life, who, suddenly seeing himself marching along on the screen, was so surprised that he could not help shouting, 'That's me there.'

Jesus's brothers want to make Him go to the feast at Jerusalem. It is the Feast of Tabernacles in the autumn before His crucifixion. They do not like to see Him hiding His talent in remote corners of Galilee. They feel it is a crying shame that He does not seek a larger public. They are tired of having to put up with the criticisms and insults levelled at their brother. They would much rather sun themselves in the glory of a universally popular and respected relation: 'His brethren therefore said unto him, Depart hence, and go into Judaea, that thy disciples also may see the works that thou doest. For there is no man that doeth any thing in secret, and he himself seeketh to be known openly. If thou do these things, show thyself to the world.'

Jesus knows that He is going to the feast: but His brothers' demand reminds Him of the time when Peter tempted Him to leave the way of the Cross. This is the same temptation that Satan offered Jesus at the beginning of His ministry, when he led Him up to a pinnacle of the Temple and tried to persuade Him to throw Himself down. He will not go to the feast in the way that His brothers would like, to make Himself popular and to enhance His family's reputation; He will go to be hated by everyone. That is why He lets His brothers go on ahead. John adds briefly, 'For neither did his brethren believe in him.' Do *we* believe in Him?

Do we believe in the Jesus who says to His brothers, 'The world cannot hate you; but me it hateth, because I testify of it, that the works thereof are evil'? Or are we not all secretly on the side of the brothers, who admittedly love Him and are glad to call Him their brother, but only so long as He will go to the feast with them in the way that they want? Are we not tempted time and again – and let us be quite honest about this – to demand, in the spirit of His brothers, that Jesus should come to the feast with us? This is the Jesus who is good enough to go to the feast with us, and help to adorn our national and family celebrations. This is the Jesus who is good enough for our baptisms, confirmations and funerals. It is convenient for us that He should accompany us so far but no further. This is the Jesus who is good enough to be worn as a badge at all sorts of festivals, or political and church parades. Do you suppose that Jesus is pleased that in many lands the funeral obsequies for the late Pope[1] were highly political, with perfidious diplomacy well to the fore? Can Jesus be pleased that services of thanksgiving are now being held – and not only

[1] Pius XI, *d.* 1939.

Roman Catholic ones – because Andalusian shepherds and factory workers in Barcelona have once more been trodden in the mud? This is the Jesus that we try to drag to our feasts: but He stays away: 'Go ye up unto this feast: I go not up yet unto this feast; for my time is not yet full come.'

Those of us who are troubled about idolatry entering into the Church – and it is found not only in the Roman Catholic Church – can comfort ourselves with the thought that Christ is not present in every place where His name is used as a password. If we call Him by name at the beginning and end of our festivals and a hundred times in between, that is no proof that He is present. His name may be taken in vain, but never Christ Himself. It is Jesus, not His brothers, who decide where, and how and when He will be at the feast. Do not despair of Jesus. You have no right to despair of Him, for after all, when His time came He did go to the feast, in order to reveal the wickedness of the world and of a Church that had become worldly. As a result He was hated and crucified. He died for truth, love and justice, and that is our comfort and support.

The second group at the Feast of Tabernacles is the people, who, say the Pharisees, are accursed and know nothing of the law, and should therefore be silent. These unsuspecting people really are ignorant, and know nothing of the designs of their leaders, and can therefore say, 'Thou hast a devil: who goeth about to kill thee?' These timid people do in fact keep silent and, when they speak, only murmur and mutter: 'Howbeit no man spake openly of him for fear of the Jews.' How helpless and weak they are; they mutter and do nothing. They are a reed blown to and fro by the wind, influenced first by one man, then by another. 'And there was much murmuring among the people concerning him: for some said, He is a good man: others said, Nay; but he deceiveth the people.' Could any two opinions of a man be more divergent? 'Then said some of them of Jerusalem, Is not this he whom they seek to kill? But, lo, he speaketh boldly, and they say nothing unto him. Do the rulers know indeed that this is the very Christ?' They will believe anything, but then the people always were credulous. They will shout, 'Hosanna!' or 'Crucify Him!' with equal enthusiasm. Then we find them wavering again: 'Howbeit we know this man whence he is: but when Christ cometh, no man knoweth whence he is.' They vacillate now as they have done for thousands of years. 'Many of the people therefore, when they heard this saying, said, Of a truth this is the Prophet. Others said, This is the Christ. But some said, Shall Christ come out of Galilee? Hath not the scripture said, That Christ cometh of the seed of David, and out of the town of Bethlehem, where David was? So there was a division among the people because of him.'

The people are not unanimous on any one point: there is great discussion about Jesus, but no decision. And so they are unsuspecting, weak, anxious and divided because they discuss Jesus, but will not let themselves follow Him. It is time we realised that people who do nothing but discuss Christ are bound to waver and vacillate. A nation which has scorned and rejected Christ for decades is bound to be spineless, together with its leaders. So long as we go on arguing about Christ, we will not be sure of ourselves in anything we think or say or do. It is quite extraordinary how many people I have met in the past week who have been discussing Christ for years, with no result, and who are sinking ever deeper into a quagmire of argument and speculation. I should like to take them by the scruff of the neck, and shake them and say, 'For goodness' sake, stop this chattering about Christ and take one little step, however diffident or even laughably small it may be, along His path. One inch in this direction is worth more than a thousand miles of discussion about Him: "If any man will do his will, he shall know of the doctrine, whether it be of God or whether I speak of myself." ' If we do God's will, however shakily, we will begin to see Christ clearly. Through discussion His picture will be obscured.

If the first group, which is determined to take Christ to the feast, seems on the whole to be more like the Roman Catholic part of Christianity – far be it from me to make accusations of heresy, for I know only too well to what extent this group includes our own Church – then the second group seems to be more like the Protestants. Our Church is being crushed and undermined by endless doubting and differences of opinion about Christ. We are wasting our strength in fruitless conflict over differing points of view and losing sight of God's great day through parochial arguments: 'So there was a division among the people because of him.' That is our Protestant guilt. So even if we are pained by the behaviour of others, we would do well to rid ourselves of sanctimonious criticism of our Roman Catholic fellow-citizens. For in Jesus's eyes we all belong to both groups: 'Show thyself to the world,' 'So there was a division among the people because of him.'

And now for the third group, the chief priests and Pharisees. They are remarkably decided and unanimous about what they want. It is easier to be unanimous against God than for Him. 'The Jews' are the really active people in this chapter. They are looking for Jesus even before He appears at the feast: 'Then the Jews sought him at the feast, and said, Where is he?' Later we hear of them, 'Then they sought to take him: but no man laid hands on him, because his hour was not yet come.' However, when they realised that the people might be influenced by Him, we read, 'The Pharisees heard that the people murmured such things concerning him; and the Pharisees and the chief priests sent officers to take him.' While one group is trying to bask in His reflected glory, and the second group discusses and disagrees about Him, the enemy is at work trying to catch and kill Him.

But Jesus opposes this third group too. Did you not notice how powerless they feel against Christ, in spite of their unanimity? Did you not hear what happened when the officers whom they had sent out came back? 'Then came the officers to the chief priests and Pharisees; and they said unto them, Why have ye not brought him? The officers answered, Never man spake like this man.' If only it were given to us to speak like that! Let us pray to be able to speak in such a way that even today officers will return with their mission unaccomplished. This is Christianity's great need today. Let us pray for this one thing.

Jesus is confronted with this threefold barrier at the Feast of Tabernacles: heretical delusion, faint-hearted doubting and the hatred of unbelievers. What strange allies! But Jesus is not inactive in the face of this oddly-assorted crowd. He has been uppermost in people's minds throughout the feast, then suddenly He appears as if from nowhere. They find Him sitting in the Temple, the very heart of His enemies' stronghold, as if nothing had happened, teaching His old message, 'I have been sent from the Father in Heaven and no one can harm a hair of my head before my Father's hour has come.' And His teaching is full of authority, like the teaching of Moses. Moses was empowered to give the people circumcision, which is performed on the Sabbath, and similarly Jesus has authority from above to heal on the Sabbath. That is the substance of His teaching and He goes on to say that He is going to a place where none of them can follow Him. When we see Him teaching there in the middle of the feast, we are reminded of the twenty-third Psalm: 'Thou preparest a table before me in the presence of mine enemies.'

And then a most extraordinary thing happens. 'In the last day, that great day of the feast, Jesus stood and cried.' At the climax of the feast, Jesus addresses the public in a loud voice. He cries out at the threefold barrier. Will He get any answer back other than an empty echo? He is calling someone, but who among this crowd can hear Him? Will they not all have deaf ears, or mistaken belief, or half-hearted belief, or no belief at all? But Jesus cries out because He knows that someone will hear Him. He cries out over the broad Temple court to one man who is thirsty. His voice is searching, persuading, pleading and appealing as He cries, 'If any man thirst, let him come unto me, and drink,' as if to say, 'Is there anyone here who is thirsty? Is there anyone here who wants more of me than material for a festive banner? Is there anyone here who wants more of me than material for discussion? If there is anyone here who is thirsty, let him come unto me and drink.'

What can I do now but take up this cry of Jesus's in awe and fear and call it out today, please God also in a searching, persuading, pleading and appealing voice? Six months after that cry on the last day of the Feast of Tabernacles, the die was cast. There are occasions which are of vital importance. A few months later it may be too late. So in these times we must not grow tired of crying out, 'If any man is thirsty, let him come to Jesus and drink.' Is there anyone here who is not satisfied? Is there by chance anyone here who has drunk deeply of the waters of this world, and who is now slowly beginning to realise that everything that this world had to offer could not quench his thirst? The world is like snow: the more you try to quench your thirst with it, the thirstier you get. If there is anyone here who has that kind of thirst, let him come to Jesus and drink. Or is anyone here so moved by the troubles of others that they torment him like a spiritual and physical thirst? Perhaps one of us is distressed to learn, for instance, that some little tailor is in despair because he is being squeezed out of business by the factories? How many of us must be horrified, not like the Pharisees but in truly Christian fashion, that in the town of Basle there is an average of one divorce for every working day of the year? Or do some of us hunger and thirst after justice, and cannot help but mourn that in the past week the politics of Europe have buried truth and justice even deeper? Or is there someone here who is simply weeping at the impotence and disunity of our Protestant church? If there is anyone here who is thirsty, let him come to Jesus and drink. Where can we hope to quench our thirst if not in this crucified, hated Jesus, who was cast out because He stood for justice and love? If we no longer trust Him, what is there left but the night of despair? After reading the depressing news in our daily papers, are we not bound to turn to the gospels; for where, if not in the Bible, is there even a drop of hope for spiritual existence? If anyone is thirsty, let him come to Jesus and drink. He made His offer plain enough when He placed the cup in our midst and told us, 'Drink ye all of it.'

The man who is fortunate enough to hear this cry, that goes out to the whole world on the last day of the feast, 'out of his belly shall flow rivers of living water.' 'Rivers of living water'!

The man who accepts union with God can become a river, more than a spring that restores individuals, a great river that saves a whole region from drought. These rivers of living water are rivers of clear knowledge, rivers of active charity, of peace and joy: such rivers of living water will flow forth from him who is united with the river that flows from Jesus into our times. Jesus is alluding to that Messianic river, which, according to Ezekiel, begins at the altar of the Temple and pours down over the plain, right out to the open sea, and on whose banks grow trees which 'bring forth new fruit according to his months.' 'He that believeth on me, as the scripture hath said, out of his belly shall flow rivers of living water.'

And now one last point. Jesus's cry to anyone who is thirsty does not fall entirely on deaf ears. The end of the chapter shows us that there is at least one man there who is thirsty. And that man appears where no one would have thought of looking, among the group that represents hatred and radical unbelief. If that group contains one man who is thirsty, should we not expect to find many more in the other two groups? This one man is Nicodemus, who is thirsty in the deepest sense of the word. His need is for truth and eternal life. He has not been able to sleep for the thirst which once drove him to Jesus on a stormy night. He cannot bear to remain as he is now, and wants to become a new Nicodemus. He is seeking in Jesus the peace that not even religion in the world as he knows it has been able to give him. At first he also tried discussion with Christ. That was the first and last time, for soon he uses his lips for something other than discussing – for drinking.

The first-fruits of his coming and drinking are visible straight away. Let us picture to ourselves what happens. Nicodemus steps forward and intercedes for Jesus; a crack has appeared in the barrier. However awkward and timid it may be, it is a real step in imitation of Christ. Nicodemus risks no less than expulsion from the party and social ostracism: 'Art thou also of Galilee?' As a result of this one step, Nicodemus becomes an example, an encouragement and a sign to the people. If there is anyone here who is thirsty like Nicodemus, let him come to Jesus and drink. 'Blessed are they which do hunger and thirst after righteousness: for they shall be filled.'

Jesus and the Woman Taken in Adultery

Jesus went unto the mount of Olives. And early in the morning he came again into the temple, and all the people came unto him; and he sat down, and taught them. And the scribes and Pharisees brought unto him a woman taken in adultery; and when they had set her in the midst, they say unto him, Master, this woman was taken in adultery, in the very act. Now Moses in the law commanded us, that such should be stoned: but what sayest thou? This they said, tempting him, that they might have to accuse him. But Jesus stooped down, and with his finger wrote on the ground, as though he heard them not. So when they continued asking him, he lifted up himself, and said unto them, He that is without sin among you, let him first cast a stone at her. And again he stooped down, and wrote on the ground. And they which heard it, being convicted by their own conscience, went out one by one, beginning at the eldest, even unto the last: and Jesus was left alone, and the woman standing in the midst. When Jesus had lifted up himself, and saw none but the woman, he said unto her, Woman, where are those thine accusers? hath no man condemned thee? She said, No man, Lord. And Jesus said unto her, Neither do I condemn thee: go, and sin no more.

Then spake Jesus again unto them, saying, I am the light of the world: he that followeth me shall not walk in darkness, but shall have the light of life. The Pharisees therefore said unto him, Thou bearest record of thyself; thy record is not true. Jesus answered and said unto them, Though I bear record of myself, yet my record is true: for I know whence I came, and whither I go: but ye cannot tell whence I come, and whither I go. Ye judge after the flesh; I judge no man. And yet if I judge, my judgment is true; for I am not alone, but I and the Father that sent me. It is also written in your law, that the testimony of two men is true. I am one that bear witness of myself, and the Father that sent me beareth witness of me. Then said they unto him, Where is thy Father? Jesus answered, Ye neither know me, nor my Father: if ye had known me, ye should have known my Father also. These words spake Jesus in the treasury, as he taught in the temple: and no man laid hands on him; for his hour was not yet come. Then said Jesus again unto them, I go my way, and ye shall seek me, and shall die in your sins: whither I go, ye cannot come. Then said the Jews, Will he kill himself? because he saith, Whither I go, ye cannot come. And he said unto them, Ye are from beneath; I am from above: ye are of this world; I am not of this world. I said therefore unto you, that ye shall die in your sins: for if ye believe not that I am he, ye shall die in your sins. Then said they unto him, Who art thou? And Jesus saith unto them, Even the same that I said unto you from the beginning. I have many things to say and to judge of you: but he that sent me is true; and I speak to the world those things which I have heard of him. They understood not that he spake to them of the Father. Then said Jesus unto them, When ye have lifted up the Son of man, then shall ye know that I am he, and that I do nothing of myself; but as my Father hath taught me, I speak these things. And he that sent me is with me: the Father hath not left me alone; for I do always those things that please him. As he spake these words, many believed on him. Then said Jesus to those Jews which believed on him, If ye continue in my word, then are ye my disciples indeed; and ye shall know the truth, and the truth shall make you free. They answered him, We be Abraham's seed, and were never in bondage to any man: how sayest thou, Ye shall be made free? Jesus answered them, Verily, verily, I say unto you, Whosoever committeth sin is the servant of sin. And the servant abideth not in the house for ever: but the Son abideth ever. If the Son therefore shall make you free, ye shall be free indeed. I know that ye are Abraham's seed; but ye seek to kill me, because my word hath no place in you. I speak that which I have seen with my Father; and ye do that which ye have seen with your father. They answered and said unto him, Abraham is our father. Jesus saith unto them, If ye were Abraham's children, ye would do the works of Abraham. But now ye seek to kill me, a man that hath told you the truth, which I have heard of God: this did not Abraham. Ye do the deeds of your father. Then said they to him, We be not born of fornication; we have one Father, even God. Jesus said unto them, If God were your Father, ye would love me: for I proceeded forth and came from God; neither came I of myself, but he sent me. Why do ye not understand my speech? even because ye cannot hear my word. Ye are of your father the devil, and the lusts of your father ye will do. He was a murderer from the beginning, and abode not in the truth, because there is no truth in him. When he speaketh a lie, he speaketh of his own: for he is a liar, and the father of it. And because I tell you the truth, ye believe me not. Which of you convinceth me of sin? And if I say the truth, why do ye not believe me? He that is of God heareth God's words: ye therefore hear them not, because ye are not of God. Then answered the Jews, and said unto him, Say we not well that thou art a Samaritan, and hast a devil? Jesus answered, I have not a devil; but I honour my Father, and ye do dishonour me. And I seek not mine own glory: there is one that seeketh and judgeth. Verily, verily, I say unto you, If a man keep my saying, he shall never see death. Then said the Jews unto him, Now we know that thou hast a devil. Abraham is dead, and the prophets; and thou sayest, if a man keep my saying, he shall never taste of death. Art thou greater than our father Abraham, which is dead? and the prophets are dead: whom makest thou thyself? Jesus answered, If I honour myself, my honour is nothing: it is my Father that honoureth me; of whom ye say, that he is your God: yet ye have not known him; but I know him: and if I should say, I know him not, I shall be a liar like unto you: but I know him, and keep his saying. Your father Abraham rejoiced to see my day: and he saw it, and was glad. Then said the Jews unto him, Thou art not yet fifty years old, and hast thou seen Abraham? Jesus said unto them, Verily, verily, I say unto you, Before Abraham was, I am. Then took they up stones to cast at him: but Jesus hid himself, and went out of the temple, going through the midst of them, and so passed by. [VIII]

Jesus does not say, 'I should like to be the Light of the world,' or 'I want to become the Light of the world,' or even 'I should like to bring a little light into the world.' He simply states, 'I am the light of the world.' It is not a wish, or a demand, but a fact. He is in fact, the Light of the world. At the moment when the Lord makes this majestic statement it becomes reality, just as a king begins to rule as soon as he ascends the throne. In the first chapter of this fourth gospel we read, 'And the light shineth in darkness,' and this has now become actual fact. We already have considerable evidence of the brightness of this Light. There spring to mind Jesus's nocturnal conversation with Nicodemus, and the events at Jacob's well, and at the pool of the sick. Another such proof is the incident with the Pharisees and the woman taken in adultery, which has been placed at the beginning of our chapter here for very good reason. Let us sum up again briefly what has been happening.

Jesus is sitting teaching at the entrance to the outer forecourt of the Temple, where the poor-boxes are. Suddenly He is interrupted by an excited group of scribes and Pharisees, bringing to Him a woman who has committed adultery, a particularly serious offence. According to the Law of Moses, the punishment for this is death by stoning. This wretched woman is dragged in front of the people who are listening to Jesus, and her misdeed is described in crude detail. Then the scribes and Pharisees ask Jesus what He has to say about it, hoping that He will pronounce a mild judgment, so that they will be able to accuse Him of disregarding the Law. But Jesus says nothing. He bends down and writes in the sand, as if the whole affair were no concern of His. Evidently He does not intend to give the answer they are trying to draw out of Him, for He realises their intention and remains silent. His enemies interpret this silence as embarrassment, and insist on an answer. What an answer they get! Suddenly He stands up, looks at the woman's accusers and says to them, 'He that is without sin among you, let him first cast a stone at her,' then He stoops down again and continues to write in the sand without another glance at them. After a while He looks up again, and they have all gone. Abashed and with guilty consciences, they have all crept away, from the highest to the lowest. In the end only Jesus and the woman remain, surrounded by His original audience. We know what follows.

This man teaching at the entrance to the Temple is truly the Light of the world, and this Light has an almost uncanny effect. First of all it judges, but not in the manner of the scribes and Pharisees whom Jesus reproaches, 'Ye judge after the flesh.' They judge according to what can be seen by the human eye. Jesus says of Himself, 'I judge no man (after the flesh). And yet if I judge, my judgment is true.' He judges from above, with the all-penetrating eye of Him whose judgment is just. He does not judge according to appearances, rather does He look into the hearts of men. That is why His light is 'sharper than any two-edged sword, piercing even to the dividing asunder of soul and spirit, and of the joints and marrow, and is a discerner of the thoughts and intents of the heart.' The man who can see what lies beneath the robes of priests truly has the right to say, 'Ye are from beneath; I am from above: ye are of this world; I am not of this world.' They thought they were performing a great feat by dragging this woman out and exposing her, this poor, sinful woman who was already branded and humiliated by her wrong-doing. But the Saviour does not excuse the woman. She is a sinner: but now His light falls not only on her, but also on her accusers, and the spotless appearance of their cloaks of virtue is dimmed. The sun in the sky often fails to bring even the worst crimes to light. But Jesus Christ, the Light of the world, discovers them all.

But we must be careful, for there is a danger here that, as on-lookers, we may begin to gloat over the discomfiture of the scribes and Pharisees. By doing so we would be falling into the very attitude that the scribes themselves showed towards the woman they had taken in adultery. That is not why we are told this story. We are told it so that we shall let the Light of the world penetrate our 'Sunday best' too. This Light wants to discover what we have brought here in secret. There must be very few people who have not come into conflict with the seventh commandment. And if not the seventh, then the eighth about stealing, or the sixth about killing, or the fifth about honouring one's father and mother, or the first about having other gods before God. Whichever commandment we may have broken, the Light of the world wants to discover it. And here I would beg you not to avoid this revealing Light, do not evade it now or your coming to church will not be blessed. Let us join in begging our Father in Heaven to let His Light penetrate our hearts and disclose to us the possibly unacknowledged wrongs in our lives, those hidden wounds which will never let us be completely happy. Let us beg Him to let the light of His countenance shine upon us and to give us submissive hearts.

A follower of Christ is distinguished not by the fact that he will one day be free from sin in the sense that he will never sin again, but by the fact that, from the day when he first comes near to Christ, he will no longer be able to persist in any sin without his conscience crying out, tormenting him, belabouring him and finally convincing him: 'I am the light of the world: he that followeth me shall not walk in darkness, but shall have the light of life.' These scribes and Pharisees certainly see themselves for a moment in Jesus's light, but afterwards avoid it. They do not want to walk in the Light. They run away like frightened rabbits caught in the beam of a motor car's headlamps. However, far from repenting, they are filled with anger and rebellion and the desire for revenge against this man who has shown them their true selves. They do not want to walk in the Light, because they prefer darkness. Instead of taking the opportunity offered them here and becoming followers of Christ, they shut themselves off all the more from the Light: 'The Pharisees therefore said unto him, Thou bearest record of thyself; thy record is not true.' That is why Jesus has to say to them later, 'Ye neither know me nor my Father: if ye had known me, ye should have known my Father also.' That is why He cannot spare them the most terrible words that He has ever spoken: 'Ye shall die in your sins.' And He repeats it twice over: 'Ye shall die in your sins: for if ye believe not that I am he, ye shall die in your sins.' Either we walk in the Light of Christ, or we love darkness more than the Light, in which case we walk in darkness and will finally die in our sins.

Dying in our sins does not mean that at the end of our lives we may suddenly die unprepared and unreconciled. These words can have another meaning: we can begin to die in our sins long before our dying day. How many good and laudable resolutions have died in our own lives, crushed under the weight of our sins! Of the people around us who are apparently living, many are dying, or have long ago died, in their sins. And that is a very sad thing. It is hard enough to see someone we love wasting away physically as the result of an illness, but it is the saddest thing of all to see someone dying in their sins. All over this town of ours people are dying in their sins. Every day we read in the 'Deaths' column of our local newspaper the names of those who have passed away. This is often an imposing list. However, if deaths in sin were to be reported in a newspaper in Heaven, the column would be very much more imposing. Yet Jesus does not want a single one of us to die in his sins, because it was for our sins that He Himself died. It is His will that we should come to recognise salvation and accept His Light. That is why He clings to hope for these people even now, although they are resisting Him. He expresses this in the words, 'When ye have lifted up the Son of man, then shall ye know that I am he, and that I do nothing of myself.'

Christ does not want anyone to die in his sins. All of you here today know that you need not die in your sins, and that you can live in the Light of forgiveness, so why do you not carry this message cheerfully and with devotion out into the streets of the town? I always think that, if things were as they should be, a large crowd such as we find Sunday after Sunday in our churches here, should have a greater effect and should produce more 'Good Samaritans.' Fewer people should die in their sins in a city such as this, full of bells and church spires. Do not say that that is what the clergy are here for – a Protestant Christian never says that. Do not make the excuse that you are too shy and ignorant to do it – Jesus would rather have us awkward than lazy, and cowardly, and ungrateful. Just see how clumsily, and not only clumsily but downright absurdly the scribes and Pharisees drag this woman before Jesus. But, although their action is prompted by evil, there is at least one merit in it, namely, that a sinner has been brought to Jesus. The evil aims of these men have been turned to good by Christ. If He can turn even the wicked blunder of these hostile Pharisees to the good of this poor soul, why should He not turn to good the mistakes that His children and servants fall into in His service?

The woman taken in adultery does not have to die in her sins. Her encounter with the Light of the world does not kill her, it wakens life in her. The Light is not only judgment, but at the same time, mercy and forgiveness. It does not only discover, it also covers up again. It not only reveals, it also revitalises, strengthens and cleanses. The power of our blood is certainly amazing enough, but the power of Jesus's blood is even greater. This adulteress has been released as a result of her meeting with the Light of the world, freed not from her sexuality but from its tyranny. Should not this woman's liberation give new courage to those of us who are similarly oppressed? The fact that she has been able to find release from the demons of unchastity must give even the least of us hope of help in such need: 'Neither do I condemn thee: go, and sin no more.' This woman has seen the truth of the words: 'Then said Jesus to those Jews which believed on him, If ye continue in my word, then are ye my disciples indeed; and ye shall know the truth, and the truth shall make you free. . . . Verily, verily, I say unto you, Whosoever committeth sin is the servant of sin, . . . If the Son therefore shall make you free, ye shall be free indeed.'

However, the Light that shines, discovers, works, heals, cleanses, helps, covers up and saves, is under attack. Its struggle with the darkness that is trying to overpower it continues day and night. We are not between the two; the Light has come to us and is fighting around us. Indeed, nowhere, I think, does Jesus speak so seriously about the power of darkness as here. Jesus calls the lord of darkness, the Devil, a liar and the father of all lies. And the lord of darkness is also at work. Jesus has every reason to know that he is working hard, because His people, the seed of Abraham and the chosen race, are led by men who will have nothing to do with the Light, although they proudly call themselves 'children of Abraham.' Darkness can gain power even over the chosen people, who have daily intercourse with the word of God, who say their prayers every hour, give a tenth of everything they have to the Church and observe two days of fasting every week. Behind the cloak of religion and in the garb of virtue, darkness finds its most dangerous accomplices. That is why Jesus says to the chosen leaders of the chosen people, 'You who call yourselves "children of Abraham" are children of the Devil. Your father is not Abraham but the Devil, the father of lies and a murderer from the beginning.' This grossly sinful adulteress has found salvation, but Jesus accuses the guardians of religion with the words, 'Ye are of your father the devil, and the lusts of your father ye will do. He was a murderer from the beginning, and abode not in the truth, because there was no truth in him. When he speaketh a lie, he speaketh of his own: for he is a liar and the father of it.'

Although He is living in a hostile land, nevertheless Christ is still the Light, and the Light has victory on its side, even though it has to fight day and night. Evil can in fact never win. We have compared the Light of Christ with the sun, and similarly we can compare evil with the moon. The moon can shine too but its light is inconstant and changeable. Admittedly moonlight can be very strong: it can deceive, misguide and ensnare because it glitters, and flows and shimmers, but it is never bright; it remains twilight. That is what the Devil is like: that is what the power of darkness is like. Nor can the moon shine of its own accord; it is dependent on the sun for its borrowed light. The power of evil is dependent in the same way. But Christ is still the Light of the world, of the whole world, even the Light of Hell and the Devil, just as the sun is the light of the moon. And only a man who walks in the Light is safe from the power of darkness. It is just as the Evangelist John says on the very first page of his book, 'The light shineth in darkness; and the darkness comprehended [or overcame] it not.'

It is interesting that Jesus does not break off the argument with

His adversaries. He goes so far as to call them children of the Devil, which only increases their hostility to boiling rage. They are impenitent to the point of saying, 'Thou art a Samaritan, and hast a devil.' Despite that Jesus does not turn away from them, for it is at this stage of incipient blindness that they need Him more than ever before. He goes on appealing to them as He says, ' "Before Abraham was, I am. . . . Your father Abraham rejoiced to see my day; and he saw it, and was glad." If your father Abraham rejoiced to see "my day," why do you who call yourselves sons of Abraham not rejoice too? Why are you so hostile? It is no use calling on your father Abraham, because I am before him.' But they do not understand how He can be before Abraham. That is a mystery even to His friends, let alone His enemies.

There is one last remarkable thing: 'Then took they up stones to cast at him.' How extraordinary the ways of God can be! At the beginning of this chapter there are stones lying ready for the adulteress, at the end they are lifted against Jesus, who has saved this adulteress from dying in her sins. In the end all stones intended for the sinner strike Jesus. And He bares His head to them. Stones will strike Him, but not at this point in the story, for the hour has not yet come. Yet strike Him they will. And when He bares His head for the poor sinner His victory over death and Hell is complete. There we have irrefutable proof that He is the Light of the world.

Jesus, on the Sabbath, Heals a Man Born Blind

And as Jesus passed by, he saw a man which was blind from his birth. And his disciples asked him, saying, Master, who did sin, this man, or his parents, that he was born blind? Jesus answered, Neither hath this man sinned, nor his parents: but that the works of God should be made manifest in him. I must work the works of him that sent me, while it is day: the night cometh, when no man can work. As long as I am in the world, I am the light of the world. When he had thus spoken, he spat on the ground, and made clay of the spittle, and he anointed the eyes of the blind man with the clay. And said unto him, Go, wash in the pool of Siloam, (which is, by interpretation, Sent.) He went his way therefore, and washed, and came seeing.

The neighbours therefore, and they which before had seen him that he was blind, said, Is not this he that sat and begged? Some said, This is he: others said, He is like him: but he said, I am he. Therefore said they unto him, How were thine eyes opened? He answered and said, A man that is called Jesus made clay, and anointed mine eyes, and said unto me, Go to the pool of Siloam, and wash: and I went and washed, and I received sight. Then they said unto him, Where is he? He said, I know not.

They brought to the Pharisees him that aforetime was blind. And it was the sabbath day when Jesus made the clay, and opened his eyes. Then again the Pharisees also asked him how he had received his sight. He said unto them, He put clay upon mine eyes, and I washed, and do see. Therefore said some of the Pharisees, This man is not of God, because he keepeth not the sabbath day. Others said, How can a man that is a sinner do such miracles? And there was a division among them. They say unto the blind man again, What sayest thou of him, that he hath opened thine eyes? He said, He is a prophet. But the Jews did not believe concerning him, that he had been blind, and received his sight, until they called the parents of him that had received his sight. And they asked them, saying, Is this your son, who ye say was born blind? how then doth he now see? His parents answered them and said, We know that this is our son, and that he was born blind: but by what means he now seeth, we know not; or who hath opened his eyes, we know not: he is of age; ask him: he shall speak for himself. These words spake his parents, because they feared the Jews: for the Jews had agreed already, that if any man did confess that he was Christ, he should be put out of the synagogue. Therefore said his parents, He is of age; ask him. Then again called they the man that was blind, and said unto him, Give God the praise: we know that this man is a sinner. He answered and said, Whether he be a sinner or no, I know not: one thing I know, that, whereas I was blind, now I see. Then said they to him again, What did he do to thee? how opened he thine eyes? He answered them, I have told you already, and ye did not hear: wherefore would ye hear it again? will ye also be his disciples? Then they reviled him, and said, Thou art his disciple; but we are Moses' disciples. We know that God spake unto Moses: as for this fellow, we know not from whence he is. The man answered and said unto them, Why herein is a marvellous thing, that ye know not from whence he is, and yet he hath opened mine eyes. Now we know that God heareth not sinners: but if any man be a worshipper of God, and doeth his will, him he heareth. Since the world began was it not heard that any man opened the eyes of one that was born blind. If this man were not of God, he could do nothing. They answered and said unto him, Thou wast altogether born in sins, and dost thou teach us? And they cast him out.

Jesus heard that they had cast him out; and when he had found him, he said unto him, Dost thou believe on the Son of God? He answered and said, Who is he, Lord, that I might believe on him? And Jesus said unto him, Thou hast both seen him, and it is he that talketh with thee. And he said, Lord, I believe. And he worshipped him.

And Jesus said, For judgment I am come into this world, that they which see not might see: and they which see might be made blind. And some of the Pharisees which were with him heard these words, and said unto him, Are we blind also? Jesus said unto them, If ye were blind, ye should have no sin: but now ye say, We see; therefore your sin remaineth.

[IX]

The man is blind, but as if that were not enough, he is poor as well. Instead of being able to hide himself from the eyes of the world, which is surely the desire of all infirm people, he finds himself forced by circumstances to exhibit his blindness to the public to attract charity. His parents are still alive but they have made a professional beggar of him. Yet the worst thing is that he did not become blind, he was born blind. Everyone knows that, and to the people passing him on their way in and out of the Temple it means that this man is burdened with a particularly sinful secret or some dark curse, very probably inherited from his parents. Later on the Pharisees fling at him, 'Thou wast altogether born in sins, and dost thou teach us?' The question that seems to come automatically to every visitor to the Temple when they see him even springs to the lips of Jesus's disciples: 'Master, who did sin, this man, or his parents, that he was born blind?' A blind beggar, born blind – what a hopeless case! He may receive quite a lot of alms. But hope? Not one brass farthing's worth.

One day Jesus passes by this beggar. And to the disciples' question we hear Him answer, 'Neither hath this man sinned, nor his parents: but that the works of God should be made manifest in him.' These words break like a ray of light through the forlorn darkness that broods over the blind man. Jesus is asserting, 'This man is here for a purpose.' Nobody has ever said anything like that to him before. Until now he has thought that other people might be here for a purpose, but not he. Until now nobody has been able to understand why such a creature should have been brought into the world at all, let alone allowed to live. According to sound common sense, a life like this is useless and only a burden to others. A life like this does not even do honour to its Maker. This poor fellow is to the Creator what a burnt loaf is to the baker, or a crooked furrow to the farmer, in the opinion of so-called 'sound' common sense. And Jesus sees this infirm man and says, 'This man is here so that the works of God may be made manifest in him.' This very man who was born blind is now to bring honour and glory to God; this same beggar is to become yet another sign of God's majesty and power. His life is in fact to acquire the highest meaning that a human life can have in this world: the works of God are to be revealed in him. This can only put our sound common sense to shame, and make us own in wonder that if such a thing is possible even in a man like this, then there cannot be any creature in God's wide world in whom the same miracle cannot be worked. How brightly the light is beginning to shine!

This gives light to many another being whose life is in darkness. We all know of such cases, some of them perhaps very close to us, where one is tempted to ask, 'Why on earth are these people here?' They cannot or will not work, but only take up other people's time, so that the obvious question is, 'Can there be any meaning in such an existence?' The answer is: 'Yes, an existence like this has a final, sacred, incontestable meaning. The works of God are made manifest in these lives, which are surrounded by God's love, mercy, forbearance and patience in order that His power and splendour may be revealed.' There is probably someone here who often feels that there is no significance or purpose in his life and who wonders, 'Why am I here? Why don't I throw my life away?' If any of you feel like this, remember that Jesus said to a beggar who was blind from birth, 'You are here so that in you, in you of all people, the works of God may be made manifest.' Since that day when God gave these words to the world there at the entrance to the Temple, there is no life under the sun that is without meaning or reason. And if the only purpose in such a life were to give healthy people cause to think again, and to thank God, and to stop taking for granted those things that are not a matter of course, then that life would not be worthless.

In fact, these words of Jesus's give a final meaning to all life. From the point of view of eternity, my life and yours are not so very different from that of this blind man. Fundamentally we are all poor and blind, and our hopes and deeds are evil from the very first. Let us not be so presumptuous as to suppose that while this blind man's life is without meaning, the lives of us normal, healthy people are full of usefulness, reason, and purpose. In the end, this world and humanity do not derive their significance from themselves, but from what God makes manifest in them. The only reason why the world has not decayed into dust, and mankind has not perished, is so that God may reveal His works in us. It is God's will and pleasure to show His patience and faithfulness in this poor humanity, blind from birth. First of all He did this by sending His prophets, and finally He sent His Son, Jesus Christ, who has made the works of God manifest in the world. We have been given Christmas, Good Friday, Easter, Ascension Day and Whitsun. And Jesus will yet show this world what perfection means. God will create a new earth and we are promised a new Heaven. The world exists today so that the works of God may be made manifest in it through Jesus Christ. This is like a window, opening to let in the fresh air from the mountains of God. Knowing the truth, we can breathe freely now that humanity and the world have a purpose: they are a vehicle for the manifestation of God's works.

Of course it is God's works and not ours that give this world its meaning. We are not here to show off, and to boast how wonderfully we have advanced in learning and technology. That it is the works of God rather than ours is shown strangely, and simply, and almost repulsively in the way that Christ glorifies the name of the Creator through this man who was born blind. Christ spits on the ground, and makes a paste out of spittle and dust: this He smears on the blind man's eyelids and tells him to go and wash in the nearby pool of Siloam. The man obeys and comes back, able to see. Far be it from us to try to explain this strange procedure, for it passes our comprehension. It is as puzzling to us as Christ's writing on the ground when He freed the woman taken in adultery. Is Christ trying to show that He, who in the beginning created the world out of nothing, and made man from dust, can perfect His work with dust and spittle? It is striking that Christ performs this cure with such ceremony. He knows that it will be followed by an official investigation, for once more it is the Sabbath. Perhaps He intends these actions to be so conclusively clear that not even the most wicked mind will be able to dispute them later on.

If what follows is not unexpected to Jesus, it comes as a great surprise to us. 'Since the world began was it not heard that any man opened the eyes of one that was born blind.' When these words of the once-blind man really come true; when the works of God are revealed in such an incomparably wonderful way as here; when such a miracle occurs, then we would naturally expect rejoicing among the people, who are allowed to witness it. But that is not the case. Now a thorny hedge of human meanness suddenly grows up around this wonderful act of God. How can we explain that? It is because human beings are usually embarrassed when God sets to work: it has never been otherwise. God's actions have always made things difficult for men. The people through whom God has worked on earth have always become a source of discomfort to their fellows, beginning with Abraham down to John the Baptist, and that other John to whom God sent prophetic visions while he was in exile on the island of Patmos. His work in the world through Jesus Christ was a great vexation to everyone, particularly to Herod and the priests, Caiaphas and Pilate. So, when we long for a revival of the Church and complain about the godlessness of our generation, let us be quite clear about what we mean as we pray for a new Kingdom of God. When the final revelation of God's works begins, many people will be frightened instead of rejoicing. The affairs of our church communities and councils will no longer run so smoothly. When the Spirit of God begins to move, even the most religious of men will find their peace and serenity disturbed, and their interests threatened, and will begin to resist, with strife and storms as a result. For God's opportunities are so often an embarrassment to us.

And now let us return to our blind man who has received his sight. His neighbours are the first people to show embarrassment.

They ask him whether it is really he or his double. Instead of rushing up and shaking him by the hand, or breaking out in joy and gratitude, they cross-examine him and ask him how, when, where and who? And when he mentions the name of Jesus they feel guilty, for He is the man whom they wanted to stone. And now it occurs to them that it was the Sabbath when Jesus healed this man, just as it was when he cured the impotent man by the pool of Bethesda. Surely the devil must be behind this? The Pharisees must hear about this. And soon the whole affair is like a court case. When God acts, in these times and this world, the dock is always ready; for miracles are an embarrassment to us.

The Pharisees' embarrassment is no less great. They are annoyed because this wretched man, whom a short time ago they accused of being of the Devil (ch. VIII), has healed a man commonly known to be blind. This cure cannot possibly be of God. They resort to every kind of cunning to disprove what has happened. First of all they interrogate the man who has been healed and try to confuse him. Finally they send for his parents and ask them, 'Is this really your son?' 'Yes.' 'Was he born blind?' 'Yes.' 'Has he received his sight?' 'Yes.' The parents have to confirm everything.

The parents are affected too. This blind child has been a source of embarrassment to them ever since he was born, but never so acutely as now that he has gained his sight. Until now they have occasionally been ashamed or hurt, when they saw passers-by cast meaningful glances at him, and whisper to each other. What meanness and unkindness the mother of such a child has to suffer from other people! Having a child like this must often have grieved these parents. But now that he has been healed by God's hand, they are not only embarrassed and ashamed, they are afraid. At least they have been spared that so far, but now they are frightened because the authorities threaten to banish them from the Temple, a fate worse than exile. Banishment and excommunication have always threatened those who are identified with the miracles of God. The parents' embarrassment has reached such a pitch that they almost disown their child now that he has received his sight, which they would never have done while he was blind. They defend themselves with the desperate words, 'He is of age; ask him: he shall speak for himself.' They would like to wash their hands of the whole affair. The effect of God's intervention in the life of a child is often sorrow and anxiety for the parents. It cannot have been easy to be the mother of St Augustine, nor a trifle to confess to being the father of Martin Luther: and similarly it is difficult for these parents to admit that they are the father and mother of this man who has been healed. The great anxiety that he caused them previously is now increased a thousand-fold, for he has been the subject of a miracle, and has become an embarrassment to his fellow-men.

And what about the man who has been healed? How often he must have been embarrassed in the past because of his affliction! But he was never so embarrassed then as he is now that he can see, for his case is unheard-of and dangerous. He is seeing the world for the very first time, and is like a child that must talk about everything it sees. It is dangerous for him to see the world, yet he sees even more. He sees Heaven too and he sees Jesus for the first time. To see Heaven and Jesus is very dangerous.

The blind man has always been lonely, but now that he has seen Jesus he becomes all the more lonely, with the loneliness of those whose eyes have been opened. What is more important is that he becomes a believer. As the darkness of his senses disappears, it is wonderful to see how one window after another opens, and how the night of the spirit and his distrust of people fade. He becomes a believer and a professor of his faith. Today Basle is celebrating the opening of its new university buildings, a great event for professors and students as well as the citizens of the town, at a time when believers and 'professors' are so urgently needed. This man who has been healed becomes a believer and a professor of Jesus Christ. But now these people who were the professors of their time, constantly repeating, 'We know . . . We know. . . ,' try to throw dust into the newly-opened eyes. They call themselves professors, yet they want to close the eyes and mouth of this man because he has begun to see too much. But

God will not allow it. The man remains a follower of Jesus Christ, a professor in word and deed. In fact the greater the danger the more definite he becomes. At first we hear him say, 'A man that is called Jesus healed me.' Then, in spite of their contempt, he says to the Pharisees, 'He is a prophet.' Later, when they revile Jesus in front of him, he states fearlessly, 'If this man were not of God, he could do nothing.' Finally he comes to believe in Jesus and worships Him, and says, 'Lord, I believe.' Through the grace of God this man confesses Jesus Christ. That is how God's works are revealed in man. It is God's work when he can say, 'I can see,' and again it is God's splendid work when he can say, 'I believe.' They threaten him, but he professes his faith and so in the end is banished from the Temple. The so-called professors expel the only true professor and believer in Jerusalem. That sort of thing always happens when Christ begins to open people's eyes. When the work of God is revealed in a man, he is expelled by society, as he no longer fits in. That is what has happened here.

Christ is at work today too and His works are still being revealed in men. It is not evening yet: it is not yet the night when no man can work. There is still time to make your decision. But the night is coming when it will be too late and nobody will be able to work any more. However, it is still day and so, in the original text, in connexion with the man who was born blind, the Lord says, 'We must work . . . while it is day.' The same words are an invitation to His disciples and His followers, for all time.

In saying that we must work, Christ means that we must let God work in us; that we must let our eyes be opened and, if necessary, become lonely for Christ's sake, or even become unpopular and be cast out from society. Up till now this man has let himself be led because he was born blind. Now that he can see, he allows Christ to lead him where He will. This helps to explain Christ's glorious work in the world today: He creates men who allow themselves to be led by Him; He creates professors and believers.

The Parable of the Door to the Sheep-fold

Verily, verily, I say unto you, He that entereth not by the door into the sheepfold, but climbeth up some other way, the same is a thief and a robber. But he that entereth in by the door is the shepherd of the sheep. To him the porter openeth; and the sheep hear his voice: and he calleth his own sheep by name, and leadeth them out. And when he putteth forth his own sheep, he goeth before them, and the sheep follow him: for they know his voice. And a stranger will they not follow, but will flee from him: for they know not the voice of strangers. This parable spake Jesus unto them: but they understood not what things they were which he spake unto them. Then said Jesus unto them again, Verily, verily, I say unto you, I am the door of the sheep. All that ever came before me are thieves and robbers: but the sheep did not hear them. I am the door: by me if any man enter in, he shall be saved, and shall go in and out, and find pasture. The thief cometh not, but for to steal, and to kill, and to destroy: I am come that they might have life, and that they might have it more abundantly. [x. 1–10]

'This parable spake Jesus unto them: but they understood not what things they were which he spake unto them.' It is important for us to note most carefully right at the outset whom the Lord is addressing here. Christ is engaged in conversation with particular people; the priests, Pharisees and scribes. These are teachers and shepherds of the people, and their social, economic, intellectual and spiritual leaders. To these false shepherds the Lord explains what a true shepherd is by telling them the parable of the door to the sheep-fold. He says, 'I am the door of the sheep.' And He insists on it a second time with: 'I am the door,' and 'he that entereth in by the door is the shepherd of the sheep.' In other words, the true leader, teacher and shepherd of his people is one who goes in to the sheep by the door, that is through Jesus Christ.

Christ says of the true shepherd, 'To him the porter openeth.' The porter is God, the Father of Jesus Christ, God, the chief Shepherd, opens the door to the man who enters the sheep-fold through Christ. That man has not reached his goal by his own efforts; God Himself has called him. The seal of true leadership is that it is a gift of God, and recognised as such by both leaders and led. Fortunate indeed is the land that has leaders, teachers and shepherds appointed by God, shepherds who are called.

That brings us up against the most important consideration that must occupy our minds today, the first Sunday of the new year, namely the question of true leadership. In the year that we have just begun, the decisive question for us as Christians and Europeans will be: have we in Church and State, in economics and politics, in civilian life and the armed forces, leaders, teachers and pastors who are true shepherds, shepherds who reached their positions through the door and through Jesus Christ? Have the leaders, teachers and shepherds of our own nation been called by God, so that they feel themselves responsible to God for all their actions? Dare we ask the question, 'Have we leaders, teachers and shepherds by the grace of God or by the grace of the party or the purse? Has the porter opened the door to our shepherds, or was it some influential relation?' Nations which have shepherds who are deputies of God are living nations.

All this reminds us of our Christian duty on the first Sunday of the new year. The Lord does not give us time for vain and gloomy meditation about the future. The Lord Himself reminds us of our real duty as a community to our own and to all nations: to pray for God's gift of true leadership in this coming year.

Pray in the first place that in the Church we may have leaders and teachers who are true shepherds, particularly in our own Church. Pray for shepherds who can proclaim God's Word with such conviction that their sermons will have something of that authority shown on the first page of the Bible where we read, 'God said, Let there be . . . and there was.' Pray that from now on sermons will no longer be aimlessly heard and delivered, but that they will inspire decision and action for the honour of God. But to speak and hear like this is a gift that can only be bestowed on us by the porter's opening the door: that is to say, through God's gracious condescension, His almighty presence and powerful intervention. If that does not happen, and the wind of Heaven remains still, and the door of Heaven stays shut, or, more precisely if we shut ourselves off from Heaven, then there can be no new year, nor ever will be. All of us who call ourselves Christians must feel concern and shame, that year after year things remain as they always were, in spite of the fact that the door has been opened, and Christmas has come. So pray that the words of the clergy may acquire conviction, and we shall pray that you may hear them in this new year. Pray for shepherds, in the pulpit, with no fear of men, who will bow before nothing but God's word. Pray for shepherds of the soul, who have not smuggled themselves into the fold, but who have come to the sheep through the door and who are inspired by the certainty of their own salvation to proclaim salvation to the world. Pray for shepherds in and out of the pulpit, whether they have specific office or not; pray for everyone in God's vineyard; pray that in the near future God will pour out a new pastoral spirit over His community. Soon it may be too late.

And further, pray that Christ will awaken shepherds in schools and universities, shepherds who know that 'the fear of the Lord is the beginning of wisdom,' and who take their place at the desk or lectern in the full knowledge of their responsibility to God. Pray that our people may have teachers who come to the sheep through the door.

Pray that God will awaken shepherds among our economic leaders, financiers, captains of industry, company chairmen and directors, who have entered in by the door and who know that they are responsible to God for every penny at their command. Pray that in our industrial life there may be shepherds who have come to the sheep through God, knowing that a powerful position implies not only privilege but duty.

Pray, too, for true shepherds in politics. Do not say that politics has nothing to do with religion. There is nothing that is not included in the Word of God. Pray for shepherds in politics, who are ordained and empowered by God, and who are prepared to accept and wield authority in full understanding of the true Biblical sense of the word.

Finally, pray that our husbands, brothers and sons who are on military service may have superiors who know that the way to the sheep leads through the door. The more I speak to men on leave and read letters from soldiers, the more I realise what responsibility there is in military command, and what an influence a single N.C.O. or officer can exercise for good or evil. The other day I heard of a lieutenant who goes to church on Sundays, even when it is not compulsory, and who has given a small group of soldiers the courage to do the same. I read a letter from the wife of a labourer to her husband's colonel, thanking him for sending her husband back from military service a much better man. Therefore pray for shepherds in the services too, who have gained their rank and position by way of the true door.

But now this leads us to the question: if that is so, is there anyone in our democracy who has not been called to be a leader, teacher or shepherd, however obscure his position may be? What about mothers and fathers? They are called to be shepherds to their families, and even if they have only one little sheep to guard, both they and the child are to be pitied if they do not approach him by way of the door. I know an old lady, living alone like so many others, in a ground-floor flat, who talks to all the neighbouring children who run in and out past her door. Quietly and cheerfully she plays her part as shepherdess to the children, as God has bidden her. So we are all called to act as shepherds, if only to a friend who is weaker than ourselves. And surely every one of us knows of somebody who needs the helping hand of a shepherd. 'Am I my brother's keeper?' The answer is yes. Let us not become idle and lazy, but pray ceaselessly that God may make us a 'nation of shepherds,' a nation of Jesus Christ's shepherds, who come to the sheep through the door.

And now God shows us a true shepherd at work. There is a relationship based on mutual trust between a nation and true leaders, teachers and shepherds. Of the true shepherd we read, 'The sheep hear his voice.' Thus it is again a matter of hearing. A nation of shepherds of Jesus Christ has no taint of that deadly mistrust, where each man suspects that everyone else is working only for his own interests. A burnt child dreads the fire. Sheep who have often met the wolf in sheep's clothing are bound to become distrustful in the end. Only where the leaders of a nation have entered in to the sheep through the door can the sheep have confidence that what is spoken, written and promised by authority is founded on truth and faith. Pray, therefore, that soon it may be said of our nation, 'the sheep hear his voice.'

Not only do the sheep know their true shepherd, but conversely a true shepherd knows his sheep, each one by name. How touching are the words, 'and he calleth his own sheep by name, and leadeth them out.' These sheep used simply to be numbers; now they have names. Our generation is in danger of becoming nameless. But we want to have names, and we want to trust the great Shepherd: we do not want to be a nation of numbers, and will not rest until each one of us has a name again. That is what the great Shepherd wants: 'He calleth his own sheep by name, and leadeth them out.'

And we also read of the great Shepherd, 'And when he putteth forth his own sheep, he goeth before them.' True leaders, true teachers and true shepherds go before their sheep, because the great shepherd goes before: in leading their flocks they follow Him. These words are particularly applicable to us university people, who have had the special privilege of continuing our studies longer than others. We have not received our university education so as to be able to fleece and slaughter the sheep for our personal benefit, but in order to guard, and tend them and lead them out to pasture. He is a bad shepherd who abuses his position by sending others on ahead where sacrifice is called for, and who will only lead the way when it is in his own interest. So pray for shepherds who will lead the way in self-sacrifice, and who know, through the great Shepherd, the meaning of the words: 'And when he putteth forth his own sheep, he goeth before them.'

In return, the true shepherd will receive the gift of true followers 'And,' it goes on to say, 'the sheep follow him: for they know his voice. And a stranger will they not follow, but will flee from him: for they know not the voice of strangers.' Today, not without reason, we have a certain reserve towards all things foreign. And there is a widespread fear that we may some day be ruled by foreign masters. This is no bad thing as long as it is a conscious defence against open or secret anti-Christian powers and godless shepherds and false leaders. But we cannot help suspecting that this exaggerated fear of foreign influences and ideas, that is prevalent here and there, is a sign of a guilty conscience rather than watchfulness. A nation whose leaders and teachers are true Christians has not the same reason to fear foreign infiltration as has a nation that lacks the spirit of true leadership. Only when we are our brothers' keepers in our hearts can we be truly on our guard against dangers from without. If we protect our weaker brothers as God means us to do, we are giving our country the best possible safeguard. But a ruling class that has estranged itself from its own people lays itself open to the judgment implied in God's words, 'a stranger will they not follow. . . .'

But now a further question. 'Is what Jesus shows us here not too good to be true?' Even if we were only discussing a fine ideal, we should not want to despise it, for it would at least be worthy of respect, and it is as well not to laugh at people with such ideals. But what Christ says here is in fact more than an ideal; in Jesus Christ, the great Shepherd, it is a miracle and reality. It is the miracle of the imitation of Christ. The Apostle Paul never tires of describing it to us, although it is not easy to describe in terms which everyone can understand. It is high time for us to realise exactly what Christ means when He says, 'I am the door,' and when He calls people to enter by the door. Entering into Jesus Christ means letting oneself become part of Jesus's death and

Resurrection. In another place the Apostle says of Christians that they were baptised into the death and Resurrection of Jesus. 'We are always bearing about in the body the dying of the Lord Jesus, that the life also of Jesus might be made manifest in our body.' And he says, 'If any man be in Christ, he is a new creature.' We could put it like this: as we are all called to be shepherds of Jesus Christ, so are we all called first of all to become sheep of the great Shepherd. If a man first becomes a true sheep of Jesus Christ, then he can become a shepherd. Christ became a lamb and let Himself be sacrificed. By so doing He became the great Shepherd of all nations, and of all time, and no man can become a true shepherd other than through the Cross of Christ. We are concerned here with final and mysterious reality, the miracle and mystery of our salvation through Christ. There the Cross is the source of inspiration for the true shepherd; the Cross is the way and the door to the sheep. We can understand now that the door we are speaking of is very narrow, like the way that leads to it and through it, and that there are very few who can take that way. But let us pray to the Lord that in all nations and especially in ours these few will become many.

There is another way into the sheep-fold than through the door. We can bypass the Cross of Christ and ignore the door. Christ uses very harsh words to describe this other method of entering, whether it be in priest's garb or under the cloak of philanthropy. He calls it entering as a thief and a robber. The way round the Cross is the way of selfishness and complacency. The way round Christ's sacrifice, so often taken with the best of intentions, finally leads time and again to fratricide. The man who has passed by Christ crucified, however good his reasons, has always fallen into the abyss of his own self-sufficiency and pride, and has become a thief and a murderer. Like everything else, this has an application in society from top to bottom, from large-scale robbery and murder to the poor man who robs someone even poorer and beats him to death. 'Verily, verily, I say unto you, He that entereth not by the door into the sheep-fold, but climbeth up some other way, the same is a thief and a robber.

... The thief cometh not, but for to steal, and to kill, and to destroy.'

The times in which we live are so 'thievish' and murderous that they stand in opposition to Christ's offer: 'By me if any man enter in, he shall be saved, and shall go in and out, and find pasture.' One thing we can be sure about at the beginning of the new year is that the nations are faint and 'scattered abroad, as the sheep having no shepherd'. Why is this? 'Wide is the gate and broad is the way' that leads past Christ, and many there be that take that way. Let us pray to the great Shepherd that these many may become few, for it is God's gracious will that many, indeed all, should enter in by the door.

So again we hear the call of Christ: 'I am the door.' How good it is of God not to leave us standing, shivering, in the gateway of the new year but to call to us like a cheerful shepherd, 'I am the door.' There really is a door! With these words the future is opened, and whoever wants to go through the open door need never be afraid again. So here is a future. Are we going to go through the door, or are we going to smuggle ourselves past it into the new year, as we have so often done before? If so, there will be no real new year for us. Or are we going to pray, for once, from the bottom of our hearts, for courage to risk the step over this decisive threshold? If we enter this new year through the door, we shall thereby be able to face everything that the year may bring. And even if this year should bring death to us, through the door of Christ we can even go into death and not be lost. 'I am the door; by me if any man enter in, he shall be saved, and shall go in and out, and find pasture.'

The Parable of the Good Shepherd

I am the good shepherd: the good shepherd giveth his life for the sheep. But he that is an hireling, and not the shepherd, whose own the sheep are not, seeth the wolf coming, and leaveth the sheep, and fleeth: and the wolf catcheth them, and scattereth the sheep. The hireling fleeth, because he is an hireling, and careth not for the sheep. I am the good shepherd, and know my sheep, and am known of mine. As the Father knoweth me, even so know I the Father: and I lay down my life for the sheep. And other sheep I have, which are not of this fold: them also I must bring, and they shall hear my voice; and there shall be one fold, and one shepherd. Therefore doth my Father love me, because I lay down my life, that I might take it again. No man taketh it from me, but I lay it down of myself. I have power to lay it down, and I have power to take it again. This commandment have I received of my Father.

There was a division therefore again among the Jews for these sayings. And many of them said, He hath a devil, and is mad; why hear ye him? Others said, These are not the words of him that hath a devil. Can a devil open the eyes of the blind?

[x. 11–21]

You will probably agree with me that these familiar words about the good Shepherd, have a special significance today. The wolf is on the prowl; his howling keeps us awake at night, and even in the daytime he will not leave us in peace. We might call this the day of the wolf. But the words spoken by Christ are for all time and apply today as much as ever: 'I am the good shepherd.' The wolf appears under many different names and in various guises. To most of us he simply means war, with all its implications:

hunger, cold, homelessness, refugees, degradation, and servitude of the body and the soul. We are afraid of all these wolves, which surprise and scatter the sheep. And Christ understands our fear, and He knows that we shall be frightened when this happens. That is why He insists: 'Fear not. "I am the good shepherd." '

At least the appearance of the wolf has had one good result, in so far as it has shaken this self-confident generation out of its complacent apathy. The howling of the wolf has caused many a sheep to start looking for its Shepherd. We have reached the stage where the nations feel an increasingly acute need for a greater, almighty protector. Psalms XC and XCI, which tell of the protection of the highest, and a refuge for ever and ever, are today again among the most widely read in the Bible. The whole world is prepared to accept God as its chief Guardian. Even heads of state call on the Almighty, though their appeals do not always do Him credit. You might say, therefore, that the chances of the Gospel of the good Shepherd are now improving. The good Shepherd has become popular again, as a general safeguard against frost, nakedness, hunger and danger.

But the heathen have always had their tutelary gods and goddesses. They set up their protective deities on their huts like lightning conductors. There is an uncomfortably pagan element in the acceptance of God, merely as the protector of our public or private property. But the God of the Bible is not like that. He does not give His followers any guarantee that they will live together, comfortably and permanently, in their homes. The man who comforts and teaches may have a willing audience, but let him not base his comfort on the Word of God. We cannot employ the good Shepherd as a reliable watchman, or hang Him round our necks like an amulet.

Yet He says, 'I am the good shepherd.' But the meaning behind these words is not what people like to hear. It is not we who can have Him: it is He who wants to have us. We are not to use Him for our ends: rather does He want to have us at His disposal. There is no mention of our property and its protection. Christ is talking from first to last of what belongs to Him, of His property and His possessions. Not for nothing does He differentiate clearly between Himself and the hireling, 'whose own the sheep are not'. The sheep are His. He is no hireling, He is the owner and as such calls the sheep His own. And as owner He is not prepared to be deprived of any part of what belongs to Him. That is the difference between servant and master. The servant protects the sheep, but in the end he runs away because his own life is worth more to him than the animals in his care. That is his right as a hireling. But the shepherd who owns the sheep does not run away. He is prepared to protect what belongs to him with his very life. That is what 'I am the good shepherd' means – 'I am the master of the flock.' We are reminded of the psalm, 'The Lord is my shepherd.' Yes, our Shepherd is the Lord.

So the Shepherd no longer appears as a harmless figure. We can see in this parable a strong hand, as it were, stretching out to us, and all that we have, and summoning us to give ourselves up. This hand has been stretched out for a long time, but too often we have eluded its redeeming grasp. God's hour may not be convenient for us, but it is conceivable that there are a few people here this morning, for whom God's hour has struck, and who did not shrink from the morning cold, because they have heard the call of the good Shepherd and because the hand of the Lord is ready to receive them. When someone surrenders to the good Shepherd, it is a miracle at which the angels in Heaven rejoice.

But why should this Lord and Shepherd be interested in us? What does He want of us, and what does He see in us? What does He expect of us? Does He not know how unrewarding man is? And does He not know how tainted we are with sin? Of course He knows. He understands His people perfectly, and yet He is always pursuing them. It is not our strength, nor our riches, nor our goodness that attracts Him: quite the contrary; it is our poverty and need, our imperfection and weakness: in a word, our sin. It is our sin that urges Him to be our Shepherd. What a strange Shepherd! He does not think of His own advantage, but of the lost condition of the sheep. That is why this Shepherd will not rest until He has gathered them into His fold. He has no equal among the shepherds of this world. St Luke writes of Christ the Shepherd: 'Then drew near unto him all the publicans and sinners for to hear him. And the Pharisees and scribes murmured, saying, This man receiveth sinners and eateth with them. And he spake this parable unto them, saying, What man of you, having an hundred sheep, if he lose one of them, doth not leave the ninety and nine in the wilderness, and go after that which is lost, until he find it? And when he hath found it, he layeth it on his shoulders, rejoicing. And when he cometh home, he calleth together his friends and neighbours, saying unto them, Rejoice with me; for I have found my sheep which was lost. I say unto you, That likewise joy shall be in heaven over one sinner that repenteth, more than over ninety and nine just persons, which need no repentance.'

For hundreds who are satisfied with themselves, there are a few who feel discontented. If there is one man here today who feels that he would like to get up and walk out because his life seems impossibly bungled, and who sees no hope of changing, to him I should like to say that the Good Shepherd, that true master of the lost sheep, has been waiting for him, in particular, until this very day. This Shepherd, who seeks what is lost, did not Himself become one of the lost for nothing. He has no equal among shepherds, in that He becomes a Shepherd on the Cross. Five times in this short extract we read, 'I lay down my life for the sheep.' However much our inclination draws us to a general protector, there is no one that we could prefer to the Shepherd on the Cross. This Shepherd on the Cross has been defeated and His flock scattered. If what we want is a powerful earthly guardian, this defeated Shepherd is no use to us, and our best course is to turn our backs on Him in disappointment. This crucified Shepherd is a source of irritation to all those who seek their own ends and are intent on security and power. It is conceivable that you have come here this morning only to be irritated and to refuse the Shepherd. Even so, the Word of God will have had its deciding and dividing effect. Here, before the defeated and crucified Shepherd, the decision is made whether you will go to the right or the left, with the sheep or the goats, with the blessed or with the damned. This is the place where ears are not only opened, but also where they close irrevocably: 'There was a division therefore again among the Jews for these sayings. And many of them said, He hath a devil, and is mad; why hear ye him? Others said, These are not the words of him that hath a devil.'

However, the man who has the grace not to turn his back on the crucified Christ, but stays here, can learn the greatest mystery of all time: the defeated Man, wounded and bleeding, whose cry from the Cross is utterly forlorn, does not die unnecessarily, but because He wants to in obedience to His Father's will. It is by His Father's instructions that He hangs there helplessly. His death is His sacrifice rather than His fate: 'No man taketh it [my life] from me, but I lay it down of myself. I have power to lay it down, and I have power to take it again.' But it is the will and command of the Father that all men should benefit by this supreme sacrifice. So the Shepherd of the lost has to descend into the deepest abyss, and climb to the highest peak, and go to the outermost edge of God's domain. This sacrifice is 'for the sheep.' Because the condition of the sheep is so serious, lost even unto death, the Good Shepherd decides to descend into death. Because the sheep are so far lost, the Good Shepherd decides that He must follow them into hell. His will to possess is so great and persistent that He is not deterred either by death or by hell from asserting His claim: 'I am the good shepherd: the good shepherd giveth his life for the sheep.'

Yet three days after the Shepherd is defeated and His flock scattered, He is alive again. The Father does not leave the Shepherd in death and hell: on Easter day He wakens Him in splendour and installs Him as the Shepherd of all nations and of all time. What seems utter degradation in the sacrifice on the Cross, has now become the fulfilment of authority and triumph in the office of Shepherd. Now that He is beyond the grave, He is all the more the Good Shepherd and rules in power. And He never dreams of giving up His claim to all the nations of the earth.

On the contrary, His Shepherd's call is more uncompromising than ever: 'And other sheep I have, which are not of this fold: them also I must bring, and they shall hear my voice; and there shall be one fold, and one shepherd.'

From the moment when He is risen we see the Good Shepherd at work throughout Easter. First of all He seeks out and reunites the small flock, who were so cruelly scattered when their Master died. And by the first evening of Easter He has brought together every single one of them. The next step is unexpected and astonishing. The eternal Shepherd and High Priest intends to gather unto Himself His own, from all the nations, by investing as shepherds those who first wholly gave themselves up to Him, so that while they are sheep they are also shepherds. To Peter, who was the most lost of all the disciples (apart from the one who was condemned to final perdition), to him of all people is given a special office: 'Feed my lambs. . . . Feed my sheep.' And even Paul, who was once one of the Pharisees, those false shepherds who finally closed their doors to Christ, is saved like a brand from the burning and installed as a shepherd of the people. And all the disciples receive the command, 'Go out into the world and make all people my disciples: teach them and baptize them.' Again it is conceivable that one of you has come here this morning only to hear the call of the eternal Great Shepherd: 'Help to feed the sheep, you to whom it is given to be yourself a sheep, help to feed the lambs.' For the Good Shepherd has other sheep in other folds whom He will bring too.

After my last sermon, I received a letter expressing the terrible opinion that it is no longer any use pointing out to men in business, politics and the services, how far they are responsible to God, because it is too late. The writer thought that these people have shut themselves off from God, and that the sooner they perish the better. That is a very serious thing to say, and we cannot easily ignore it. The Bible shows that such a thing is possible. But since God is the judge, it is not for us to decide when and where it is no longer any use, nor for whom it is too late. As long as that night 'when no man can work' has not yet come, we as Christians have the right and duty to hope that our Lord and Shepherd has other sheep in other folds than those we already know of. We have no reason to presume that in any one place there are no more sheep left for whom the Good Shepherd died. We can take it for granted that there are still sheep in the most unexpected places. Indeed, when the day of the great gathering draws near, we shall be amazed at the places from which the sheep come running.

Admittedly the letter-writer was right in saying that it does not follow that if you are called to be a messenger of Jesus Christ you will be victorious and meet with little resistance. In this world today the Christian community encounters the greatest possible opposition. Failure, shame and suffering await it. It will never be able to deny that it is the community of the man who died on the Cross. Does not the Good Shepherd Himself say, 'Behold, I send you forth as sheep in the midst of wolves: be ye therefore wise as serpents, and harmless as doves.' Both we who live in faith, without seeing, and those isolated sheep, scattered here and there, who know only that the Good Shepherd knows them but who do not know one another, must not forget Christ's words, 'I am the good shepherd, and know my sheep, and am known of mine.' We must always remember that He insists on what is His, for He gave His life for the sheep. Those who have heard this call can go comforted towards that last great day of which we read, 'When the Son of man shall come in his glory, and all the holy angels with him, then shall he sit upon the throne of his glory: and before him shall be gathered all nations; and he shall separate them one from another, as a shepherd divideth his sheep from the goats.' The judge of the sheep and the goats is the same as He who says, 'I am the good shepherd: the good shepherd giveth his life for the sheep.'

The Parable of the Sheep

And it was at Jerusalem the feast of the dedication, and it was winter. And Jesus walked in the temple in Solomon's porch. Then came the Jews round about him, and said unto him, How long dost thou make us to doubt? If thou be the Christ, tell us plainly. Jesus answered them, I told you, and ye believed not: the works that I do in my Father's name, they bear witness of me. But ye believe not, because ye are not of my sheep, as I said unto you. My sheep hear my voice, and I know them, and they follow me: and I give unto them eternal life; and they shall never perish, neither shall any pluck them out of my hand. My Father, which gave them me, is greater than all; and none is able to pluck them out of my Father's hand. I and my Father are one.

Then the Jews took up stones again to stone him. Jesus answered them, Many good works have I shewed you from my Father; for which of those works do ye stone me? The Jews answered him, saying, For a good work we stone thee not; but for blasphemy; and because that thou, being a man, makest thyself God. Jesus answered them, Is it not written in your law, I said, Ye are gods? If he called them gods, unto whom the word of God came, and the scripture cannot be broken; say ye of him, whom the Father hath sanctified, and sent into the world, Thou blasphemest; because I said, I am the Son of God? If I do not the works of my Father, believe me not. But if I do, though ye believe not me, believe the works: that ye may know, and believe, that the Father is in me, and I in him.

Therefore they sought again to take him: but he escaped out of their hand, and went away again beyond Jordan into the place where John at first baptized; and there he abode. And many resorted unto him, and said, John did no miracle: but all things that John spake of this man were true. And many believed on him there. [x. 22–42]

'Ye are not of my sheep' because 'my sheep hear my voice.' There is a hair's breadth division between these two thoughts. The Lord is differentiating between the people He calls His sheep and those to whom He says, 'Ye are not of my sheep.' The former believe in Him, the latter do not. The former hear His voice and follow Him, the latter are deaf and turn away. This line of demarcation does not run merely through this short extract from the Bible, but through the whole of the writings of the Old and New Testaments. We think of Cain and Abel, both born of the same womb; Jacob and Esau, both nurtured under the same roof; Judas and Peter, both called to be disciples by the same Master; we think of one criminal to the right of Christ, and one to the left; we think of Whitsun and some people filled with the Holy Ghost, while others mock at them in ignorance or malice, 'These men are full of new wine.' And on the last day 'there shall be two men in one bed . . . Two women shall be grinding together . . . Two men shall be in the field; the one shall be taken, and the other left.'

This dividing line between belief and unbelief is the only boundary that matters to God and His cause. Only these two camps are of importance to Him: the one where His voice is heard, the other where it is not heard. Everything else that divides men – language, nationality, race or creed – may be important in our eyes; for God and His cause, however, our frontiers are neither conclusive nor binding. In God's eyes there is neither Jew nor Greek, neither slave nor freeman, neither man nor woman; here there are only human beings, people who either hear the voice of the Good Shepherd or 'believe not.' Just as God says, 'My thoughts are not your thoughts, neither are your ways my ways,' so He might equally well say, 'My frontiers are not your frontiers, neither are your barriers my barriers: on the contrary, inasmuch as Heaven is higher than the earth, so are my boundaries higher than yours.' We have met together this morning so near to one another, and yet torn and divided as only human beings can be, troubled by sympathies and antipathies, and confused by the play of lies and counter-lies; we are driven to and fro by blind hatred and equally blind love; mocking laughter from the abyss is almost audible. We can only share in world events by sympathy; yet let us for Heaven's sake collect ourselves and reflect quietly, so as not to lose sight of God's final and eternal decision, on our preoccupation with our temporal and temporary boundaries. Let us face the old, ever untimely, yet always timely, question, 'Whom do you belong to? Which side are you on? Whose property are you? Are you a sheep of the Good Shepherd or are you one of those who are told, "Ye are not of my sheep" ?' Whatever earthly events may distract our spirit, or whatever the coming day or week may bring, nothing is, or must be, more important to us than the fact that the Good Shepherd went out among the nations and sends out His Shepherd's call to the lost world.

If we want to belong to the sheep, what must we do? What sort of arrangements are we to make; what steps are we to take? Fortunately we do not have to think out this question for ourselves, for Christ Himself gives us the astonishing answer, which is disquieting or pleasing according to the circumstances. Christ says that the Father gave Him the sheep: 'My Father, which gave them me, is greater than all.' The Lord says the same again in the prayer in the garden of Gethsemane, where He prays to the Father for those 'which thou gavest me,' and thanks Him that He has lost none of those given Him by the Father except 'the son of perdition; that the scripture might be fulfilled.' In every single sheep that is added to His flock Jesus sees a gift from His Father in Heaven. The Good Shepherd did not gather the flock by Himself, nor did He create it; the Father gave it to Him.

But if the Great Shepherd says this of Himself, how much more do His words apply to us who are called to the office of shepherd at home or in the community! I shall never forget the words of a mother, who was greatly distressed that her children had turned out badly, and who said to the clergyman as she lay on her deathbed, 'There was nothing I could do but pray for them. No mother can ensure her children's salvation, and,' with a side-long glance at the clergyman, 'no parson can save his parishioners.' It is Someone else who does that, the One who makes His choice when, and where, and as it pleases Him. Nor can any of us decide for himself whether he will belong to the flock or not. The only possible course for us is to pray, to seek and to knock. But Someone else opens the door. He grants the gift of finding to him who seeks; He gives it to him who prays. The gift is everything. And no one who is accepted into the flock of Jesus Christ can say, 'I have earned it.' Here we can only give thanks and praise in gratitude that the Father has sought us from childhood, that He has shed the light of His countenance upon us, and that He has called us when our hour has come. 'For thou hast possessed my reins: thou hast covered me in my mother's womb. . . . Thine eyes did see my substance, yet being unperfect; and in thy book all my members were written, which in continuance were fashioned, when as yet there was none of them.'

The Father's gift of grace is not shrouded in obscurity. The Father tells the Son whom He is going to give Him, and the Son recognises them, and can say, 'I know them,' 'I know my own.' And the recognition is passed on from the Shepherd to the sheep, so that they can know themselves and one another, and so that none of them need any longer end his days in solitary darkness. There are ways of distinguishing between one who is a sheep and another who is not. The sheep are blessed with a receptive ear. 'My sheep hear my voice.' This helps us to decide whether we and other people belong to the sheep. Sermons begin to mean something, so that one sermon a week is soon not enough. What sheep can go for seven days without pasture and drink? Those whom the Father has given to the Son soon find themselves thirsting for the Word of God, and dependent on the voice of the Shepherd, for whom they develop a very personal need. His sheep recognise His voice, so that they can distinguish between it and the voice of a stranger. The sheep are also endowed with a special deafness to the voice of a stranger who is not a shepherd. And if any one of you has to admit uneasily, 'It is not like that with me yet; I can live for weeks and months without the voice of the Good Shepherd,' then I can assure you that this very uneasiness is in itself an initial sign that you have actually heard His voice, and are on the way to being a sheep of the good Shepherd.

When His sheep have heard His voice in the right way (there is also a wrong way), then something happens. The sheep are ready for action, they are prepared to make decisions, they begin to obey and follow Him. That is the second sign by which a sheep is recognised: 'My sheep hear my voice, and I know them, and they follow me.' In view of the state of Christianity in the West, we should be urgently concerned to be granted the kind of hearing that entails unconditional following. In the past many a Christian has claimed to be a 'hearer of the word,' but when it came to the point, he did not act and did not follow. It was the wrong kind of hearing. But when they hear His voice in the right way, 'the sheep follow him.'

Where does He lead them? Inevitably Psalm XXIII comes to mind. The Good Shepherd leads His sheep into green pastures, and beside still waters and in the paths of righteousness. But in the same psalm we read that He also leads them 'through the valley of the shadow of death,' and into the presence of their enemies. The Good Shepherd leads His sheep into battle, which no sheep likes. Every word that He says about His sheep, from now on, points to danger and temptation, distress and death. 'And I give them eternal life; and they shall never perish, neither shall any pluck them out of my hand. My Father, which gave them me, is greater than all; and none is able to pluck them out of my Father's hand.' It is important to notice what the Good Shepherd does not promise His sheep. He gives them no assurance that, whatever happens, they will remain alive on this earth; He does not guarantee them an abundance of food, and warm clothing, and secure homes; He does not offer them a life in comfortable circumstances; the Good Shepherd does not promise His sheep what we used to mean by 'peace.' On the contrary. They must know and realise that they are the property of the One who said, 'I lay down my life for the sheep,' but who also said, 'My sheep follow me.' 'Whosoever will save his life shall lose it: but whosoever will lose his life for my sake, the same shall save it.' He does promise them one thing, however – eternal life.

They will never perish, not even if they have to lay down their earthly lives. No one can snatch them out of His and His Father's hands, not even those who have the power to tear them away from house and home, and wife and children. That is the third distinguishing sign of the sheep: they have the certainty of eternal life.

'I give them eternal life.' That means nothing to those who do not belong to the sheep; like Heine they gladly leave Heaven 'to the angels and the sparrows.' But it does mean something to the sheep; to them this promise signifies a power stronger than any force on earth, banishing the fear of the threat of death.

Christian courage is rooted in this. The Good Shepherd can give His sheep such a clear certainty of eternal life, that their life on earth, and its loss or preservation, becomes relatively unimportant beside eternity. A man who was obviously puzzled asked me this week how we can completely change our ideals and deepest convictions almost over-night. Christ gives us the explanation here: our ideals and deepest convictions were formerly related to earthly values, and therefore not rooted in eternity. In the past there has been a lot of fighting for what is true, good and noble, and a lot of work in the name and service of the progress of humanity, which was all very commendable; but our efforts began to fall flat because they had no roots. We believed, but our belief was of this world; we hoped, but our hope was of this world; we loved, but our love was of this world. Our deepest convictions were like a flower whose roots have been nibbled at by grubs or insects. It can bloom until the roots have been bitten right through, and then the flower soon withers and dies. Pledging ourselves to God's cause is effective only when that pledge is firmly rooted in the belief in eternal life. It is not enough to live for an ideal: we must be prepared to die for it. And we can really die for God's cause, if we know that we shall never perish, and that no one can pluck us from the hand of the Shepherd, because He gives us eternal life.

In order to understand this last point, we have to turn our attention again towards those to whom the Lord says, 'Ye are not of my sheep.' There are pious people and church officials, who could also belong to the chosen of God, but they do not want to. That is important, for while admittedly it is not in our power to be called to belong to the Shepherd's flock, we can reject the call, and so forfeit our membership. That is what happens in our story. John begins with the significant statement, 'And it was . . . the feast of the dedication, and it was winter.' The feast of the dedication of the Temple is being celebrated. Ever since 165 B.C. Israel has observed this feast on 25 December and throughout the following week. The festival was instituted to commemorate the heroic battles of the so-called Maccabees. That was in the days when the Emperor Antiochus Epiphanes IV subjugated nation after nation, pillaged land after land, desecrated the Temple with heathen worship, and tried to exterminate the belief in God. The Maccabees rose up with the battle-cry, 'Live honourably or die honourably!' and by force of arms threw off the yoke of the desecrator of their Temple.

At this festival of the dedication, Jesus encounters the spiritual leaders of the nation. A crusading mood prevails among the people and their priests; they are full of enthusiasm for the purity of faith in memory of the heroic Maccabees. On account of the cold and winter rain, Jesus is walking up and down in the porch of Solomon, when a number of these pious zealots suddenly challenge Him. The Lord answers them patiently but, say what He will, they will not listen to Him. He refers them to His works, which He has performed before their very eyes, but these miracles do not convince them that He is the Messiah. They do not want to see the works of a Shepherd who gives His life for His sheep; what they want is a Messiah after the pattern of the Maccabees, who roused the people to rebellion. Their Messianic dream is of a general who will free them from the domination of the Romans.

Nowadays we can understand only too well these people, in their militant mood, rejecting a Shepherd who lets Himself be crucified. A God who fights His battles like a shepherd, and with sheep, is no more popular today than at the feast of the dedication of the Temple. That is where the hidden danger lies for us: it is so easy to whip up a crusading mood over the shameful wrongs of the world and, in so doing, to deny the Shepherd and no longer hear His voice. Because Jesus stands before them in lowliness, these pious fanatics at the feast regard His claim to be the Saviour as blasphemy, and reject Him. The heroes of the times of the Maccabees would turn in their graves if they heard a mere Shepherd daring to say, 'I and my Father are one.' The thought of a Messiah come to suffer and to die inflames the irritation of the priests to fury. They take up stones to kill Him, but He escapes from them because His hour has not yet come. Yet it will come soon, for the fact remains. He is the Shepherd. He fights His battles as a shepherd and His followers are sheep. The sheep is the most defenceless of all domestic animals: the horse has its hooves, the bee its sting, the cat its claws and the goat its horns, but the sheep has nothing but its shepherd. It is not by chance that the sheep has always been the sacrificial animal, led to the slaughter. But it is with sheep that the good Shepherd fights His battle, with sheep that He gains His victory, and with sheep that He builds His eternal Kingdom. 'My sheep hear my voice, and I know them, and they follow me: and I give them eternal life; and they shall never perish, neither shall any pluck them out of my hand.'

The Raising of Lazarus

Now a certain man was sick, named Lazarus, of Bethany, the town of Mary and her sister Martha. (It was that Mary which anointed the Lord with ointment, and wiped his feet with her hair, whose brother Lazarus was sick.) Therefore his sisters sent unto him, saying, Lord, behold, he whom thou lovest is sick. When Jesus heard that, he said, This sickness is not unto death, but for the glory of God, that the Son of God might be glorified thereby. Now Jesus loved Martha, and her sister, and Lazarus. When he had heard therefore that he was sick, he abode two days still in the same place where he was. Then after that saith he to his disciples, Let us go into Judæa again. His disciples say unto him, Master, the Jews of late sought to stone thee; and goest thou thither again? Jesus answered, Are there not twelve hours in the day? If any man walk in the day, he stumbleth not, because he seeth the light of this world. But if a man walk in the night, he stumbleth, because there is no light in him. These things said he: and after that he saith unto them, Our friend Lazarus sleepeth; but I go, that I may awake him out of sleep. Then said his disciples, Lord, if he sleep, he shall do well. Howbeit Jesus spake of his death: but they thought that he had spoken of taking of rest in sleep. Then said Jesus unto them plainly, Lazarus is dead. And I am glad for your sakes that I was not there, to the intent ye may believe; nevertheless let us go unto him. Then said Thomas, which is called Didymus, unto his fellow disciples, Let us also go, that we may die with him.

Then when Jesus came, he found that he had lain in the grave four days already. Now Bethany was nigh unto Jerusalem, about fifteen furlongs off: and many of the Jews came to Martha and Mary, to comfort them concerning their brother. Then Martha, as soon as she heard that Jesus was coming, went and met him: but Mary sat still in the house.

Then said Martha unto Jesus, Lord, if thou hadst been here, my brother had not died. But I know, that even now, whatsoever thou wilt ask of God, God will give it thee. Jesus saith unto her, Thy brother shall rise again. Martha saith unto him, I know that he shall rise again in the resurrection at the last day. Jesus said unto her, I am the resurrection, and the life: he that believeth in me, though he were dead, yet shall he live: and whosoever liveth and believeth in me shall never die. Believest thou this? She saith unto him, Yea, Lord: I believe that thou art the Christ, the Son of God, which should come into the world. And when she had so said, she went her way, and called Mary her sister secretly, saying, The Master is come, and calleth for thee. As soon as she heard that, she arose quickly, and came unto him. Now Jesus was not yet come into the town, but was in that place where Martha met him. The Jews then which were with her in the house, and comforted her, when they saw Mary, that she rose up hastily and went out, followed her, saying, She goeth unto the grave to weep there. Then when Mary was come where Jesus was, and saw him, she fell down at his feet, saying unto him, Lord, if thou hadst been here, my brother had not died.

When Jesus therefore saw her weeping, and the Jews also weeping which came with her, he groaned in the spirit, and was troubled, and said, Where have ye laid him? They said unto him, Lord, come and see. Jesus wept. Then said the Jews, Behold how he loved him! And some of them said, Could not this man, which opened the eyes of the blind, have caused that even this man should not have died? Jesus therefore again groaning in himself cometh to the grave. It was a cave, and a stone lay upon it. Jesus said, Take ye away the stone. Martha, the sister of him that was dead, saith unto him, Lord, by this time he stinketh: for he hath been dead four days. Jesus saith unto her, Said I not unto thee, that, if thou wouldest believe, thou shouldest see the glory of God? Then they took away the stone from the place where the dead was laid. And Jesus lifted up his eyes, and said, Father, I thank thee that thou hast heard me. And I knew that thou hearest me always: but because of the people which stand by I said it, that they may believe that thou hast sent me. And when he thus had spoken, he cried with a loud voice, Lazarus, come forth. And he that was dead came forth, bound hand and foot with graveclothes: and his face was bound about with a napkin. Jesus saith unto them, Loose him, and let him go.

Then many of the Jews which came to Mary, and had seen the things which Jesus did, believed on him. But some of them went their ways to the Pharisees, and told them what things Jesus had done. Then gathered the chief priests and the Pharisees a council, and said, What do we? for this man doeth many miracles. If we let him thus alone, all men will believe on him: and the Romans shall come and take away both our place and nation. And one of them, named Caiaphas, being the high priest that same year, said unto them, Ye know nothing at all, nor consider that it is expedient for us, that one man should die for the people, and that the whole nation perish not. And this spake he not of himself: but being high priest that year, he prophesied that Jesus should die for that nation; and not for that nation only, but that also he should gather together in one the children of God that were scattered abroad. Then from that day forth they took counsel together for to put him to death. Jesus therefore walked no more openly among the Jews; but went thence unto a country near to the wilderness, into a city called Ephraim, and there continued with his disciples. And the Jews' passover was nigh at hand: and many went out of the country up to Jerusalem before the passover, to purify themselves. Then sought they for Jesus, and spake among themselves, as they stood in the temple, What think ye, that he will not come to the feast? Now both the chief priests and the Pharisees had given a commandment, that, if any man knew where he were, he should shew it, that they might take him.

[XI]

'Now a certain man was sick.' We know this man and we know his sisters. His home, Bethany, is three quarters of an hour's walk from Jerusalem, a circumstance not without importance in the story. Lazarus's illness is representative of all humanity, so that we might say that not only the man in the house of his sisters is ill, but that any place where human beings live can be included in the words, 'A certain man was sick.' People lie ill in many thousands of white beds in the wards of hospitals and nursing-homes everywhere. In fact, not only individuals, but whole nations are sick. Man in general is in the same state as Lazarus. One can almost feel the weight of all the ages of humanity in this remarkable symbolic opening to our chapter.

'Therefore his sisters sent unto him, saying, Lord, behold, he whom thou lovest is sick.' Jesus loves Lazarus and his sisters too, and no doubt Lazarus loves Jesus. The essential point here is that the sisters acknowledge Christ's love for their brother. When someone we love is ill we are so often tempted to listen to the Devil's whisperings that this is proof that God does not love us. The sisters of Bethany, however, are confident: their brother may be ill but Christ loves him. Let us reassure all sick people: the hospitals are full of people who weep, and groan, and curse, and pray, but let us encourage them with the knowledge that Jesus loves Lazarus who is ill. Let us proclaim to this sick generation 'Behold, he whom thou lovest is sick.'

The two sisters do not fully realise the implication of their words. It is interesting to see how often in the fourth gospel, and in this chapter particularly, words have a deeper meaning than is at first apparent. Everything said here has a wider significance. Jesus loves Lazarus so much that He decides to return to Bethany. What exactly does that mean to Him? At the end of the last chapter we heard that Jesus escaped from His enemies. Jesus is in retreat, if not in actual flight, when He hears the news that His friend has fallen ill. He has just left Bethany, Jerusalem and Judaea, where they tried to stone Him twice. The news reaches Him just when He has evaded the clutches of His enemies. It is an indirect call for help from the two sisters. The reason why they do not actually ask Him to visit Lazarus is only too clear. They know quite well how dangerous the soil of Bethany has become for Jesus. When He receives the news Jesus stays where He is for two days, during which time it becomes clear to Him that this is not merely an appeal from Martha and Mary: His Father is calling Him back to Judaea, back to Bethany and Jerusalem where the Jews are waiting to stone Him. The disciples try to dissuade Him, but by way of answer He tells them the parable of the day that has twelve hours. His twelfth hour is indeed near, but the Father in Heaven, and not the Jews in Jerusalem, will determine when His day shall come to an end. The Father seems to have decided that Jesus must go back to Judaea now, so He turns back with His disciples, determined to see the sick Lazarus. Jesus's love for the sick Lazarus is so great that for his sake He will brave the stones and other perils that await Him in Jerusalem. In this lies the mystery of His love. He is prepared to die for the sake of Lazarus so that the old prophecy may be fulfilled in Him: 'Surely he hath borne our griefs, and carried our sorrows. . . . The chastisement of our peace was upon him; and with his stripes we are healed.'

In the meantime Lazarus has died. Jesus knows this and tells the disciples. 'Nevertheless,' He says, 'let us go unto him.' Thomas loyally suggests, 'Let us also go, that we may die with him.' When Jesus arrives He finds that Lazarus has been buried for four days. Almost as if they had prearranged it, both sisters address Him with the words they must often have repeated during those sorrowful days, 'Lord, if thou hadst been here, my brother had not died.' That is a typically human sentiment. We hear it expressed so often by those recently bereaved: 'Lord, if thou hadst been here, our loved one had not died. But thou wast not here and now he is dead.' How embarrassing it is for Jesus to have to hear this, and all the more so when it comes from Martha and Mary, who nevertheless believe in Him. It is humiliating for Him that the guests from Jerusalem take up this cry with a certain mixture of mockery and satisfaction: 'Could not this man, which opened the eyes of the blind, have caused that even this man should not have died?'

Humiliating? Yes, but something worse than mere personal degradation is evident here. No doubt you have noticed that Jesus is deeply moved while on His way to Lazarus's grave. Twice we read that He 'groaned in the spirit,' once that He 'was troubled' and once that He wept. St John does not explain the cause of His grief, but we know from other parts of the New Testament that Jesus often suffers similar emotions on His long journey to the Cross. He weeps over Jerusalem; His soul is sorrowful at Judas's betrayal, and there in the garden of Gethsemane His soul is 'sorrowful even unto death' and He prays in agony and fear. And judging by the words of our chapter there can be no doubt that Jesus is in agony here too. His sorrow makes the path to Lazarus's grave like another path to Gethsemane. He is weeping, not for Lazarus whom He raises up a moment later, but for the guests, for Jerusalem, for Israel, in short, because of everything that is going to happen.

So Jesus is prepared to die for His friend. The grave of Lazarus, before Him, brings to His mind that other grave, on which the stonemasons are working in the garden of Joseph of Arimathaea, at this very hour. Soon He Himself will be wrapped in grave-clothes and laid behind the stone. The important point is that He is prepared to accept the fact of His own fast-approaching death. All this explains His emotional struggle. It is His own, personal, solitary struggle. His way to Lazarus, and to all those who lie dead, is the way to His own death on the Cross. When He weeps the guests are quite right in saying, 'Behold how he loved him!' But what they say holds more truth than they realise. To all those lying on sick-beds and to all who mourn and say, 'Lord, if thou hadst been here, my brother had not died,' let us say, 'The Lord is with you when a loved one dies.' If there is one place where the Lord is surely present, then it is at a death-bed or by a grave. His glory is revealed even here. Jesus dies for love of the dead Lazarus.

God's way to us poor human beings is even more full of mystery: the sacred path of eternal love leads beyond the sick and dead Lazarus, beyond the hospital bed and the grave. The struggle undertaken by Christ for our sake ends in victory. He has said to the disciples, 'This sickness is not unto death. . . . Our friend Lazarus sleepeth; but I go, that I may awake him out of sleep.' Because the Father has given Him victory over the death of Lazarus He says to Martha, 'Thy brother shall rise again.' And when she acknowledges this, thinking that He is referring to the general belief in resurrection, shared by pious Jews, He speaks the decisive words, 'I am the resurrection, and the life.' Now we begin to see more clearly. 'I am the resurrection, and the life' is one of the 'I am's' which are so characteristic of St John's gospel, like 'I am the bread of life. . . . I am the light of the world. . . . I am the good shepherd. . . . I am the truth. . . . I am the way.' 'I am.' He does not merely say, 'There is resurrection and eternal life'; but, more definitely, 'I am the resurrection and the life.' The resurrection and the life are in Him so completely and exclusively, that without Him there is no resurrection and no life. Our life depends on the path that He is taking now, for love of the sick and dead Lazarus. His path is quite simply a matter of life and death.

In a moment He shows us what He means by 'I am.' He asks where they have laid Lazarus, and when they lead Him to the grave He orders them to roll away the stone. Horrified, Martha steps forward to stop Him entering, because decay must already have set in: 'Lord, by this time he stinketh: for he hath been dead four days,' but Jesus moves her aside. Standing before the grave, He looks up to Heaven and thanks the Father for having heard Him. Then He calls out, 'Lazarus, come forth,' and the dead man comes out, wrapped in grave-clothes and his face covered with a napkin. Jesus says to them, 'Loose him, and let him go.'

This account can only have meaning for us if we have understood 'I am the resurrection, and the life,' and if we consider how soon Christ Himself will rise from the dead. The stone will very soon be rolled away from His own grave, and He will be freed of His grave-clothes. Behind the open grave of Lazarus of Bethany, appears the empty grave of Easter. So we lose interest in Lazarus remarkably soon after he has been raised from the dead. He is hardly mentioned again in this chapter: like so many other actors in the Passion, he appears, points to Jesus, and disappears again. The heart of the matter is not the raising up of Lazarus but something more comprehensive, the Resurrection of Jesus. Christ does not only die; He loves Lazarus so much that for his sake He rises from the dead. What happens here at the grave of Lazarus indicates the glorious end. Jesus will not rise up like Lazarus, who becomes a mortal man again, and will some day fall ill and die once more. After His resurrection, Jesus will no longer be a human being who weeps and is afraid; He will be risen up in splendour and for ever. For ever and for everyone. He will not have risen up privately, as it were, like Lazarus; His Resurrection will have an effect beyond His own person. Christ will have risen for all who believe in Him. 'I am the resurrection, and the life: he that believeth in me, though he were dead, yet shall he live: and whosoever liveth and believeth in me shall never die. Believest thou this?'

This introduces the question of faith, implicit in the whole of this great chapter, and indeed in the whole of the fourth gospel. We could call this the chapter of faith, because it demonstrates the meaning of faith. People who could not, or would not, believe have always found this chapter in particular a stumbling block. To the thinkers of the eighteenth century it was like a red rag to a bull. Spinoza, one of the most clear-thinking of philosophers, said he would gladly give his whole system to be able to believe what is written in this chapter. 'Believest thou this?' The question that Jesus asks Martha is valid for us too. Do you believe that it is of importance to you personally that Christ is the resurrection and the life? Do you believe that when death comes you will be able to say confidently, 'Although I die, yet I shall live'? And if it has not yet come to this, will your faith be a support and source of strength to you in all the temptations and difficulties of your life? Do you believe that you can actually live in Christ? For 'whosoever liveth and believeth in me shall never die.' If only we could believe! It would be worth while to give up any system for the faith that conquers life and death. For the sick, dying, and dead, Lazarus symbolises us as we are. Everything stinks of the grave today: our marriages, our families, our industrial life and our politics. Faced with this decay, all that we can do is to believe in Him who says, 'I am the resurrection, and the life.' Then we can say with Martin Luther that the words, 'In the midst of life we are in death,' should be, 'In the midst of death we are in life.' A generation that has faith can live and die: our generation can do neither.

What a loving lesson in faith this chapter is! It is perfectly clear that all three groups, the disciples, the sisters, and the guests, believe in Him. And yet we know that their faith is going to be severely shaken. Very soon the devastating storm will break, and very little of their faith will remain visible. But in spite of the weakness that will emerge on Good Friday and Easter morning, there is no doubt here that they believe now. 'Believest thou this?' Their answer to this question does not sound complacent and bold. These men and women of the Bible know full well that faith is not to be had at will. No, faith is not kept handy in one's pocket like a handkerchief; faith is the most mysterious of all gifts, for which we can only give thanks each day, and for which we can only ask anew each morning.

'Believest thou this?' Knowing the state of our faith, Jesus does not put this question insistently. Just see how lovingly He makes allowances for His disciples' lack of faith, and how gently He prepares them for the coming storm. Jesus knows what a tender plant faith is. See how delicately He touches on the question of faith with the two mourning sisters. He Himself does not demand that we should believe. He is Lord of our faith, yet here He has become a servant of our faith. He does not want to give the impression of using force. Jesus never uses force. He does not treat the faithful as if they were on the parade ground. In fact, He coerces our faith so little that He allows some people to leave Bethany not believing in Him. He even allows some people to go away, after the raising of Lazarus to issue a warrant for His arrest, determined that He must die. Jesus is waiting until that mysterious fruit, faith, ripens. Blessed is he who does not brutally shake down the unripe fruit.

And yet this chapter asks us in all friendliness and most earnestly, 'Believest thou this?' It is not our question, it is Christ's. But let us ask it of ourselves! Let us take it away with us and ponder it in the stillness of our hearts. Christ says, 'I am the resurrection, and the life.' Do you believe this? Jesus says, 'He that believeth in me, though he were dead, yet shall he live.' Do you believe this? 'And whosoever liveth and believeth in me shall never die' – in spite of the smell of mortality around us, do you believe this? Blessed are they that do not see and yet believe.

The Anointing in Bethany and the Entry into Jerusalem

Then Jesus six days before the passover came to Bethany, where Lazarus was which had been dead, whom he raised from the dead. There they made him a supper; and Martha served: but Lazarus was one of them that sat at the table with him. Then took Mary a pound of ointment of spikenard, very costly, and anointed the feet of Jesus, and wiped his feet with her hair: and the house was filled with the odour of the ointment. Then saith one of his disciples, Judas Iscariot, Simon's son, which should betray him, Why was not this ointment sold for three hundred pence, and given to the poor? This he said, not that he cared for the poor; but because he was a thief, and had the bag, and bare what was put therein. Then said Jesus, Let her alone: against the day of my burying hath she kept this. For the poor always ye have with you; but me ye have not always. Much people of the Jews therefore knew that he was there: and they came not for Jesus' sake only, but that they might see Lazarus also, whom he had raised from the dead. But the chief priests consulted that they might put Lazarus also to death; because that by reason of him many of the Jews went away, and believed on Jesus.

On the next day much people that were come to the feast, when they heard that Jesus was coming to Jerusalem, took branches of palm trees, and went forth to meet him, and cried, Hosanna: Blessed is the King of Israel that cometh in the name of the Lord. And Jesus, when he had found a young ass, sat thereon; as it is written, Fear not, daughter of Sion: behold, thy King cometh, sitting on an ass's colt. These things understood not his disciples at the first: but when Jesus was glorified, then remembered they that these things were written of him, and that they had done these things unto him. The people therefore that was with him when he called Lazarus out of his grave, and raised him from the dead, bare record. For this cause the people also met him, for that they heard that he had done this miracle. The Pharisees therefore said among themselves, Perceive ye how ye prevail nothing? behold, the world is gone after him.

[XII. 1-19]

In our mountains there are many places where you can hear a multiple echo. In today's text St John lets us hear the echoes which resound from the grave of Lazarus at Bethany, the first from near at hand and the others from farther afield. The raising of Lazarus has had a remarkable after-effect on all those who witnessed it. It would be surprising if it were not so, for it is no everyday occurrence when a man returns to life after four days in the grave. Such an awakening call from eternity is bound to have powerful repercussions.

First of all, the echo in Bethany itself. The people of Bethany would like to show their gratitude, so they give a splendid supper for the man who raised up their fellow-citizen. This takes place, as the other Evangelists report, not in the home of Martha and Mary, but at the house of a man who was once a leper, called Simon the Leper. Lazarus and his sisters are present. Of Martha all we hear is, 'And Martha served,' as if John were implying, 'she is serving as usual. She is in her element when she is serving.' But she has never served as she is serving now. Today she is serving the man who restored her dead brother to her from the grave. In the past she may sometimes have served as a duty, but today her serving is prompted by gratitude. Her brother was dead and now he is alive again. 'And Martha served.' Who would not like to be in Martha's shoes here!

Mary is serving too, but in her own way. She has brought her most costly possession with her, a vessel containing a kind of perfume made in India, a gift worth three hundred pence. When you consider that a penny was the average daily wage for a workman in those days then, taking the Sabbaths into account, it is more or less exactly a year's pay for a workman that Mary sprinkles on Jesus's head and pours over His feet. We might regard this homage as senseless and exaggerated, if we did not know that she is paying it to the man who has restored her dead brother to her. What is a year's wages; what indeed is money and property when a dead brother has been restored to life! Nowadays people pay their dentist several times that amount merely for healthy teeth. And many a man would gladly sacrifice this sum to have a loved one, who is dead, restored to him. This is how Mary shows her gratitude. Who would not like to be in Mary's shoes here!

Lazarus is serving too. What a strange fellow he is; what an unusually silent guest! Although we learn a good deal about him in the four gospels, we never hear a single word from his own lips. Even on the occasion of this supper we read of nothing that he says or does, except that he is one of the guests and sits at table with Jesus. We know absolutely nothing of what this Lazarus ever said or did in his life; all we hear repeatedly is what others say about him and do for him. We only know that he was ill, that he died, that he ate and drank, and that Jesus loved him and raised him up. But through this complete withdrawal Lazarus becomes one of the purest and most powerful witnesses of Christ. We always think that we can serve and thank God and honour Him by what we do and give, but we can see here that someone can also be a witness of God by what he receives, and what he allows to happen to him. What an eloquent witness of Christ this strangely silent brother, Lazarus, has become because Jesus's love has been revealed in him!

In institutions, old people's homes and mental hospitals all over the world there are people like Lazarus, whose existence only means something because the love of God is revealed in them. They are the sick, the incurable, those of unsound mind, the aged and the infirm, who have existed for years or for the whole of their lives solely in order to let themselves be helped and loved, to let themselves be cared for and supported for the sake of Christ, who loved Lazarus. There are some among us this morning who are chronically ill, and who have nothing more to say for half of their lives than, 'I am sick and weak and helpless and Christ loves me.' And there are people here who for the past quarter of a century have been nursing at home a sick Lazarus, of whom all they can say is, 'He is ill and will die some day and Jesus loves him.' I beg you to take care of these sick brothers and sisters, silent witnesses of God that they are, in whom the love of Christ is practised and revealed daily and often hourly. Take care of them as if they were the apple of your eye, for they are the treasures of the Christian community. In the world today, and unfortunately in our own country too, there is a growing attitude of mind that is hostile to the helpless and incurable and is seeking their lives. This tendency originated in the field of medicine, which has become godless and, like Judas, is weighing up the usefulness of Lazarus. Lazarus is no longer to have a place at the table of the great Creator. Since there is not enough bread for the healthy and strong, we must get rid of the sick and frail by means of gas or the hypodermic. This is an attitude which, I repeat deliberately, originated in medicine and which we sometimes meet in our own circles. So let us not be mistaken: although the tendency may not yet be very strong, there is something of the Judas spirit among us too. Now is the time to give an urgent word of warning. Get rid of the aged and infirm if you like: turn them away from your table! The result will not be that the healthy have more to eat. If there is not enough bread for the sick and the crippled, there will not be enough for the healthy either. For the love that was born on the way to the greatest sacrifice will die if it cannot be poured out on the helpless, and increase and grow in strength. The natural love of mothers and fathers, brothers and sisters will be nipped in the bud, and this generation will grow as cold as ice. Drive Lazarus away from his miserable bed if you like: you will only find that your own bed grows uncomfortable, for the Lord loves Lazarus. Banish Lazarus from the table of the nations and you too will very soon be turned away, for the Lord loves Lazarus, through whom you may be blessed or judged. There must be a Lazarus. His presence at our table means life for our country. But if Lazarus is neglected, then our faith in Christ is corrupted, for Jesus loves Lazarus. Christ must have someone among us on whom to lavish His love, so He says to Judas, 'The poor always ye have with you.'

In Bethany we see three different ways of serving and thanking God. There are so many different aspects of service and gratitude in God's vineyard. One man serves by the work of his hands like Martha. Another serves by giving his most treasured possession for Christ, even though it may seem to have no practical purpose, as Mary does. This kind of service may be expressed by means of an alabaster jar, or by playing the organ in deep devotion, or by silent worship in the spirit and in truth. A third man thanks and serves Christ by simply existing, like Lazarus, to be sheltered, cared for and loved by Him. It will not do to play off one kind of service against another as Judas tries to do, for all three are equally valuable to Christ, each in its own way. The Lord protects Mary from the reproaches of Judas and says, 'Let her alone.' For us the question implied here, in all friendliness and sincerity is, 'What is the state of your service and your gratitude?' The question is not, 'How do you serve Him?' but, 'Do you serve Him at all, in one way or another?' You cannot be a Christian without gratitude.

But can we show Him gratitude? Have we cause to do so? No doubt we feel that Martha and Mary have every reason to be grateful now that their brother has been restored to them. But what if we are suffering from an illness that we have borne for years; can we thank Him then? Who can give thanks, when one of their loved ones has died and has not been restored to life, in spite of all their tears and prayers?

The answer that the Lord gives to Judas throws light on this painful question, and takes us a step further. Jesus rebukes Judas with the words, 'Let her alone: against the day of my burying hath she kept this. For the poor always have ye with you; but me ye have not always.' At this point Jesus is giving the conversation a new turn. His friends in Bethany are grateful to the Lord for what He has done for them in the past. But Jesus redirects their attention, and focuses it on what He is going to do in the very near future. They are taken up with the mercy that Jesus has shown to Lazarus. But Jesus implies that while what He has done may be great and important to them, He is going to do something even greater and more important very soon. What matters is not the raising up of Lazarus, but rather that other death and resurrection to which it points. Christ is to sacrifice Himself for them. His friends in Bethany thank God for a small gift, an insignificant gift compared with the very great one that God will soon provide, though not here in Bethany but over in Jerusalem. So He urges them not to let their thoughts dwell on the grave of Lazarus, but to prepare themselves to receive the greatest gift of all.

We should like to have to thank God for what we think He ought to have given us, in other words for small things. And if He refuses us these small things that we should like, we shut ourselves off from His greatest and most splendid gifts, and turn away from Him, in defiance and ingratitude. Because we are denied a part, we grumble and deprive ourselves of the whole. That is why Jesus tries to distract the attention of His friends in Bethany from the earthly rescue of Lazarus, and points to the true, all-embracing act of salvation that is soon to be performed at Golgotha. He wants to say to Martha, 'You are serving me now. That is very good. But there are more important things than your excellent serving, so do not take it too seriously. Soon our roles will be reversed and I shall serve you. For I have not come to be served, but so that I may serve, and give my life as payment for many.' And to Lazarus He is trying to say, 'You are serving your Lord and thanking Him by being present at a supper that has been given for Jesus Christ. But Christ will soon invite you and all the other guests to another supper, which He will prepare for all of you.' Mary is giving thanks to the Redeemer for restoring her brother to her. That is why she has broken her costly jar, and poured out its precious contents. But that is not the most important thing. The man who is sitting at supper with them will soon break a far more costly vessel: His body will be broken and the blood that will be spilled will be immeasurably more precious than her spikenard, worth three hundred pence. And the whole world will be redolent of it, just as the house is filled with the scent of the ointment. In Jesus's eyes, Mary's libation foreshadows the embalming of His body; but at the same time it symbolises the age-old custom of anointing a king when he ascends the throne. So He says, 'Let her alone.'

Consequently, we are faced with another question asked in all friendliness and sincerity: 'Are you grateful for the greatest of all gifts that has been given to us men through Jesus Christ? In Bethany a man is called back from the grave into this transient, earthly life. However, all of us who have the gift of faith owe Him infinitely more gratitude because He has redeemed us into eternal life beyond the grave. Lazarus will certainly die again, in spite of his temporary escape from death. But the man who believes in Christ shall live, even though he dies. Jesus reaches into one grave in Bethany, and draws a man back into mortal life. Soon, not here in Bethany but over there in Jerusalem, God will reach out in His majesty into all graves, of all time, everywhere. Are you grateful for this? What are three hundred working days as a thank-offering for this kingly gift? Even if you were to give thanks every day of your life, it would still not be enough. When we have done our utmost duty we shall still have to say, 'We are unworthy servants.'

The first echo of the raising of Lazarus has come from Bethany itself. The second resounds from the hills and valleys round about Jerusalem. The people are on the move. They have heard what has happened in Bethany, and want to see for themselves. Christ, the Saviour, and Lazarus, the saved, have become a sensation. The coming and going between Jerusalem and Bethany has reached such proportions that the Jewish leaders are getting worried. So far Jesus has avoided all such crowds and demonstrations whenever possible. It would not surprise us to read that He has fled. But now He allows the inevitable to take place, because His hour is near. On the next day He does nothing to prevent pilgrims from streaming out and receiving Him with palm branches in their hands, a scene familiar to us from the descriptions of Palm Sunday in the other gospels. We learn from St John that this reception is in honour of the man who has raised up Lazarus. First of all a splendid supper, then a princely gift from the hands of Mary, and now this kingly entry into Jerusalem!

But what do the people expect of Him? The people are openly proclaiming Him King of Israel now. They are taking it so much for granted that He will ascend the throne of David, that they call upon God to help Him in His reign with the words, 'Hosanna to the Son of David,' which means, 'Help the Son of David.' Why are they doing this? The people always want a king who can do things. And no one can dispute that this is such a man. The first time they wanted to make Him their king was when He fed the five thousand (ch. VI). Now He has raised up a man from the dead. They see Jesus as a man of action, which is something the people always admire. They want a man who will be able to get things done. So they proclaim Him king, and this time Jesus allows it to happen, in spite of the fact that these same people will change their minds about Him when He is standing bound before Pilate and will cry, 'Crucify him!' presuming in their disappointment that He can after all do nothing. He lets it happen and rides into Jerusalem towards His death on the Cross. He rides towards His greatest defeat, because He can do nothing, and wants to do nothing, contrary to His Father's will, because He can do nothing but obey His Father, even to death on the Cross.

His inability to do anything contrary to His Father's will is the very reason why the Father makes Him King of all kings. The people wanted a king after their own image and desires, in other words a little king. We always want a little king who can satisfy our immediate needs. However, He has become the great King, not only the king of Israel but of the Gentiles and all the nations, King of the whole human race. He has also become King of the angels and of the spiritual world. His obedience to Heaven rather than the world had made Him the King, whose name is above all other names. We must not blame the people for their mistake: even the disciples do not at first realise the significance of the entry into Jerusalem. Not until much later do they understand that the ancient prophecy has been fulfilled: 'Fear not, daughter of Sion: behold, thy king cometh, sitting on an ass's colt.'

And now the third echo of the raising up of Lazarus: this time from the Temple. The thronging of the hundreds of pilgrims on the road to Bethany has been heard there, and it has caused great consternation in the chambers of the High Priest: 'Behold, the world is gone after him.' The Jews have played with the idea of killing Him long enough: now they must act, they must crucify Him. But now, the very method that they in their blind fury have chosen to render Him powerless, God exploits to make Him all-powerful. Now the whole world will really go after Him. The word *cosmos* is used at this point in the original text. The whole cosmos will follow Him as a result of the High Priest's efforts to make Him powerless and 'harmless' by crucifixion. All the power of Heaven and earth will be His.

I should like to mention, in conclusion, a small but surprising point in our text. It says, 'But the chief priests consulted that they might put Lazarus to death.' Because Lazarus has been saved the enemies of Jesus turn their attention to him too. A dangerous position for him to be in! This living corpse, this silent, yet so eloquent witness of the glory of Christ, is a thorn in their flesh. Evidently the man who is saved through Christ begins an uncomfortable life, his life will be dangerous from now on. The enemy has always been ill-disposed towards the saved Lazarus. We have almost forgotten this in the Church now. Today we are beginning to realise again that the man who shares Christ's table leads a perilous existence. But those who have lifted a hand against the saved of Jesus Christ, and have tried to do violence to them, have had to learn what these priests learned when they sought the lives of the Saviour and the saved: the harsher their treatment of the Saviour of Lazarus, and later of His community, the more surely the whole world followed Him. Although he may be in danger, the man who can belong to the saved and can follow Christ with the crowd is blessed indeed.

The Parable of the Corn of Wheat

And there were certain Greeks among them that came up to worship at the feast: the same came therefore to Philip, which was of Bethsaida of Galilee, and desired him, saying, Sir, we would see Jesus. Philip cometh and telleth Andrew: and again Andrew and Philip tell Jesus. And Jesus answered them, saying, The hour is come, that the Son of man should be glorified. Verily, verily, I say unto you, Except a corn of wheat fall into the ground and die, it abideth alone: but if it die, it bringeth forth much fruit. He that loveth his life shall lose it; and he that hateth his life in this world shall keep it unto life eternal. If any man serve me, let him follow me; and where I am, there shall also my servant be: if any man serve me, him will my Father honour. Now is my soul troubled; and what shall I say? Father, save me from this hour: but for this cause came I unto this hour. Father, glorify thy name. Then came there a voice from heaven, saying, I have both glorified it, and will glorify it again. The people therefore, that stood by, and heard it, said that it thundered: others said, An angel spake to him. Jesus answered and said, This voice came not because of me, but for your sakes. Now is the judgment of this world: now shall the prince of this world be cast out. And I, if I be lifted up from the earth, will draw all men unto me. This he said, signifying what death he should die. The people answered him, We have heard out of the law that Christ abideth for ever: and how sayest thou, The Son of man must be lifted up? who is this Son of man? Then Jesus said unto them, Yet a little while is the light with you. Walk while ye have the light, lest darkness come upon you: for he that walketh in darkness knoweth not whither he goeth. While ye have light, believe in the light, that ye may be the children of light. These things spake Jesus, and departed, and did hide himself from them.

But though he had done so many miracles before them, yet they believed not on him: that the saying of Esaias the prophet might be fulfilled, which he spake, Lord, who hath believed our report? and to whom hath the arm of the Lord been revealed? Therefore they could not believe, because that Esaias said again, He hath blinded their eyes, and hardened their heart; that they should not see with their eyes, nor understand with their heart, and be converted, and I should heal them. These things said Esaias, when he saw his glory, and spake of him. Nevertheless among the chief rulers also many believed on him; but because of the Pharisees they did not confess him, lest they should be put out of the synagogue: for they loved the praise of men more than the praise of God.

Jesus cried and said, He that believeth on me, believeth not on me, but on him that sent me. And he that seeth me seeth him that sent me. I am come a light into the world, that whosoever believeth on me should not abide in darkness. And if any man hear my words, and believe not, I judge him not: for I came not to judge the world, but to save the world. He that rejecteth me, and receiveth not my words, hath one that judgeth him: the word that I have spoken, the same shall judge him in the last day. For I have not spoken of myself; but the Father which sent me, he gave me a commandment, what I should say, and what I should speak. And I know that his commandment is life everlasting: whatsoever I speak therefore, even as the Father said unto me, so I speak.

[XII. 20–50]

Jesus once again urges the people most earnestly to walk while they have the Light for, He says, 'Yet a little while is the light with you.' It becomes evident now that many of the rulers believe in Him but do not confess their faith, because they are afraid of being expelled from the synagogue, and because they love 'the praise of men more than the praise of God.' At the same time we learn that the majority of the people do not believe in Him in spite of the many miracles He has performed, culminating in that greatest miracle of all in Bethany. The Lord realises that the gloomy prophecy of Isaiah has been fulfilled: 'He hath blinded their eyes and hardened their heart.' Just when all this becomes clear to Him, and He sees His way to the people barred as if by an iron curtain; when He finds the heart of Israel steeled against Him and when it has become apparent that 'He came unto his own, and his own received him not.' now Jesus finds Himself tempted. This is St John's version of the Agony in the Garden of Gethsemane, and he gives us a background to the account given by the other gospels of Christ's struggle against temptation.

Jesus is on His way out of the Temple, having entered it in triumph on Palm Sunday. He is leaving it for the very last time. As He reaches the forecourt of the Gentiles, certain Greeks seek Him out. They address Philip and say to him, 'Sir, we would see Jesus.' Would Philip be so good as to arrange for them to speak to Jesus? Strangely enough Philip does not dare at first to do as they ask, and turns to Andrew. Finally the two of them pluck up courage to tell Jesus what the strangers want. They are obviously proselytes from Greece. In itself this is an insignificant incident. However, it is obviously a surprise for Jesus, coming as it does at this moment. Just imagine what this strange coincidence might mean. The door to the Temple and to His own people has just been slammed shut and now it seems as if another door might open to Him: here are some Greeks wanting to see Him. Could this not be a friendly sign from the Father? Does it not look like a lead? Perhaps these Greeks are messengers from above, sent by His Father to say, 'Turn your back on the Jews and go over to the other nations. What does it matter if the way to one stubborn people has closed? The wide door to the Gentiles is standing open for you. Do these Greeks here not appear to be a delegation, from all the waiting nations who are beckoning you to come over and help them? Shake the dust from your feet, take up your staff and leave Jerusalem: the world is wide and there is plenty of room in the guest-house of the nations.'

Yet it is not God, but the Tempter, who is approaching Jesus. It is a false lead, like the one at the beginning of Christ's Ministry, described by Matthew, when the Devil led Him to the top of a very high mountain, and, showing Him the world and all its kingdoms, whispered to Him, 'All these things will I give thee if thou wilt fall down and worship me.' The visit of the Greeks confronts Him with the temptation to take another way out than that which leads to the Cross. It is undoubtedly the will of the Father that Jesus should go out to all the nations, and He will open up the way for the Son, but not before Israel has crucified Him. Israel must, and will, go to the extreme of executing its King. Because it is the Father's will that this is the way that leads to the salvation of all nations, Jesus is prepared to take it in voluntary filial obedience. But could not the arrival of these Greeks be a sign from the Father? Is the Father at the very end going to spare Him this final, inconceivable step after all? Did not this same Father once call out to Abraham at the very last moment when he was about to sacrifice his son, and give him a ram instead? Is it possible that these Greeks are a similar last-minute sign from God, who may yet be going to send Him out to the nations without a Cross? That is the temptation. It explains the strange shyness of these Greeks, who do not dare to address the Lord personally, as if they had some subconscious suspicion that they are involuntary tools of darkness. It also explains the reluctance of Philip, who does not dare to interrupt Christ's journey without Andrew's support, remembering only too well the words that greeted Peter when he tried to divert his Master from the way of the Cross: 'Get thee behind me, satan: for thou savourest not the things that be of God, but the things that be of men.' We would be fully justified in trembling before a Tempter who has such cunning at his disposal. Jesus however sees through this subtle move and immediately takes counter-action. Only Jesus could discern Satan behind the disguise of an angel of light. He answers that the time will certainly come when He will draw unto Him all men, Jews and Gentiles, who will let themselves be drawn. Then He will be able to send out His disciples with the splendid words, 'Go ye therefore, and teach all nations.' But this great hour has not come yet. First of all He has to be lifted up on to the Cross. He must fight through and suffer His dark hour before His hour of glory comes.

At this moment of temptation a parallel from nature comes to His aid. Unless a grain of wheat falls into the earth and dies, it will not bear fruit. It can only do so by an act of sacrifice. Admittedly other grains of wheat are ground into flour and made into bread instead of being used as seed. They are far from useless, but they 'abide alone' and do not multiply. Fertility and reproduction are given only to the grain of wheat that lets itself be buried in the earth, and decay and die. Jesus could go to the Greeks now, and carry on His ministry among them and bring them many blessings, but the will of the Father directs otherwise. Like the seed-corn He must first be buried in the earth and die. And so He obeys the Father even to dying on the Cross, turning a deaf ear to the Devil's suggestions. He will not 'abide alone.' His spiritual children will be as numerous as the stars in the sky and the grains of sand on the sea-shore, and His dear blood will be the seed that will be carried out among all the nations. Where this seed falls, God's field will be tilled and God's harvest will ripen. By staying in Jerusalem He is doing more for these Greeks than He would by going to them now. He becomes the Lord of all nations by remaining within the confines of Israel instead of going out into the wide world. He is ensuring the salvation of all the nations, including the Greeks, by dying in obedience to His Father's will, rather than trying to prolong and extend His influence on the earth, and that without abandoning Israel. 'And I, if I be lifted up from the earth, will draw all men unto me,' that is, all those who will let themselves be drawn. But first He must be lifted up: first of all the grain of wheat must die.

Surprisingly enough, Christ next applies what He has just said of Himself to His community. The Church, which owes its life solely to His death and Resurrection, will never be able to forget that it is the Church of Him who chose the way of the grain of wheat. The course of the Church must conform to the pattern laid down by the grain of wheat. In the Church of Jesus Christ, not only the head but also the members must go through death to life. 'He that loveth his life shall lose it; and he that hateth his life in this world shall keep it unto life eternal.'

In their application to the Church, these words about the grain of wheat that wants to draw after it into death and life all those who believe in Christ, can throw light on a problem that has occupied my thoughts a great deal in the last few years. We are living at a time when the Church in every part of the world seems, humanly speaking, to be dwindling. This state of affairs gives rise everywhere to the question: 'What is to be done?' How can we preserve our Church? Would it not be possible to help our enfeebled Church back on to its feet, let us say by means of a boldly designed plan, more or less like the hotel plan that revived our hotel industry, or like the drive for more intensive cultivation that is occupying us in these years of war? Is it not urgently necessary to regain ground for the Church by means of a campaign of this kind? Thoughts like this crop up in our minds in our anxiety for the Church. But going by our text for today, can we say that the Bible expresses similar thoughts? Is it not possible that Christ intends to maintain and build up His Church by quite different methods, not by expansion in our sense of the word but, who knows, perhaps in the very opposite way, though the idea may not appeal to us. In the history of the Church, Christ has quite often called a handful of people who were prepared to set little store by their own lives. Could not Christ, as in the time of Gideon, renew His Church again today with three hundred people, sending thirty thousand back to their homes?

Whether we like it or not, the Church is certainly dwindling according to the will of God. In this way God is pointing out so clearly that we can no longer shut our eyes to the fact that it is not men but Christ who maintains the Church. He may use us: but He may also send us away in order to achieve His purpose. We do not like that at all. But it is written here that His community is called to follow the path that He takes, and His way is the way of the grain of wheat, not the quick, technical way of organization, but the slow and elementary way of growth: 'If any man serve me, him will my Father honour.' The Father may honour him, but that does not mean that men will do the same. Honour in God's eyes is often dishonour among men. But a man who no longer fears the scorn of men and who risks being rejected by them and cast out by the pious is worthy of the Father's honour. The only honour recognised by the Church of Christ crucified is dishonour in the eyes of the world. A handful of men, who have ceased to fear excommunication and long to be honoured in Heaven, are worth more to the Kingdom of God and therefore also to the maintenance of the Church, than any festival pomp and packed churches. What good are churches full of people who love their lives more than anything else? But the way leads through death: 'If any man serve me, let him follow me; and where I am, there shall also my servant be: if any man serve me, him will my Father honour.'

But are we not treading on dangerous ground here? Do not the lords and masters of this world talk in the same way? Do they not also say, 'If you do not risk your lives, you will never save them'? Do they not demand that their subjects should be prepared to stake everything? Certainly, but not every cause for which people give up their lives is God's cause. One can also give up one's life for the Devil and his work. Therefore we have to decide whether we are risking our lives for Christ and His cause, in imitation of Him, or whether we are listening to the voice of a stranger and swearing by the name of a stranger.

But who dares to say that he will become one of those who are expected to despise their lives for Christ and His cause? It is little wonder that in the last half-century we have not dared to sing the last verse of Luther's hymn which contains the words: 'Let them take my body, my property and my honour, my wife and children; they can take all I have, yet they will gain nothing.' It runs against the grain to give up our lives like this. Under certain circumstances a man or woman may be inspired to die for some great leader or great cause of this world. A man can never be eager to hate his life and give it up for Christ and His Kingdom. This is where natural zeal fails, even that reckless willingness to die on the battlefield, and it is better so. The Russian author Turgenev used to tell the story of how, when a fire broke out on a steamer off Stettin, he kept his head, and comforted the weeping women and encouraged the men. The truth of the matter is, however, that the captain found it necessary to reprimand this large young man for pushing his way into a life-boat in front of women and children, all the while moaning, '*Mourir si jeune!*' Merezhkovsky, who relates the incident, remarks, 'Who knows how he himself would behave when in danger of his life? Who dares to judge the behaviour of someone faced with death? The fact that Turgenev was so terribly frightened is much less serious than his lying about it so shamelessly later on.' When it comes to dying for Christ our flesh will cry out, '*Mourir si jeune!* I am too young to die!' Then we shall find that we have the same human weakness as Peter. Our courage will fail. But thank God that Christ has accepted us as we are, even though our nature resists the way of the grain of wheat with every fibre of its being. Christ became like one of us and in His weakness even He has to confess, 'Now is my soul troubled.' This hour of torment has been sent to tempt Him to waver. 'And what shall I say?' The nature He has accepted for our sake is beginning to falter. In this state of distress He seeks refuge in prayer, which is first of all the prayer of a human being who does not want to die: 'Father, save me from this hour.' Are the Greeks a way out for Him after all? Does the Father mean to spare Him and save Him? But then He pulls Himself together and we hear Him say, 'But for this cause came I unto this hour.' He came to this hour because the Greeks are to have life and all the other nations too, and because He must ensure their salvation by taking the way of the grain of wheat. And now He overcomes the weakness of His nature with its uncertainty and fear, and in his new-found glory and strength the victorious cry escapes His lips, 'Father, glorify thy name.'

That is Christ's prayer and the prayer of His community, as their hour of trial approaches. The prayer of Christ, and all Christian prayer, is not so arrogant and unrealistic as to ignore the emotions and weaknesses of the flesh as if they did not exist. On the contrary, these human weaknesses play an integral part in prayer: 'Father, save me from this hour.' But that is followed by: 'Father, glorify thy name.' The other Evangelists' version of this is, 'O my Father, if it be possible, let this cup pass from me: nevertheless not as I will, but as thou wilt.' In view of the Church's present situation, what can we do but join in this struggle and prayer of Christ's and call out likewise, 'Father, save us from this hour.' but adding, 'Father, may thy name be glorified.' 'Father, spare us yet again: be patient once more with us and with our children. But if it must be, then "glorify thy name."'

At this moment of humiliation, which Christ undergoes for our sake, the Father acknowledges Him, just as He did at the beginning when Jesus was baptised in the river Jordan. Luke says at this point that an angel appeared from Heaven, strengthening Him. John says, 'Then came there a voice from heaven, saying, I have both glorified it and will glorify it again.' The people feel that they must find a natural or supernatural explanation of this. Some say that it was an angel and others that it was only thunder. But Jesus has heard His Father's voice answering Him in His hour of temptation, and He is satisfied. 'I have glorified my name in Israel and I shall glorify it again among all the nations and once more in Israel when your hour has come.'

The Father's acknowledgment decides the issue and the battle is won. You can feel the jubilation in Christ's words, 'Now is the judgment of this world: now shall the prince of this world be cast out.' The description of the Devil as 'the prince of this world' occurs only in the gospel of St John, here and in two other places. The prince of this world is now to be dethroned and cast out. It is striking and significant that Christ should say this, for He means that a decision has been made, and that from now on certain events must take their course. The prince of this world has been deposed, but though he can no longer rule he still has considerable scope for his work. The Cross has dethroned him. From being the prince he has become a tool and a servant, whose powers have been circumscribed, a kind of minion or petty official sent to trouble the nations. Another Prince is enthroned on the right hand of the Father, and to Him has been given all the power, not only in Heaven but also on the earth. That is why this hour of sore temptation ends with the victorious cry, 'Now shall the prince of this world be cast out.'

Jesus Washes His Disciples' Feet

Now before the feast of the passover, when Jesus knew that his hour was come that he should depart out of this world unto the Father, having loved his own which were in the world, he loved them unto the end. And supper being ended, the devil having now put into the heart of Judas Iscariot, Simon's son, to betray him; Jesus knowing that the Father had given all things into his hands, and that he was come from God, and went to God; he riseth from supper, and laid aside his garments; and took a towel, and girded himself. After that he poureth water into a bason, and began to wash the disciples' feet, and to wipe them with the towel wherewith he was girded. Then cometh he to Simon Peter: and Peter saith unto him, Lord, dost thou wash my feet? Jesus answered and said unto him, What I do thou knowest not now; but thou shalt know hereafter. Peter saith unto him, Thou shalt never wash my feet. Jesus answered him, If I wash thee not, thou hast no part with me. Simon Peter saith unto him, Lord, not my feet only, but also my hands and my head. Jesus saith to him, He that is washed needeth not save to wash his feet, but is clean every whit: and ye are clean, but not all. For he knew who should betray him; therefore said he, Ye are not all clean. So after he had washed their feet, and had taken his garments, and was set down again, he said unto them, Know ye what I have done to you? Ye call me Master and Lord: and ye say well; for so I am. If I then, your Lord and Master, have washed your feet; ye also ought to wash one another's feet. For I have given you an example, that ye should do as I have done to you. Verily, verily, I say unto you, The servant is not greater than his lord; neither he that is sent greater than he that sent him. If ye know these things, happy are ye if ye do them. I speak not of you all: I know whom I have chosen: but that the scripture may be fulfilled, He that eateth bread with me hath lifted up his heel against me. Now I tell you before it come, that, when it is come to pass, ye may believe that I am he. Verily, verily, I say unto you, He that receiveth whomsoever I send receiveth me; and he that receiveth me receiveth him that sent me.

When Jesus had thus said, he was troubled in spirit, and testified, and said, Verily, verily, I say unto you, that one of you shall betray me. Then the disciples looked one on another, doubting of whom he spake. Now there was leaning on Jesus' bosom one of his disciples, whom Jesus loved. Simon Peter therefore beckoned to him, that he should ask who it should be of whom he spake. He then lying on Jesus' breast saith unto him, Lord, who is it? Jesus answered, He it is, to whom I shall give a sop, when I have dipped it. And when he had dipped the sop, he gave it to Judas Iscariot, the son of Simon. And after the sop Satan entered into him. Then said Jesus unto him, That thou doest, do quickly. Now no man at the table knew for what intent he spake this unto him. For some of them thought, because Judas had the bag, that Jesus had said unto him, Buy those things that we have need of against the feast; or, that he should give something to the poor. He then having received the sop went immediately out: and it was night.

Therefore, when he was gone out, Jesus said, Now is the Son of man glorified, and God is glorified in him. If God be glorified in him, God shall also glorify him in himself, and shall straightway glorify him. Little children, yet a little while I am with you. Ye shall seek me: and as I said unto the Jews, Whither I go, ye cannot come; so now I say to you. A new commandment I give unto you, That ye love one another; as I have loved you, that ye also love one another. By this shall all men know that ye are my disciples, if ye have love one to another.

[XIII. 1-35]

A new phase has begun for Jesus and His disciples, but only Jesus knows it at present; His disciples are not aware of it yet. That is why the disciples do not and cannot understand what Christ is saying, and why this chapter is so full of questions and mystery. Is it not always so when God does something new? Is it not characteristic of His work that it is secret and hidden from human eyes at first? God's plans are made long before anyone on earth can conceive of them. It is often tens, or hundreds, or even thousands of years before we are allowed to learn something of the decisions that have been made in Heaven. God's intentions are often obscurely alluded to, or suggested, in prophecies but they do not become generally evident until very much later. It was only after the Resurrection of Christ that the early Christian community began to read and understand the Old Testament with opened eyes. When Christ says to Peter, 'What I do thou knowest not now; but thou shalt know hereafter,' His words are applicable both throughout this chapter and to all who ever served Him, from Noah to Abraham and Moses and all the prophets down to John the Baptist. None of them understood Him; they all had to wait until the great light of Easter broke through the darkness of thousands of years, and the day of understanding dawned for all the nations.

Nor are things otherwise in our small, personal experience. Time and again we are led along paths whose destination we do not know. God sends us sorrows to which we can scarcely reconcile ourselves. 'Thou shalt know hereafter' are words often heard at the grave-side. The same is true of events in the world today. Many a catastrophe is obscure and puzzling to us. We do not know where God is guiding our country. His intentions are unfathomable at present. At the same time it can only strengthen our faith to know that whatever is in store for us has already been decided in Heaven. If we had ears to hear we could listen to the angels rejoicing at the ultimate victory of truth, justice and love. So these words apply particularly to our generation: 'What I do thou knowest not now.' And there will be a 'hereafter' for everyone who does not throw away his faith.

And what is this new phase into which Jesus and His disciples have entered, and which Jesus knows about but His disciples do not? The decision that His hour has come has been made. He has so often eluded His pursuers: now He will no longer flee from them, for He knows that very soon He will go to the Father. He knows too that the Father has given all things into His hands.

This knowledge endows Him with an untroubled serenity. Admittedly, as in so many of the previous chapters, we read that He is 'troubled.' But this time another word is added. Previously we have always been told that His soul was troubled: here however it says that He is 'troubled in spirit.' His soul no longer falters. That moment has arrived in the Passion of the Lord when He becomes majestically calm, and His trembling and fear of what is to happen have left Him. That is the new phase. His eyes are now firmly fixed on the Cross and its glory. Thus there is a joyful feeling of fulfilment underlying this chapter which foreshadows the words that He will cry out from the Cross in a few days' time: 'It is finished.' The certainty that He will finish His task is a source of strength to Jesus. We see Christ as a leader already rewarded for a victory that is certain but not yet gained.

Now we can begin to understand the paradox of this chapter, that Jesus appears in lowliness and at the same time in majesty. We see Him as a servant, going about a menial task with an apron tied round Him. But at the same time He is the Lord and Master from first to last, radiant with an heavenly splendour. In this chapter about the washing of His disciples' feet He is called 'Lord' no fewer than eight times, twice He is referred to as 'Master' and once as the 'Son of man.' 'Ye call me Master and Lord: and ye say well; for so I am.' And immediately following the departure of Judas we hear Him say, 'Now is the Son of man glorified, and God is glorified in him.' He says this knowing quite well that His glorification will not become apparent until Easter Sunday. We can comprehend the lowliness of Christ only if we never forget that He is the Lord. He will soon be taken prisoner, but He will remain the Lord. They will take Him before the High Priest and strike Him, but He will not cease to be the Lord. They will drag Him into the judgment hall before Pilate, but there He will be the Lord more than ever. He will be scourged, nailed to the Cross and jeered at. But there is one thing that they will never be able to alter nor prevent: He is the Lord and will remain the Lord, the Lord of all lords. At His most humble He is invested with the greatness of God and no one shall rob Him of that.

Now we can also understand Jesus's words to His disciples. They are also called both to lowliness and grandeur. 'For I have given you an example, that ye should do as I have done to you.' They too are to perform humble duties in the world. As servants they cannot be greater than their Master. He has washed their feet and so they should not be ashamed to perform similar services. Jesus gives His Church the role of service. But we would be misunderstanding the Church's lowliness if we were to forget for a moment that it is the Church of Christ. The disciples will not understand Him yet, nevertheless He is their Master and they are His disciples. They will fail Him in His impending struggle, yet they will be His disciples. One of them, Peter, their leader, and the strongest and most gifted of them all, will even deny Him. But in spite of his fall, Peter will remain His disciple, because Christ is to die for them all in a few days. He will send out these disciples of His to all the nations, and their calling will be very great, because whoever accepts them will be accepting Him: and whoever accepts Him will be accepting the Father in Heaven. It will be their privilege to set out on their way to the nations at the command of God Himself. Whoever accepts or rejects them will be accepting or rejecting Christ and therefore God. 'Inasmuch as ye have done it unto one of the least of these my brethren, ye have done it unto me.' Christ speaks of His Church and of His own as highly as this, but not so much because the disciples are great in themselves as because He is their Lord and Master. 'If a man desire the office of a bishop, he desireth a good work.'

Only one man does not desire this 'good work.' Judas does not want to rise to greatness through lowliness. He refuses to be assigned the part of servant. He does not want the sort of Master who washes people's feet: he wants a Church that rules. But whenever the Church tries to rule in the earthly sense, it comes under the shadow of Judas. Jesus sends him away from the group, having waited until the very last when the Temple door has finally shut, and He realises that Israel has hardened its heart against Him. He orders him to carry out quickly what he intends to do. Here again Jesus is master of the situation. This expulsion of Iscariot means that Jesus has all the more pleasure in the rest of the disciples, who will now, without exception, be and remain His.

The first unusual and mysterious thing that Jesus says about the calling of the disciples is that their duty is to serve; but in their service lies their greatness. And the Lord says another, equally astonishing, thing about the eleven who remain: 'Ye are clean.' They are clean because He is going to die for them. They are clean for the very reason that the blood of Jesus cleanses us all of sin. It is just as if Jesus were generously sharing out the treasures and rewards of the Cross to His disciples. Jesus is cleansing the disciples of their sins like an employer giving his staff wages in advance. He is giving them now what He will win and suffer for them on the Cross. 'Ye are clean.' Jesus might say this to any man, just as He says it to His disciples. 'Look at yourselves closely: what a lot there is in you displeasing to both God and man! All the same you are clean, because it is for you that the decision has been made: it is finished!'

The third and probably greatest word that Jesus says to His disciples is that they are called to love: 'A new commandment I give unto you, That ye love one another; as I have loved you.' Men are to love one another, not just anyhow, but as Christ loves His own. That is a new conception. The disciples have not understood why Christ talks of a 'new commandment': after all, even in the days of the New Testament everyone knew the commandment that one should love God and man. What is this new idea? It is that there will soon be a Christ who loved the world so much that He died for it on the Cross. Soon there will be people who can love one another, because of what Christ has fulfilled on the Cross. The opportunity for such love has filtered through to earth from Heaven, and this aspect of love is new on earth. And yet in the first chapter we heard that 'there is no new thing under the sun.' That is true; but only with reference to men and not where God's splendid works are concerned. There is a new kind of love under the sun now, because Jesus came to dwell under the sun, to love us unto death. And that is why men can now love one another too. Christ says, 'Love one another; as I have loved you,' to His disciples, who up till now have been quarrelling about who should take first place at table, and each of whom has always wanted to be the most important in the Kingdom of Heaven. Just as from now on there will be men who will live though they die, and who will be clean though they are wretched sinners, so there will be men in whom the impossible will be wrought by God: although, like all other men, they are egoists by nature, they will love one another just as Christ has loved us, with a love that is stronger than death. Now there really is something new under the sun, something unknown before, and that is the love that died for the world under Pontius Pilate. An inexhaustible spring of love has thus broken forth. This spring of love will be plentiful enough for all peoples, countries, and continents and all ages unto eternity. 'A new commandment I give unto you, That ye love one another; as I have loved you, that ye also love one another.'

But now, let us return to the washing of the disciples' feet. Do we really understand it? We may think we have understood it immediately, but probably we have not understood it at all. We may think that Christ is being kind to the disciples when He kneels in front of them and washes their feet. This seems to be a very moving and friendly gesture. Even the disciples want to take it in this touching way at first, and Peter indignantly refuses the favour. He considers it undignified and thinks that Christ is going a bit too far. He feels that he cannot possibly accept such a service from Christ, but then understanding comes to him and he has to confess that this is not so much a case of Christ's lowliness and poverty as of his own. The washing of feet indicates a need on the part of the person who is washed. This service fulfils an urgent spiritual need for Peter. It would be his misfortune if, instead of humbly accepting, he were to reject it and say, 'I do not need it.' Jesus washes Peter's and the other disciples' feet because they walk on the earth. The words once cast at the serpent, 'Upon thy belly shalt thou go, and dust shalt thou eat,' have particular application to the disciples' feet. Even the feet of Christians become dusty when they stand and walk on the earth.

Whenever our feet touch the earth they become dirty and therefore need to be washed. This simple fact serves Christ as a parable, taken from everyday life in those times. To be basically clean in those days people bathed; but for perfect cleanliness their feet needed repeated washing because they wore open sandals. So Jesus says to His followers, 'You are clean, for you are washed; you are baptised in my name. That is irrefutable and final. But your feet constantly need washing, even though you are bathed, and in the same way you constantly need purification in spite of the fact that you are baptised Christians.' We may be Christians once and for all, nevertheless we need regular confirmation of the fact. We may have received forgiveness for our sins once and for all, nevertheless we frequently need to be forgiven anew because we go on sinning day after day. We may have entered irrevocably into the love of Jesus Christ, nevertheless we need His love for us to be renewed again and again. That is why Jesus has added the Sacrament of Holy Communion to that of Holy Baptism. It is regularly celebrated by the community because our need for it is ever present. At the Holy Communion we are reminded of that unique purification achieved for us on the Cross for all time, and which we cannot and do not have to achieve for ourselves. At the same time, however, we bring to the Lord's Table the sins that we are always committing, so that He may do for us what He did for the disciples when He washed their feet. So when we regularly give each other the Holy Communion, we are doing exactly what Jesus bids us do when He says, 'For I have given you an example, that ye should do as I have done to you.'

With few exceptions the Christian Church does not make a regular ritual of washing feet, and I think rightly so. The washing of feet symbolises the regular confirmation of our purity and its purpose is amply served by the Holy Communion. When Jesus begins to wash His disciples' feet, Peter sees in it at first only the humility of his Master and refuses to accept this sacrifice from Him. However, Jesus reminds Peter of his own need for humility and points out the necessity of accepting, otherwise he will have 'no part' with Jesus. And His words bring home to us the importance of attending Holy Communion. The Lord is telling us that we need it as baptised Christians. Not that we are allowed to conclude from this that someone who never goes to Holy Communion is therefore no Christian and excluded from the Christian community. We do not want to make a law of taking Holy Communion. But it must be a matter for concern that there are so many Christians who are content to be baptised and think that they need nothing more. Staying away from Holy Communion is a very bad thing. The obstinate excuse that 'one can be a good Christian without it' is to be deprecated. Christ surely knows why He says to Peter, 'If I wash thee not, thou hast no part with me.' I often wonder if there is not some hidden connexion between our neglect of the Holy Communion, and our poverty of love and hardness of heart. Could that be why the new commandment is so weak and ineffective in the community? Is it perhaps because we are too careless or too proud to let our feet be washed, that our love is always so cold and narrow?

A conversation I had with an experienced lay-preacher the other day surprised me to a certain extent, and gave me much food for thought. He was relating his experiences to me, and told me that when he meets people to whom life has been cruel, and who are so embittered and crushed that they are no longer capable of love, he usually advises them to go often to Holy Communion all the same. He tells them that in this way the battered garden of their lives will be replanted. Because of the war, so much crushed and hardened ground is being restored to usefulness in our drive for increased cultivation. Yet there is crushed and hardened ground not only in our parks and outside our houses, but also inside, in marriages and families up and down the country. There are so many gardens of life in which no flower blooms any more, and no bird sings, and in which the fruit of charity will never ripen again. Come and let these barren gardens be replanted, for Christ wants flowers to bloom and birds to sing in them again and the fruits of brotherly love to thrive. For 'By this shall all men know that ye are my disciples, if ye have love one to another.'

Christ knows us by our faith: for Him faith, and faith alone, is decisive. That is why this gospel continually exhorts us to believe. Our faith determines our attitude to God. The world, however, does not know us by our faith; it has not the eyes to see it. But there is one thing that 'all men' can see and are receptive to: and that is our love. Humanity needs this love and hungers after it. 'By this shall all men know that ye are my disciples, if ye have love one to another.'

On Going to the Father

Simon Peter said unto him, Lord, whither goest thou? Jesus answered him, Whither I go, thou canst not follow me now; but thou shalt follow me afterwards. Peter said unto him, Lord, why cannot I follow thee now? I will lay down my life for thy sake. Jesus answered him, Wilt thou lay down thy life for my sake? Verily, verily, I say unto thee, The cock shall not crow, till thou hast denied me thrice.

Let not your heart be troubled: ye believe in God, believe also in me. In my Father's house are many mansions: if it were not so, I would have told you. I go to prepare a place for you. And if I go and prepare a place for you, I will come again, and receive you unto myself; that where I am, there ye may be also. And whither I go ye know, and the way ye know. Thomas saith unto him, Lord, we know not whither thou goest; and how can we know the way? Jesus saith unto him, I am the way, the truth, and the life: no man cometh unto the Father, but by me. If ye had known me, ye should have known my Father also: and from henceforth ye know him, and have seen him. Philip saith unto him, Lord, shew us the Father, and it sufficeth us. Jesus saith unto him, Have I been so long time with you, and yet hast thou not known me, Philip? he that hath seen me hath seen the Father; and how sayest thou then, Shew us the Father? Believest thou not that I am in the Father, and the Father in me? the words that I speak unto you I speak not of myself: but the Father that dwelleth in me, he doeth the works. Believe me that I am in the Father, and the Father in me: or else believe me for the very works' sake.

Verily, verily, I say unto you, He that believeth on me, the works that I do shall he do also; and greater works than these shall he do; because I go unto my Father. And whatsoever ye shall ask in my name, that will

I do, that the Father may be glorified in the Son. If ye shall ask any thing in my name, I will do it.

[XIII. 36–38; XIV. 1–14]

It takes a great deal to bring men to the stage that the disciples of Christ have reached. They are not only 'troubled,' as the translation puts it; the original Greek text uses a very strong word which means 'shocked.' Peter and Thomas and the others are thoroughly shocked, and with good reason. They have followed Jesus, burning their boats, and blowing up the bridges behind them, so to speak. Never has a group of men been so closely united with their master as are these disciples. The loyalty of Jesus's followers is incomparable on earth: it is unique because their Master is unique. And now He has disclosed to them that He is about to go where they cannot follow Him as yet. That means that they must part from Him. The reason why they are so deeply shocked is that separation from their Lord is absolutely unthinkable to them.

Now Jesus uses a word which He knows will penetrate even the perturbation into which the disciples have been thrown. This word recurs like a key-note throughout the gospel of St John: 'faith.' He tells them to believe. And if in these parting chapters He says it particularly often and with particular urgency, what He means is, 'If you have not known the meaning of faith so far, you will learn now.' They are shocked now but there are other shocks in store for them. Peter, the rock, will hear the cock crow three times, and then break down. But it is in such hours of shock that the meaning of the word faith is revealed in its true splendour. They will be so shocked that the very ground will tremble and open up beneath their feet; so shocked that they will learn that faith is no human faculty or achievement, but a support and source of strength in times of disaster. So Christ's call to them to believe is as much a last saving offer as a command. 'You *can* believe now. This much I can offer you; "Ye believe in God, believe also in me." '

'Believe in God.' That sounds strange coming from Jesus. He

says, 'Believe in God,' as if God were a stranger to Him, and as if He were going to begin to talk about 'the Lord God.' What He means is that they should believe in the God of the ancients, the God of their fathers; believe in the God who, in the days of Abraham, Jacob and Moses, gave His help and support to His people. This is the God who once opened a way across the Red Sea, the God who made the walls of Jericho fall down, the God who saved the men in the fiery furnace, and who delivered Daniel from the lions. 'Believe in God.' But Jesus knows how easy such belief in the 'Lord God' can become, and how readily men are prepared, in referring to the past, to utter high-sounding confessions of faith that commit them to nothing. We are quick to say, 'I believe that God cast down the walls of Jericho,' but the situation is very different when we stand in front of a wall and have to believe that God can break it down! That is why the Lord goes on to demand faith in Himself as He stands before them here and now, unavoidable; for in His eyes faith is the decisive factor: 'believe also in me.' He demands (and offers them) faith in Himself, just when He is on the point of becoming hidden from their eyes, when the words of the old prophecy will soon be fulfilled in Him: 'He hath no form nor comeliness; and when we shall see him, there is no beauty that we should desire him.'

Very soon they will no longer be able to see Him, for it will be impossible; they will only be able to turn away their faces from Him in horror and yet at the moment when He is expecting the Cross almost immediately, He demands (and offers them) faith in Himself. There are some among us this morning who know what shock means. All of you who are shocked because God is hidden from us in our day and age, who feel you have to cry out to this veiled God, and who must be under the impression that all Christ said and did has ended in a pool of blood and scorn, all of you must, and at the same time can, believe in Him. And believing in Christ crucified means quite simply being convinced that both the works of Christ and His victory are of significance today and that, however it appears, there will never be a world that does not bear the sign of Him who said to His disciples, 'Believe also in me.'

It is moving to see how concerned the Lord is to make this parting easier for the disciples. He uses the best method of dealing with shocked people. He portrays the whole greatness and splendour of His Father's dominion to them. In speaking of the Kingdom of Heaven His words are almost elementary, rather like a mother explaining it to her little children. He calls the Kingdom of Heaven 'my Father's house,' and says that it is very spacious with 'many mansions' in it. His Father's house is not confined to this world: it is spacious in Heaven too. He might be saying, 'Do not think so little of the might of my Father that your eyes remain fixed on this tiny earth. Just as a thousand years are like a day in His sight, so a thousand tons are like a match-box to Him.' It would be unimaginative of the disciples to think that, now that the Lord has spent thirty years on this earth, His effectiveness must be restricted to it. They must not be so selfish as to want to keep Him back from the rest of the rooms in the great house of His Father on the other side, which are waiting for His return. He must not neglect these for the sake of the small earth. If He goes over there now He will not forget His disciples for one moment. He will continue to work for them even there, and to be and remain their Helper and Saviour. 'I go to prepare a place for you,' for, 'in my Father's house are many mansions.'

But while He has many mansions on the other side, the world must be and remain all the more His dwelling. Christ came to earth in order to win it, and to declare it once and for all, His Father's domain. So if God has many dwellings in Heaven, there must all the more be many dwellings of God on this earth. If only we could be given something of that child-like confidence behind the words: 'In my Father's house are many mansions.' How very like the disciples we are when we give ourselves up to despair, because some small door has closed to us and some small opportunity is lost. How easily we are depressed by the fact that there are nations, who for years have been trying to close the door and who are interested only in expanding their earthly boundaries, but have no desire for a dwelling in the house of the Father. How quickly we give up hope, yet all the time the Father is busy opening other doors that have seemed closed for centuries. If only we could believe that God alone holds the key to every door and every dwelling in Heaven and on earth! We lose courage because some little man or other gives orders to pull down a church to make room for a military monument, or even to transform a church into a war-museum, and we forget that it is easy for God to open ten new church doors for every one that may be closed by men. Certainly many doors are being closed today by men and nations everywhere, but faith knows that God is at work among the nations, opening many more doors. In the long run no nation will succeed in keeping the door closed, because it is the command and will of God: 'Go and break into the domains of all the nations and raise up the signs of God's dominion.' Something of this confidence is shown in a story about Luther when his cause and the work of the Reformation were not going well. Luther was asked where he would be if his protector were to desert him and scatter his people. After a moment's thought, Luther answered, 'Under Heaven.' Truly there are many mansions in the house of the Father, both in Heaven and on the earth.

Christ has not the slightest intention of abandoning the world, however, even though the time has come for Him to remove to the other side of His Father's house. The disciples may not be able to follow Him for the moment, but for Christ the way back to the disciples and back to the world always remains open and passable. In going over to the other side Jesus is not leaving His Father's house; it is just as if He were moving from one room to another. He remains under the same roof. Jesus's coming into the world has finally brought Heaven and earth together, and the way from one to the other stands open. Now that God has opened it, neither man nor devil can close it. Therefore Christ talks of going away and in the same breath announces that He will return: 'And if I go . . . I will come again, and receive you unto myself; that where I am, there ye may be also.' The time will surely come when all the barriers between the dwellings on this side and those on the other will be completely broken down. But the time of perfect union is not here yet. Until His return, His own have to wait and endure in the dwellings on earth. As Christians on this side we must be faithful. The splendid knowledge that He has gone to prepare a place for us does not justify our premature forsaking of the dwellings that have been assigned to us here. On earth we must hold fast to Heaven. Like an earthly king who demands that his soldiers should hold every foot of ground, the Lord of all the dwellings in Heaven and on earth expects His own to cling to Heaven. Holding fast to the belief that the earth is God's, and that it has become His through Christ, is the precise duty of Christians in this poor world. It is essential for our country that there should be a large number of people who cling to Heaven. For the sake of the family in which God has placed you, and for the partner in marriage whom He has given you, you can and must cling to Heaven. Now that God Himself has entered into the dwellings of this world, let us no longer abandon them to the devil. We must wait patiently until He returns to take His own unto Him: 'that where I am, there ye may be also.' How wonderful it will be when the barrier has gone and when the words of Psalm XVII will be fulfilled: 'I will behold thy face in righteousness: I shall be satisfied, when I awake, with thy likeness.'

Until Christ returns, believers must be content with knowing where Christ has gone and His reason for going: 'Whither I go ye know, and the way ye know.' Thomas, who is more shocked than anyone at Christ's impending departure, promptly answers, 'Lord, we know not whither thou goest; and how can we know the way?' He receives Christ's famous answer: 'I am the way, and the truth, and the life: no man cometh unto the Father, but by me.' We are in the habit of considering these great and beautiful words on their own. Let us for once study them in relation to their context, which is of no little importance. Let us notice particularly the time when Jesus speaks them: it is immediately before His Crucifixion, so that first and foremost they postulate belief. Christ says, 'I am the way.' He says this even as He sees the hour approaching, when no way will be visible any longer; for the disciples seem to think that the Cross is the end of every way, and that literally everything will stop. They can see no future, but terrible desolation and trackless desert. But just at what appears to be the terrible end of all ways, Christ is the Way that leads from the dwellings of Heaven to the earth, and from the earth to Heaven. Today the earth is separated from Heaven by a sea of guilt and tears, yet ever since Christ, with His eyes on the Cross, said, 'I am the way,' we have known that there is always a way for God. Even as He hangs on the Cross, He is that same God whose feet do not shrink from the depths of the sea. He goes on to say, 'I am the truth.' This He says on the eve of that day of utter darkness, when lies will triumph over Him as they have never been able to do before. We have a saying that 'lies have short legs.' That is not really true: except in the case of Christ lies have very long legs indeed. They are capable of long strides and can conquer the world. But here is a place where their activity is confined. It is the end of all lies when Christ, in expectation of death on the Cross, says, 'I am the truth.' And finally he says, 'I am the life.' Twenty-four hours later He is laid, a corpse, in the grave. Yet now He says, 'I am the life.' The words that He speaks there apply just as much today, when Death is reaping a rich harvest in so many parts of the world. Believing in Christ means holding fast to the fact that He is the Way where there is no way any longer; that He is the Truth when He is hanging on the Cross; and that He is the Life even when death is everywhere.

The whole question here is one of faith, and this is brought out in the conversation between Christ and Philip. Jesus challenges the faith of His disciples with a few provocative words, in the face of which there is only belief or unbelief: 'If ye had known me, ye should have known my Father also.' Whereupon Philip answers, 'Lord, shew us the Father, and it sufficeth us.' Jesus says to him, 'Have I been so long time with you, and yet hast thou not known me, Philip? he that hath seen me hath seen the Father.'

So fundamental is faith where the Lord is concerned that even these men who have seen everything with their own eyes, heard everything with their own ears, touched Him with their own hands, and have eaten and walked with Him, can conceive who Christ is only through faith. Hence the question to Philip, 'Believest thou not that I am in the Father, and the Father in me?' And the words to all the disciples, 'Believe me that I am in the Father, and the Father in me.'

When you have been given faith in Jesus, and can conceive that He is the 'way, and the truth, and the life,' then you can begin to look at events in the world, particularly in our own time, with eyes of hope. When you know how God works, and can recognise His ways in Christ, then for you a bright light from Heaven is thrown on the life of the nations. Then you know what stands written over all ages, including our own: this watchword is divided into three parts, which run, 'Christ is the Way through every wilderness; the Truth in darkness; and Life in death.' When you believe in Christ, not only do you see the world and events in it in a new perspective, but you also begin to act instead of sitting back as an onlooker. It is true that when you believe in Christ you no longer do many of the things that you did before. But it is equally true that when you come to believe, you begin to do many things that you formerly left undone. Faith gives rise to action and such action is not insignificant. Christ did not go just to prepare a resting-place for His own in eternity, but to increase His activity from there through the disciples, who remained behind: 'He that believeth on me, the works that I do shall he do also; and greater works than these shall he do; because I go unto my Father. And whatsoever ye shall ask in my name, that will I do, that the Father may be glorified in the Son.' What an inconceivable wealth of promise lies in these words! Think for a moment of this shocked little group of men who are listening to Him, and then remember that some weeks later these few men baptise about three thousand believers in one single day. This is the kind of work that He will do through His own, after He has gone to His Father. Think how He confined

Himself within the narrow boundaries of Palestine, then remember how His disciples carried His message to all the nations, so that His community soon spread far beyond the limited frontiers of that country. That is how His followers will do 'greater works' than those that He did Himself. But for all its richness and splendour, this promise of Jesus's leaves us with a difficult question to answer: Where are these works that Christ in Heaven wants to perform among us? How is it that our deeds today are always so small and weak and trivial? Is it not because we believe in our own strength rather than in Christ acting through us from above? But why do we not believe? We have heard that the disciples were shocked when the Lord offered them faith, and demanded it at the same time. This raises the serious question: Have we perhaps not been shocked?

I often wonder whether the difficulties that we are experiencing today in this town and this country have shocked us or not. Admittedly a few of the pillars, which supported us, have collapsed, and a few little walls, on which we used to lean, have begun to give way. That has spread a certain amount of anxiety among us, but broadly speaking we are not really shocked. It may be argued that one often meets people who are in despair. Certainly, but a man who is in despair is still a long way from being shocked to the roots of his being. On the contrary, man's stubbornness lies at the root of most despair. Men fall into despair because they want to stick obstinately to their own will in defiance of God. So the basis of our despair today is our own resistance to God. However, as well as these stubbornly defiant people in despair, there is in our country today a host of complacent people. How self-satisfied we are still! How often we rely on our 'glorious' history, to which we ourselves have contributed so very little by our own efforts, yet our history for the last hundred years consists mainly in our having been spared the hardest blows. Too often we behave like the one spoilt child in the family of nations.

The call to faith cannot be heard where this stubborn despair and this imperturbable self-confidence are prevalent. Neither the defiant man nor the self-confident man wants to believe. This means that that other call: 'Let not your heart be troubled,' can never be heard either. On the contrary, what Christ says to defiant and smug people is, '*Let* your hearts be troubled! It is high time that your hearts were troubled, otherwise you will some day have a most unpleasant awakening.' But where shock has entered in, like the thaw in springtime, the encouraging call can be heard clearly: 'Let not your heart be troubled: ye believe in God, believe also in me. . . . I am the way, and the truth, and the life.'

The Promise of Another Comforter

If ye love me, keep my commandments. And I will pray the Father, and he shall give you another Comforter, that he may abide with you for ever; even the Spirit of truth; whom the world cannot receive, because it seeth him not, neither knoweth him: but ye know him; for he dwelleth with you, and shall be in you. I will not leave you comfortless: I will come to you. Yet a little while, and the world seeth me no more; but ye see me: because I live, ye shall live also. At that day ye shall know that I am in my Father, and ye in me, and I in you. He that hath my commandments, and keepeth them, he it is that loveth me: and he that loveth me shall be loved of my Father, and I will love him, and will manifest myself to him. Judas saith unto him, not Iscariot, Lord, how is it that thou wilt manifest thyself unto us, and not unto the world? Jesus answered and said unto him, If a man love me, he will keep my words: and my Father will love him, and we will come unto him, and make our abode with him. He that loveth me not keepeth not my sayings: and the word which ye hear is not mine, but the Father's which sent me.

[XIV. 15–24]

The whole world needs the Comforter. The sick in hospital, who are tormented by the knowledge that they can do nothing to help themselves; and healthy people too, who have to learn how terribly little we are able to help ourselves, even though we are in good health; women who have recently had to take leave of their husbands, and men who have had to leave their wives and children behind in doubtful security; those who have found themselves a safe spot in the heart of the country, which may not be safe after all, and those others who have decided to stay at their posts here, come what may; the children who slip into their parents' beds because they have been frightened by the noise of lorries passing in the night; the statesman at the microphone, calling upon the nation to act in a calm and responsible manner; those who have just received news that one of their loved ones has died on active service, and all those others who are waiting in uncertainty, hour after hour, wondering if the unimaginable horror of war will break over them. Every single one of us needs the Comforter.

In this instance Christ is talking to the whole world only inasmuch as it has begun to believe in Him, or at some future time will come to believe in Him and will become His. That is to say, He is speaking to His own, to His disciples and His community. For not only the world in general, but Christendom too, needs the Comforter. The community of Christ is nowhere promised that it will be allowed to sit back in safety while the storm rages outside through the ages. The community has its full share of the distress caused by general catastrophes, such as the world is experiencing today. But it has more than its due share of distress, and therefore its need of comfort is particularly great. Indeed Christians may be distinguished by the fact that their need for comfort is greater than anyone else's. It does not take a war or some other national disaster to put them in need of comfort: they need it at all times, when there is perfect peace no less than when danger threatens and other people are afraid too. The community is glad of comfort when others think they can afford to smile indulgently at these remarkable people, who dash off to church every Sunday, sing hymns of faith and comfort, and cannot bear to be without the consolation and support of their faith, even on week-days. Whether in war-time or not, there are a great many men and women who find strength to live in Christ's words: 'I will pray the Father, and he shall give you another Comforter, that he may abide with you for ever.'

The community needs special comfort because it has knowledge of God. The man who knows God begins to hunger for comfort. All he can do is to take to God his distress and questions, which are the painful result of the stress and strife of the world. Sooner or later he is bound to ask in anguish: 'Why?' This question arises not only in the mind of the unbeliever, but also in the mind of the believer and child of God. Consider how often the Psalms contain this naive question of troubled belief. Children often ask their fathers: 'Why?' 'Why not?' 'How much longer?' 'Where?' 'What for?' Children's questions? Yes, but never be ashamed of asking them: it would be very strange if we never had any 'children's questions.' The man who can remain detached from these dark times like a Stoic or an Indian fakir is not a true believer: the true believer is the man who runs to the Father like a child, calling out in his great anxiety for the world; he needs the Father and cannot live without Him. So as children of God we need special comfort because, although we know about God's love, there are so many things that prevent us from recognising it: indeed world events obscure His love for us and we can see love in its purity only in Jesus Christ. We need comfort because, while we know about God's love and omniscience, the history of the world unfolds so senselessly, and we can only see God helpless and crucified. Finally, we are especially in need of comfort as believers, because not only do we know about God in Heaven but also that the earth is His, and we have caught a glimpse of the new Heaven and the new earth in which righteousness dwells, yet at the same time we have to see the earth lapsing into its old ways again and again. Is this not enough to make anyone ask questions? Is it not enough to distress anyone? Christ's answer to this is: 'Blessed are they that mourn: for they shall be comforted.' For the Lord has said, 'I will pray the Father, and he shall give you another Comforter, that he may abide with you for ever.' God comforts the believer by giving him courage to hold fast to his belief in the great promises that He has made to this poor earth. The Christian owes an exceedingly important duty to the world. Now is the time for him to remain true to it and to stay at his post: he must trust in the Word of God and not let these great promises be belittled, distorted or even suppressed. This is the time to spread them abroad. Now Christians have been given a light that must in no circumstances be hidden under a bushel. Now they must be a city on a hill, a comfort and a shining light to all those who have an eye to see and a heart to feel. The 'other Comforter,' who will abide with us for ever, will lift us up every time we are cast down by events in the world, and will overcome the despondency which can so easily undermine our belief in the victory of God. The 'other Comforter' can unite the community and its shepherds into that one flock of which the prophet says, 'Hast thou not known, hast thou not heard, that the everlasting God, the Lord, the Creator of the ends of the earth, fainteth not, neither is weary? there is no searching of his understanding. He giveth power to the faint; and to them that have no might he increaseth strength. Even the youths shall faint and be weary, and the young men shall utterly fall: but they that wait upon the Lord shall renew their strength; they shall mount up with wings as eagles; they shall run, and not be weary; and they shall walk, and not faint.'

The Bible uses the word 'Comforter,' but the word *parakletos*, in the original Greek text, means something stronger and more definite. Actually a paraclete is one called to help or support. It is characteristic of the community of Christ that it knows that it cannot live alone, depending only on itself, and that it is not 'self-supporting,' but that it needs a helper, a support, or paraclete. It has always known this. But it is my impression that, in the last few years, we have begun to see this much more clearly. It is beginning to dawn on an ever-increasing number of people that we cannot manage without support and help from above. Indeed this seems to me to be a symptom of our age and of its particular need. God has begun to take us to task and to show us that, contrary to our belief, we cannot stand alone. He takes away our independence, in which we had placed so much trust and hope. And God will go on humiliating us until everybody realises that godless self-sufficiency which we have been preaching long enough for our own glorification is quite empty. We are indeed fortunate when we can not only see the extent of our need but can also see, and be comforted by, the support that Christ asks of

His Father for His own. Christians are lucky because they have believed all the time and have known about this support. They are luckier, by far, than those who fell in love, to the point of infatuation, with what they fondly imagined was their self-sufficiency. The evil day comes as a bitter surprise to these people. How unbelievably difficult it must be to have needed no help for years because everything was going so well and now to find oneself painfully obliged to look around for God's support. A good many people do not succeed in reorientating themselves, so nowadays there is great need for people in such difficulties, who will never be able to find their own way back. There is the work of a Good Samaritan to be done, that can only be performed by the community, which has enjoyed the support of the eternal Comforter for so long. As a child of God you cannot keep your comforting knowledge to yourself. Wherever you go you will find people who are in despair, because they are incapable of finding the way from their godless self-sufficiency to the comfort of dependence. They resort to cursing and blasphemy because they have forgotten how to pray. How fortunate we Christians are, but what an obligation we are under because Christ says to us, 'I will pray the Father, and he shall give you another Comforter, that he may abide with you for ever.'

But this Greek word for comforter has a further, more particular, meaning. A paraclete is an advocate or intercessor, summoned as a protector when legal help is required, and this is just the kind of assistance that the believer needs. Surely it must strike us how insistently and repeatedly in these valedictory chapters the Lord demands the keeping of His Commandments, the observance of the Divine law, and respect for His Word: 'If ye love me, keep my commandments.' 'He that hath my commandments, and keepeth them, he it is that loveth me.' 'If a man love me, he will keep my words. . . . He that loveth me not keepeth not my sayings.' But can we as Christians hear these demands without inevitably seeing ourselves on trial at the bar of the eternal court of judgment? Can we hear them without realising at once that it is we who are the accused? The community of Christ sees itself in a permanent state of judgment, accused by God's Word and command. It can neither justify nor defend itself. That has always been the greatest need of the Christian community, and particularly so in these days of great reckoning. Christians are incapable of ignoring guilt, and so they cannot look upon these troubled times as an undeserved stroke of fate. They know that it is is not unmerited, not the raging of blind furies, but rather the work of far-seeing justice. The events in the world today are the fruition of many years of unexpiated and unforgiven wrong-doing; they are the result of violations of the law, from the smallest transgressions to law-breaking on a national scale. Much wrong is being done now, but also right: however mysteriously, a part of God's justice is being fulfilled. Admittedly only His own are capable of understanding that; the world cannot see it. Seeing in faith is given only to that company among whom the 'other Comforter' has made His abode, and which lets itself be guided by this 'Spirit of truth,' as Jesus calls it. Only the Spirit of truth, the Holy Ghost, is able to reveal these deeper implications to man.

There is something inexorable about the Spirit of truth. He delves deep, and we must not protest nor try to avoid His searching light, for it is beneficial and necessary to dig down to the truth. And what exactly does the Spirit of truth reveal to us? Where does He lead us? He leads us to recognise the fact that what is happening in the world today is the result not only of general guilt, but also, and above all, of our own, personal guilt. This Spirit is the Spirit of truth because, without respect for persons, He discloses what is to our detriment, and convinces us once and for all of our own guilt. The Christian community in all the nations of Europe is saying today, '*Mea culpa, mea maxima culpa.*' 'It is my fault, mine is the greatest guilt.' It is typical of this world to cry out, 'It is your fault, yours is the greatest guilt; other people are to blame, wicked people; it is God's fault!' Christians, however, say (and this is also typical), 'We are to blame. It is my fault and ours if today thousands of innocent children are starving.' A murderous spirit has been abroad among us for a long time, and we have seen it grow, yet failed to resist it in time. It is my fault and yours, our greatest failure of all, that we have let it mature and grow strong. And so Christians let themselves be brought to repentance by what is happening on the earth today. They confess now that they have not kept God's commandments. They alone can do that. The community of Christ sees itself before the throne of God, accused of being morally responsible for the war. The community alone can see this: the world cannot and never will. The world can only fill its newspapers with protestations of its own innocence, laying the blame on others. For the world has not got the Spirit of truth, and hates Him for the wrongs He exposes. The world can only bear the wrongs of others to be exposed: its own actions must be applauded and condoned.

This is where the community needs the Paraclete, for it is inconsolable and completely dependent on God's comfort. It is conscious of its immense guilt. We Christians can produce no defence: we are literally as helpless as orphans. We are at the mercy of the prosecutor, and entirely dependent on our protector and advocate, who, we must not forget, has said (and where would we be if He had not said it!), 'I will not leave you comfortless [or orphans]: I will come to you.' We have merited death; and if we had to die, our punishment would be just. In our situation there is only one Protector, and that is the One who says, 'You shall not die; "because I live, ye shall live also."'

I feel that if everybody were to face the truth about themselves today and admit it, the world situation would improve. Nothing less than repentance can lay the foundation for a better world. Why is it that in every country only a small and despised group of Christians is able to accept this way of life? This never fails to disturb us. One of the disciples is evidently troubled about it too: 'Judas saith unto him, (not Iscariot,) Lord, how is it that thou wilt manifest thyself unto us, and not unto the world?' He is puzzled, but Jesus gives him the answer. He tells him rather reproachfully that he must think about himself, and leave God to take care of the world. Judas should make an honest effort to love Christ and keep His Word, until the day when Christ and the Father will come and make their abode with all those who are waiting. 'Jesus answered and said unto him, If a man love me, he will keep my words: and my Father will love him, and we will come unto him, and make our abode with him.' The promised day will eventually come. 'Behold, the tabernacle of God is with men, and he will dwell with them, and they shall be his people, and God himself shall be with them, and be their God.'

The Testament of the Son

These things have I spoken unto you, being yet present with you. But the Comforter, which is the Holy Ghost, whom the Father will send in my name, he shall teach you all things, and bring all things to your remembrance, whatsoever I have said unto you. Peace I leave with you, my peace I give unto you: not as the world giveth, give I unto you. Let not your heart be troubled, neither let it be afraid. Ye have heard how I said unto you, I go away, and come again unto you. If ye loved me, ye would rejoice, because I said, I go unto the Father: for my Father is greater than I. And now I have told you before it come to pass, that, when it is come to pass, ye might believe. Hereafter I will not talk much with you: for the prince of this world cometh, and hath nothing in me. But that the world may know that I love the Father; and as the Father gave me commandment, even so I do. Arise, let us go hence.

[XIV. 25–31]

Let us remember for a moment that at this point the Lord is taking leave of His disciples. He comforts His own by telling them what He is leaving to them. He sounds like a dying father, who is able to tell his frightened children that he has been mindful of them, and made provision for them. It is with good reason that the title of Testament is given to the contents of the Bible. Our text is concerned with a very real testament, revealed by the Lord to His children and heirs. Of course it will not entail money and property, for Christ leaves His own very poor in goods and chattels, promising them His peace instead. By that He means everything that they will need for living and dying: 'Peace I leave with you, my peace I give unto you.'

Christ has left behind peace for the nations. The words of the angels that Christmas night have become true: 'And on earth peace.' The peace of God is here; Christ has given and bequeathed it to His disciples. We know that at the present time this sounds just as incongruous as talking about life out there in the cemetery, standing beside a coffin, where you can almost smell decay through the heady scent of the flowers. To talk about peace in this world is tantamount to talking about life on your death-bed. It is bold; but why not be bold? Why should we be so cowardly as to capitulate before the so-called facts? After all is it not a fact that Christ has said, 'Peace I leave with you, my peace I give unto you'? Admittedly no one but the Son could have said that to the world, and now, if we dare to take up His message and spread it abroad, we feel that we should have the voices of angels or archangels, and that the whole army of the heavenly host should join in with trumpets and call out into this hate-filled, dying world: 'Christ has given us His peace.' But if we have neither the voices of angels, nor trumpets, at our disposal, we must simply say it with the poor voice of the ordinary man, who himself stands in the middle of this hostile world, and who himself never knows when his turn will come, nor when the horror of war will touch him; we must simply say weakly, but, please God, in faith, 'Christ has said, "Peace I leave with you, my peace I give unto you."'

But if there is anything that we know about peace today, it is that we must be on our guard when people talk about it. The word 'peace' can be applied to so many and varied things, and what is peace to some is often war to others. Christ knows that only too well, and so He speaks about peace very carefully, saying expressly, '*My* peace I give unto you,' and in order to avoid any misunderstanding he continues, 'not as the world giveth, give I unto you.'

For the world gives a kind of peace too. It is not true to say that the world is so poor and bad that it is incapable of bestowing peace on us. For example, when the ancient Greeks spoke of peace (as they often did), they meant human peace, closely connected with physical well-being. Indeed they even worshipped a goddess of peace, Irene, and portrayed her in statues. However it is interesting that they often represented her accompanied by a little boy. It might easily have been a picture of Mary with the child Jesus. But the boy was the child Pluto, and the Greek god Pluto represented prosperity, riches and wealth. So that is what they regarded as peace – a time that was favourable for making money and growing rich. So we might well ask, 'When the nations of Europe call so eagerly for peace, is it this goddess with the child Pluto that they want?' Is that not what we are longing for to a very great extent? To be left undisturbed to make money? And do you suppose that that would be peace? A period of general prosperity? If the aspirations of the present generation go no further than to be left to plant their cabbages, and cook their dinners undisturbed, does that amount to peace? Men could give us that kind of peace. It might be brought to us by an uncle from America. But would it really be peace? Christ says, 'Peace I leave with you, my peace I give unto you: not as the world giveth, give I unto you.'

The Romans too talked a lot about peace and personified it in the goddess Pax. Round her head she wore a laurel wreath, the emblem of worldly honour and fame. We Europeans have also known such 'times of peace,' times of general worldly success, when we have placed a laurel wreath upon the temples of humanity and boasted of how wonderfully far we have progressed. Have not we too paid fanatical homage to the goddess Pax, with her crown of laurels? And is that what the nations are longing for again? A time of egotism and self-adulation, a time of record-breaking and of cheap fair-booth laurels?

The kind of peace with the child Pluto and the laurel-wreath, that is, peace to earn money and fame, has not seldom been called 'peace' in the community of God as well. Within the Church today there is a good deal of yearning for peace, which signifies a return to the flesh-pots of Egypt, rather than a hungering and thirsting after that righteousness, from which the fruit of true peace springs. Similarly a continuous battle between false and true prophets rages throughout the Old Testament. And the cause of the struggle is differing conceptions of peace. The false prophets preached the sort of peace that encouraged human laziness. On the other hand, the true prophets had to raise their voices again and again, in the midst of prosperity and plenty, and, whether it pleased the people and their master or not, had to cry out in warning, 'You talk of peace, peace, peace and yet there is no peace.' The Lord is taking up this protest against false peace when He says to His disciples, 'Peace I leave with you, my peace I give unto you: not as the world giveth, give I unto you. Let not your heart be troubled.'

The little boy at whose birth the angels proclaimed peace on earth is far from being the child Pluto. The boy Jesus certainly does not personify earthly prosperity and wealth; on the contrary, He is born into a poor family, wrapped in simple garments and laid in a manger. What God calls peace is completely different from what we mean when we long for peace. And this Prince of Peace, who gives His peace to the disciples, does not wear a laurel wreath: very soon He will wear a crown of thorns. Poverty and defencelessness are always in evidence around the King of Peace, from the night when the angels sang till the time when the sun was darkened in the middle of the day. It is not the peace of the rich and famous, but the peace of the outcast and despised that Jesus leaves as an inheritance for the disciples. It is the peace of those from whose brows the last laurel leaf of worldly honour has fallen; it is the peace of the poor sinners who kneel naked and ashamed before God. Among us this morning are some people who have reached the stage where they cannot bring gold, frankincense and myrrh to the Christ-child but only a poor, guilty and tormented heart. It is to you that the Lord has left His precious inheritance. For you the Lord's departing words have particular significance: 'Peace I leave with you, my peace I give unto you: not as the world giveth, give I unto you. Let not your heart be troubled, neither let it be afraid.'

But why should the hearts of the disciples be troubled and afraid? They have every reason for it of course, for their Master is now standing on the very threshold of His Passion. The time will soon come when the disciples will see the One who guarantees them peace delivered into the hands of His enemies. For a short time it will seem as if the evil enemy has finally triumphed, which will be terrifying . To all intents and purposes it will look as if peace were finally at an end, and the world irrevocably sinking back into eternal hatred. But 'Let not your heart be troubled, neither let it be afraid. . . . for the prince of this world cometh, and hath nothing in me.' The prince of this world is coming: the Lord sees his terrible approach; he comes with great power and cunning. Let him come! 'He hath nothing in me.' Consequently he also has no power over those whom Christ here makes indisputable heirs of His peace. Christians who are faithful to Him, and to no other, can say after Him, 'Though the world be full of devils . . . "the prince of this world cometh, and hath nothing" in us.' If a man enters with wholehearted faith into the death of Christ, then the accuser cannot harm him, either in time or eternity. Because the early Christians knew that they were universal heirs of this peace, they were able to declare that they looked forward to the Day of Judgment. Indeed the man who has only Christ's promise of peace will be shown mercy and protected from the accuser at the Last Judgment. The man who has this peace needs no other.

In this world, where there is not a foot of land where peace reigns, where every clod of earth is a battlefield and every drop of water a scene of violent contention; in this world, where there is a permanent state of war on land, on the sea, and in the air, the possibility of peace that the Lord reveals to His disciples certainly seems neither reasonable nor self-evident. Peace does not grow wild, so to speak, but has to be cultivated and established, and so it is with the peace that the Lord leaves to His own: first of all it had to be made. The peace that the world can make is only imperfect from the very first. We can control our primitive natures and temporarily restrain the normally rebellious state of our hearts, just as a fire brigade might keep under control a fire which it cannot extinguish completely. But all this contrived peace is ineffectual for, unlike our rebelliousness, it does not reach to Heaven. After all, our revolt is ultimately against Heaven, so that only someone to whom it is given to establish peace between Heaven and earth could give us the perfect peace to put an end to our total war. Therefore all peace that is not between Heaven and earth is always of short duration. In the end it is Christ to whom it is given to bring about perfect peace between Heaven and earth. It happens when He finally says, 'It is finished.' The great work that is finished on the Cross is the uniting of Heaven and the ends of the earth, and this is when we can truly say that all strife is at an end. The nations of the earth are not at war because peace does not exist, but because the nations despise and reject it instead of accepting it in faith. This peace is Christ's doing the result of His act of obedience. And His act was not reluctant, not forced and unwilling but done in voluntary obedience and for love of the Father: 'But that the world may know that I love the Father; and as the Father gave me commandment, even so I do. Arise, let us go hence.' Arise, let us go hence! It sounds like a shout of command in the night. Go where? To the Cross, to battle, to victory!

We are to inherit what He wins for us there. The man who snatches this inheritance as a prize for himself, hoping to enjoy it in some idyllic corner of the world, will be a selfish heir, and rejoicing in inheritance is a mean thing. It is the will of God that we should be grateful, not jubilant, heirs. And we shall be grateful if we realise that we are not allowed to enjoy this inheritance for ourselves, but that it is given to us so that we may share it with others. We owe it to the world. If we are to execute faithfully the testament of the Lord, revealed to His own on His departure, we should be a light of peace among the nations of the world. What does Paul say to the Ephesians? 'And your feet shod with the preparation of the gospel of peace.' What does Isaiah say? 'How beautiful upon the mountains are the feet of him that bringeth good tidings, that publisheth peace; that bringeth good tidings of good, that publisheth salvation; that saith unto Zion, Thy God reigneth!' And what does the Lord Himself say? 'Blessed are the peacemakers; for they shall be called the children of God.'

The Parable of the Vine

I am the true vine, and my Father is the husbandman. Every branch in me that beareth not fruit he taketh away: and every branch that beareth fruit, he purgeth it, that it may bring forth more fruit. Now ye are clean through the word which I have spoken unto you. Abide in me, and I in you. As the branch cannot bear fruit of itself, except it abide in the vine; no more can ye, except ye abide in me. I am the vine, ye are the branches: He that abideth in me, and I in him, the same bringeth forth much fruit: for without me ye can do nothing. If a man abide not in me, he is cast forth as a branch, and is withered; and men gather them, and cast them into the fire, and they are burned. If ye abide in me, and my words abide in you, ye shall ask what ye will, and it shall be done unto you. Herein is my Father glorified, that ye bear much fruit; so shall ye be my disciples.

As the Father hath loved me, so have I loved you: continue ye in my love. If ye keep my commandments, ye shall abide in my love; even as I have kept my Father's commandments, and abide in his love. These things have I spoken unto you, that my joy might remain in you, and that your joy might be full. This is my commandment, That ye love one another, as I have loved you. Greater love hath no man than this, that a man lay down his life for his friends. Ye are my friends, if ye do whatsoever I command you. Henceforth I call you not servants; for the servant knoweth not what his lord doeth: but I have called you friends for all things that I have heard of my Father I have made known unto you. Ye have not chosen me, but I have chosen you, and ordained you, that ye should go and bring forth fruit, and that your fruit should remain: that whatsoever ye shall ask of the Father in my name, he may give it you. These things I command you, that ye love one another.

If the world hate you, ye know that it hated me before it hated you.

If ye were of the world, the world would love his own: but because ye are not of the world, but I have chosen you out of the world, therefore the world hateth you. Remember the word that I said unto you, The servant is not greater than his lord. If they have persecuted me, they will also persecute you; if they have kept my saying, they will keep your's also. But all these things will they do unto you for my name's sake, because they know not him that sent me. If I had not come and spoken unto them, they had not had sin: but now they have no cloke for their sin. He that hateth me hateth my Father also. If I had not done among them the works which none other man did, they had not had sin: but now have they both seen and hated both me and my Father. But this cometh to pass, that the word might be fulfilled that is written in their law, They hated me without a cause.

But when the Comforter is come, whom I will send unto you from the Father, even the Spirit of truth, which proceedeth from the Father, he shall testify of me: and ye also shall bear witness, because ye have been with me from the beginning.

[XV]

The message of this chapter is, 'God is love.' But He is love in His own way. Today we should like a God who would show His love in an obvious and convenient way. However, He bestows His love as He thinks fit and this is all for the best. If every man could choose how God should show His love, the result would be very much the same as if men could decide the weather to suit themselves. But God shows His love in one particular place of His own choosing and at one particular time which He has ordained. He proves to men in a quite definite, individual, unique and inimitable manner that He is love. We simply have to bow before God's decision. The man who refuses to be reconciled to this will doubt, all his life long, that God is love; he will argue for the rest of his days that he can see nothing to prove it. But the man who has once submitted to God's imperious attitude will be able to understand and experience that 'God is love.'

In this fifteenth chapter John shows us the way in which God chooses to be love. Like I Corinthians XIII, this chapter might justifiably be called 'The Hymn of Love.' When He wants to describe God's love, Christ takes the vine as an illustration. But He gives us to understand straight away that the Vine He is talking about is a special kind of vine, and not like any other. He calls it the 'true vine' as opposed to all others: that means the one and only Vine, with which no other can compare: 'I am the true vine, and my Father is the husbandman.' The Father who caused all other vines to grow has planted this one 'true vine' on the earth with a definite intention. Let us consider the extraordinary thing that Christ is saying. God's love is so great that He even plants it on this earth in the form of Jesus Christ, the true Vine. And make no mistake, the husbandman does not plant superficially: He makes eternal love put out the strong roots of the vine, not shallow, fibrous ones. Through the Incarnation of Christ the love of God has been brought from Paradise as a living and vital plant, so to speak, and deeply rooted in this lost world. We were driven out of Paradise long ago: but now it has pleased the husbandman to give us love, the most beautiful plant in Paradise, with the intention that it should from henceforth grow on the earth. Since the birth of Christ, God's love has dwelt on earth and it is there for the whole world to know. From now on the world will have no excuse for not recognising that God is love. He is. But He is love in His own way, which He shows to the world in Jesus Christ. Accept it, for Jesus is offering it to you when He says, 'I am the true vine, and my Father is the husbandman.'

But where is this love to be found? How can we tell that it is here? Christ gives us the answer in this parable: 'Do not look too far, do not look for it anywhere in the world nor in others, seek it in yourself.' In this parable Heaven throws back the question about God's love like an echo to the people who are shouting it out into the wide world and up to the stars. Now it is Heaven that is asking, 'Where is God's love? What have you done with it? Have you really not felt that it wants to dwell in you?' The vine has branches and Christ says, 'I am the vine, ye are the branches.' And just as the living sap is forced into the vine's branches, Christ gives us God's eternal love and drives it into the people who have become part of Him. The love of God is to be found where men cling to Christ and depend on Him as closely as a branch clings to, and lives on, the vine: '*L'amor che muove il sol e l'altre stelle*'; 'the love that moves the sun and the other stars.' These are the words of a man overwhelmed by the greatness of God's love. But love was greatest of all where it came down from the stars, to this small planet, and began to move men.

There is truly cause for wonder here. It is certainly a miracle that God even plants His love on this earth; but when a man can become a branch on that 'true vine,' then the greatest miracle of all, the miracle of grace, has happened. We human beings, however, have not the final power to become such a branch. Just as it is the vine that feeds and bears the branches, so it is Christ who gives poor, half-savage man the honour of becoming as closely united with Him as the branch with the vine. It is Christ alone who transforms us from useless, wild shoots into noble, fruitful branches. We are confronted here with the sacred mystery of Divine choice, which stoops to us men, seeks us out and pityingly takes us into living communion with God: 'Ye have not chosen me, but I have chosen you, and ordained you, that ye should go and bring forth fruit, and that your fruit should remain; that whatsoever ye shall ask of the Father in my name, he may give it you.'

In fact this relationship into which Christ draws the people of His choice is so close that He even calls them His friends. Men becoming friends of God! If He had only said that we were to be His servants, that in itself would have been enough, indeed almost too much for us to accept. But He goes further than that: He calls us friends, even though He knows all about us and our shameful confession, echoing Peter, 'Lord, thou knowest all things.' He knows all about the deeply-rooted hostility to God that grows, tough and obdurate, in the depths of our hearts. Yet He calls us His friends! Jesus Christ calls us friends of God! Only He could do that. Just as He says, 'See,' to the blind; 'Walk,' to the lame; 'Be clean,' to the leper; and, 'Arise,' to the dead, so here He says with the full authority of His Father's command, 'Henceforth I call you not servants; for the servant knoweth not what his lord doeth: but I have called you friends; for all things that I have heard of my Father I have made known unto you.'

Let the man who can, comprehend this. We can only be astonished, joyful and thankful. There is something deeply satisfying in being a friend of God's. We feel something of that most pure and utter joy that reigns among the angels in Heaven whenever a sinner on earth repents and is converted: 'These things have I spoken unto you, that my joy might remain in you, and that your joy might be full.' Such is the love of God and its appearance on earth. The Father in Heaven offers His friendship to those whom He knows are His enemies. So the love of God for men is perfect love for His enemies, love for the sinner.

The friendship that God offers to men is no cheap thing for Him, however; He has to pay dearly for it. Offering friendship to one's enemies is a costly and risky thing and calls for sacrifice: 'And it came to pass, as Jesus sat at meat in the house, behold, many publicans and sinners came and sat down with him and his disciples. And when the Pharisees saw it, they said unto his disciples, Why eateth your Master with publicans and sinners? But when Jesus heard that, he said unto them, They that be whole need not a physician, but they that are sick.' He sits down with the 'sick,' where the world is at its most sordid, and has estranged itself most from Heaven. In fact, He associates with sinners to a quite unbelievable extent: 'And when they were come to the place which is called Calvary, there they crucified him, and the malefactors, one on the right hand, and the other on the left.' Finally, as great as this, is the price that He pays for the friendship that He offers to sinners: 'Greater love hath no man than this, that a man lay down his life for his friends.' Now we can see why, in talking of God's love for sinners, the Lord takes the vine as a comparison when there are so many plants to choose from. The vine is the symbol of His blood that He shed for us. Every time that He calls us to His Table He is sitting with publicans and sinners again, because the whole do not need the physician. That is what is meant when He says, 'I am the true vine, and my Father is the husbandman.' That is what God's love is like: it goes to the Cross for us.

It is not only God who has to pay dearly for this friendship; it is not cheap for men either. The branches do not grow on the vine for decoration, nor are they there for their own benefit. The function of the branch is to bear fruit, and so, 'Every branch that beareth not fruit he taketh away; and every branch that beareth fruit he purgeth it, that it may bring forth more fruit.' 'Herein is my Father glorified, that ye bear much fruit; so ye shall be my disciples.' Shall be my disciples! But surely we are that already? Have we not just heard that we are His disciples by grace? But we shall not be His true disciples until we bear fruit. We are His friends: that is the gift bestowed on us by grace. But we shall not be His true friends until we bear a lot of fruit. We are branches on the Vine: but we shall not be true branches until we are productive. 'Every branch that beareth fruit he purgeth it, that it may bring forth more fruit.'

He purges, or cleanses, the branches. 'Now ye are clean through the word which I have spoken unto you.' These words anticipate the moment of purification on the Cross. Once he is a friend of God's, a man becomes cleansed and is able to shed his burden, with a sigh of relief, having found the place where he can lay it down. So as a friend of God's, he need no longer waste half of his energy trying to be reconciled with God and men. God has brought about his reconciliation already. Now he need no longer waste his time with worrying about himself. Stop thinking about yourself for once. God has brought about your reconciliation with Himself, so that you may be free to think about your brother. God wants to make your way to your brother as quick and easy as possible by lightening your burden. All this gives us another parallel to a particularly striking aspect of the vine: the pulsating force, like the sap in the vine, which drives a man to seek out his brother. The man who is cleansed begins to feel the love of Christ driving and urging him on.

'*L'amor che muove il sol e l'altre stelle.*' It is love that moves the sun and stars. And now the miracle is that it moves men!

The meaning of this was brought home to me again the other day, when I was visiting the sick in hospital. A man who had been ill for a long time was telling me what he had observed during his illness. He maintained that there are two kinds of nurses. The first kind can tell at a glance whether you are comfortable, and even if you have slept well, or if you are thirsty, in pain, or worried about something. You never have to ask them for anything or complain: they have a way of nodding in understanding, so that one feels that they know everything. Then there is the other type of nurse and doctor. These, he said, are certainly proficient, and he did not mean to be ungrateful for all the care and attention he had received for so many years. But this type cannot sense things: you have to tell them. It is as if they had something missing. Yet they are not failing in their duty. What exactly is it that this sick man noticed during his years of suffering? He saw that some people work under the impulse of joy, gratitude and love, while others, although they do their job efficiently, are not urged on by love, joy and gratitude, but are sustained and impelled by the consciousness of duty. It might be put in another way: the first kind go about their work as friends of God, inspired by Christ; the other kind do their work of themselves, perhaps at best for love of mankind, but not activated by that compulsion that comes from the Vine. It does not depend on official dress, nor on title nor uniform. You can be a clergyman yet not be actuated by the friendship of God. It all depends on friendship with God. That is what Christ means when He says, 'He that abideth in me, and I in him, the same bringeth forth much fruit: for without me ye can do nothing.'

More and more fruit. Where love is concerned Christ is prepared to give richly and lavishly. He will not let His own go short. For Christ knows all about this world's poverty and need of love. That is why He wants to pour love into this poor world day after day, through thousands upon thousands of small human channels and branches. And you, who know about the friendship of God, are the branches. Let us not be modest in this matter of more fruit. Let us be downright shameless when we ask for it. For we are not asking for ourselves, nor are we demanding anything foolish; we are asking for the one thing that this world needs, the one thing that moves the sun, and moon, and stars, and also the men and affairs of this world, and that is the love of Heaven. Hence the boldness of Christ's words: 'If ye abide in me, and my words abide in you, ye shall ask what ye will, and it shall be done unto you.' 'That whatsoever ye shall ask of the Father in my name, he may give it you.'

'He that abideth in me, and I in him.' The word 'abide' crops up more than half a dozen times in this parable. We have no power to give ourselves discipleship, friendship and union with God; but we can squander and forfeit it. This can happen in either of two ways, which are carefully outlined to us here. Firstly, our function as a branch may only be ornamental, and how often we are in danger of being mere decoration in the house of God, covered with fine foliage, but without fruit. Or we can lose God's friendship by breaking away from the Vine and trying to produce fruit without it, on the principle that we can live a good and fearless life without the help of the Church, or the Bible, or prayer, or God, or the Vine. No doubt we can do a lot without these things, but in that case, as Christ points out clearly here, what we produce is not fruit. We are then no longer acting under the impulse of eternal love: all that we do is condemned to perish: 'Every branch in me that beareth not fruit he taketh away.' Certainly we cannot bear fruit by constantly repeating, 'Lord, Lord.' On the other hand, 'If a man abide not in me, he is cast forth as a branch, and is withered; and men gather them, and cast them into the fire, and they are burned.' So the same warning applies both to the friends of God who bear no fruit and to the friends of men without God: 'If ye keep my commandments, ye shall abide in my love; even as I have kept my Father's commandments, and abide in his love.' 'This is my commandment, That ye love one another, as I have loved you.' 'Ye are my friends, if ye do whatsoever I command you.'

It must strike every attentive reader of the Bible that the fourth gospel does not give an account either of the Sermon on the Mount or of the sermon by the lake. I should like, however, to call this fifteenth chapter John's 'Sermon on the Mount.' The principles of the Sermon on the Mount recorded by Matthew, and of the sermon by the lake recorded by Luke, are contained here, in their essentials, if not completely and word for word, but with the one difference that in John the relationship to God is unmistakably emphasised from the very beginning. In this way John prevents our taking these words as a moral code independent of Christ. It is made quite clear that the Father is the husbandman, Christ the Vine and we the branches. Christ is in the middle: Christ is the mediator and go-between. Christ is the 'transformer,' through whom the love of God becomes love for one's neighbour, and friendship with God becomes friendliness towards men. And now there is one last thing to be said about the love of God on earth, something that cannot be said of any other kind of love: it is eternal. It 'abides'; it 'never faileth.' It abides whether it is acknowledged or not. It abides even if it receives neither thanks nor reward. Indeed, it abides even if it not only receives no thanks, but also if it reaps downright ingratitude. It abides even if, far from awakening love in return, it arouses hatred and mockery. Because in the eyes of God it is originally love for His enemies, so between men also it becomes love for one's enemies: 'If the world hate you, ye know that it hated me before it hated you. If ye were of the world, the world would love his own: but because ye are not of the world, but I have chosen you out of the world, therefore the world hateth you. Remember the word that I said unto you, The servant is not greater than his lord. If they have persecuted me, they will also persecute you.'

Here once again we have reason to be astonished, in an age when injustice is gaining ground and love is growing cold in so many people. The love that has been planted in the world in Jesus Christ will never grow cold. It is strong enough to let itself be hated. That is why it is stronger than hatred and death.

The essence of the love of God, which in Christ became love for one's neighbour, is this: it may be hated, persecuted, stoned, scorned and crucified but it remains victorious. 'And now abideth faith, hope, love, these three; but the greatest of these is love.'

Sorrow to be Turned into Joy

These things have I spoken unto you, that ye should not be offended. They shall put you out of the synagogues: yea, the time cometh, that whosoever killeth you will think that he doeth God service. And these things will they do unto you, because they have not known the Father, nor me. But these things have I told you, that when the time shall come, ye may remember that I told you of them. And these things I said not unto you at the beginning, because I was with you. But now I go my way to him that sent me; and none of you asketh me, Whither goest thou? But because I have said these things unto you, sorrow hath filled your heart. Nevertheless I tell you the truth; It is expedient for you that I go away: for if I go not away, the Comforter will not come unto you; but if I depart, I will send him unto you. And when he is come, he will reprove the world of sin, and of righteousness, and of judgment: of sin, because they believe not on me; of righteousness, because I go to my Father, and ye see me no more; of judgment, because the prince of this world is judged. I have yet many things to say unto you, but ye cannot bear them now. Howbeit when he, the Spirit of truth, is come, he will guide you into all truth: for he shall not speak of himself; but whatsoever he shall hear, that shall he speak: and he will shew you things to come. He shall glorify me: for he shall receive of mine, and shall shew it unto you. All things that the Father hath are mine: therefore said I, that he shall take of mine, and shall shew it unto you.

A little while, and ye shall not see me: and again, a little while, and ye shall see me, because I go to the Father. Then said some of his disciples among themselves, What is this that he saith unto us, A little while, and ye shall not see me: and again, a little while, and ye shall see me: and, Because I go to the Father? They said therefore, What is this that he saith, A little while? we cannot tell what he saith. Now Jesus knew that they were desirous to ask him, and said unto them, Do ye enquire among yourselves of that I said, A little while, and ye shall not see me: and again, a little while, and ye shall see me? Verily, verily, I say unto you, That ye shall weep and lament, but the world shall rejoice: and ye shall be sorrowful, but your sorrow shall be turned into joy. A woman when she is in travail hath sorrow, because her hour is come: but as soon as she is delivered of the child, she remembereth no more the anguish, for joy that a man is born into the world. And ye now therefore have sorrow: but I will see you again, and your heart shall rejoice, and your joy no man taketh from you. And in that day ye shall ask me nothing. Verily, verily, I say unto you, Whatsoever ye shall ask the Father in my name, he will give it you. Hitherto have ye asked nothing in my name: ask, and ye shall receive, that your joy may be full.

These things have I spoken unto you in proverbs: but the time cometh, when I shall no more speak unto you in proverbs, but I shall shew you plainly of the Father. At that day ye shall ask in my name: and I say not unto you, that I will pray the Father for you: for the Father himself loveth you, because ye have loved me, and have believed that I came out from God. I came forth from the Father, and am come into the world: again, I leave the world, and go to the Father. His disciples said unto him, Lo, now speakest thou plainly, and speakest no proverb. Now are we sure that thou knowest all things, and needest not that any man should ask thee: by this we believe that thou camest forth from God. Jesus answered them, Do ye now believe? Behold, the hour cometh, yea, is now come, that ye shall be scattered, every man to his own, and shall leave me alone: and yet I am not alone, because the Father is with me. These things I have spoken unto you, that in me ye might have peace. In the world ye shall have tribulation: but be of good cheer; I have overcome the world.

[XVI]

The world is overcome: this world, which has come to represent everything evil to us and whose oppressive weight lies heavily on our shoulders, has been overcome. Who says so? Who is it that dares to make such a bold, indeed improbable, assertion? Is he mad? Or is this some innocent person saying that he has overcome the world; someone who does not know what the world is, and therefore does not know what he is talking about, and who is consequently not to be taken seriously? No, it is not just anyone: it is Christ who tells us, 'Be of good cheer; I have overcome the world.' And because it is Christ speaking, it would be advisable not to turn a deaf ear to His call. Indeed, we would be well advised to sit up, and listen more closely to see what He means.

In this long chapter Christ makes it quite clear what He means when He says, 'the world.' And so it is important that we should read the whole chapter if we are to grasp the significance of this beautiful, triumphant, final sentence. Jesus is continuing to take leave of His disciples and of the world that does not want Him and cannot bear Him. He speaks of His coming crucifixion just as a mother-to-be might speak of her confinement. It will be a terrible day of anguish. He knows that 'a woman when she is in travail hath sorrow, because her hour is come.' For Him, and even more for the disciples, this day will bring indescribable sorrow, which already weighs heavily upon them even in anticipation: 'And ye now have sorrow.' This sorrow will become even greater: 'Ye shall weep and lament'; so great in fact that He does not yet want to tell them everything in detail, because it would be too much for them to bear: 'I have yet many things to say unto you, but ye cannot bear them now.' Yes, the revelation of the world's final treatment of Jesus will distress the disciples deeply: 'These things have I spoken unto you, that ye should not be offended.' The world can and will know nothing of Jesus, and is able to crucify Him without scruple. Whatever there is of baseness and vileness in the world comes to a head in the Crucifixion of Christ. There the world stands unveiled and unmasked. A world that can perpetrate the crime of Good Friday is capable of anything. And this is the world of which He says: 'Be of good cheer; I have overcome the world.'

But that is not all. Not satisfied with striking the Shepherd, the world will also attack His flock: 'They shall put you out of the synagogues,' Christ warns His disciples and through them His whole community. Yes, the world has worked itself up to such a pitch that it will persecute and punish the disciples in the name of God: 'Yea, the time cometh, that whosoever killeth you will think that he doeth God service.' Even church-goers, ministers, and priests will take part in the persecution of Christ's community on earth. That will happen because the world is blind, because it does not know who God is, neither God the Father nor God the Son. You can be quite sure that if ever Christians are persecuted here, clergymen will be in the front ranks of the oppressors, and will throw the biggest stones of all. Then clergymen will be the first to encourage the persecutors of the community and bless their actions. And they will think that they are doing God a service. 'And these things will they do unto you, because they have not known the Father, nor me.' And the world will rejoice triumphantly at the persecution of the community. No sign of justice will be visible any more. The world will call white black, and black white. Blasphemy will take the place of divine worship and the works of the Devil will masquerade in the guise of the works of God. And the persecuted community will then be utterly forsaken and alone. It will appeal to God to come and intervene. But Christ will not be there: He will be in Heaven, for He is going to the Father and parting from His disciples, leaving them behind on earth. Christ's description of the world here is similar to what we read in Matthew x. It is a world of completely false standards, a world that punishes good and rewards evil, describable only by the word 'darkness.' It is a world in which everyone who calls himself a disciple of Jesus has good cause to be afraid: 'In the world ye shall have tribulation; but be of good cheer; I have overcome the world.' This world which crucifies Christ and destroys His community is the very world that Christ declares He has overcome. Faced by this frightening aspect of the world, He says to His own, 'Be of good cheer.' We would do well to follow one stage further the significant idea which Jesus expounds here, and which runs through the gospel of St John right from the beginning. Christ shows us the world from a third side. What John means when he talks of 'the world' is that part of the world which we would rather not see. In times of oppression the disciples realise that they carry the world and its reflexion in themselves. Sorrow will fill their hearts, and at times will overcome them. And they will never be strong enough to resist the coming full-scale attack of the world. They will know times when they will no longer comprehend the ways of God, so that they will begin to doubt and waver. And instead of standing fast, they will all flee. Christ cannot even depend on His disciples. The hour will strike when not only God Himself will be crucified and His own be put to flight, but His own will also fail Him, and God will have no strongholds left on the earth: 'Behold, the hour cometh, yea is now come, that ye shall be scattered, every man to his own, and shall leave me alone.' That is the Christian world as Christ sees it, even in His disciples. Nevertheless He says with all the more conviction, ' "But be of good cheer; I have overcome the world." I have overcome this world, which can and will crucify me, and which can and will scatter my disciples, who will deny and forsake me, for they are willing in the spirit but weak in the flesh.' Defeated and forsaken on every side, He declares Himself victor in the battle: 'But be of good cheer; I have overcome the world.' How can He maintain this in face of the overwhelming facts which so obviously indicate the opposite? How can He claim to have overcome this threefold world of darkness?

He says it quite simply because He is Christ. In other words, quite simply because He has been sent into this world with the special mission of conquering it. The world may well crucify Him: but it is the Father who has the first and last word. It can crucify Him only because that is the strange and mysterious way in which the Father has decreed that He shall overcome the world. That is how the Father intends to fight the decisive battle in this struggle, and how it has pleased Him to overcome the world. This unique and autocratic way of overcoming the world does not in the least correspond to the means to which we men resort to overcome opposition; indeed it is such a 'slap in the face' for all who win earthly victories, that no one should be surprised to find himself confronted here by something completely incomprehensible. God does not overcome the world by armed force, but by letting it defeat and kill Him, by giving His chosen Son whom He loves and letting Him be put to death. But after three days God raises His defeated Son from the dead and sends Him back to His executioners: 'A little while, and ye shall not see me: and again, a little while, and ye shall see me.' God allows the world to achieve its fearful aim to begin with and lets it kill Him. But then He intervenes, reverses the victory of the world, and over the opened grave He proclaims the victory of His defeated Son. God has turned the evil intentions of men into good. By one magnificent move the Father has transformed the defeat of His Son into victory, and the victory of His enemies into defeat. And it is this crucified, yet risen, Christ who says to His own here, 'In the world ye shall have tribulation; but be of good cheer; I have overcome the world.' He has overcome it where it is at its darkest and most worldly, where sin and death triumph in their invincible majesty. The Father has given the Son the upper hand and it is the Son who says to the disciples, 'I have overcome the world.' And we can believe even this when it is He who says it. We could not accept it if anyone else came along and said that he had overcome the world. One who has risen from the dead has the right and the authority to convince us when He says, 'I have overcome the world.'

And then He will have to leave His own, 'leave them in the lurch,' as it were. They will be alone like orphans and at the mercy of the Prince of this world. And the Prince of this world will laugh and jeer; he will persecute Jesus's followers, who have been forsaken by God and men, until they 'weep and lament'; and he will kill them and boast about it into the bargain. But again Jesus is not just anyone at all: He is the Son. The Father has decided to take the Son unto Himself, so that it definitely looks very much as if His community on earth were completely forsaken, delivered up and abandoned to the Prince of this world. But here too the Father has decided otherwise. He does not call His Son to Him intending to leave the community on earth helpless; the result is the very reverse. The departure of the Son from the earth and His ascension into Heaven will not weaken the flock, but strengthen it; it will not scatter it, but draw it together all the more into a united community. God means to gather, guide and direct the scattered sheep. 'It is expedient for you that I go away: for if I go not away, the Comforter will not come unto you; but if I depart, I will send him unto you.'

The Father has decided that the disciples shall be compensated for the departure of the Son from the world, by the generous gift of the Holy Spirit. The Holy Spirit will come to be a Comforter to the persecuted, banished and destroyed community. The community certainly has grounds to be afraid; but it has equally good reason not to despair, for it has a powerful ally in the struggle against the heretic and the Devil. Christ makes the definite promise that the Holy Spirit will come to the persecuted community, so that it will never be 'left in the lurch,' and He fulfils His promise at Pentecost. If only we could comprehend the wonderful mystery about the Holy Spirit that Christ tells us here! He says that the Holy Spirit will be the advocate and judge of the oppressed community. The Holy Spirit will actually defend the community in its defencelessness, and will appear both to accuse and to judge in the citadel of the Prince of this world. 'And when he is come, he will reprove the world of sin, and of righteousness, and of judgment.' The world never wants to recognise its guilt, but the Holy Spirit will prevent the world's ever being able to excuse itself on the ground of ignorance. Since the Holy Spirit has been poured out, the world knows what sin is and will to eternity have no excuse. And God does not allow unrighteousness to have the last word. In spite of the rapid increase of unrighteousness, since the Holy Spirit has been sent to the community, righteousness is not defeated and dead. It answers the call again and again. The world can never more be at peace, because the Holy Spirit is abroad and punishes it repeatedly through its conscience. And while the poor community is groaning beneath the yoke of the Prince of this world, the Holy Spirit as Comforter shows that in reality he is judged. That is the meaning of these mysterious words: 'And when he [the Holy

Spirit] is come, he will reprove the world of sin, and of righteousness, and of judgment: of sin, because they believe not on me; of righteousness, because I go to my Father, and ye see me no more; of judgment, because the prince of this world is judged.' The Prince of this world is judged! However much he may pose as judge and victor, he has nevertheless been judged. A few weeks ago, when I read these words on a walk in the mountains, I felt that I should like to rush down into the valley and call out to the people, 'Be of good cheer, all you who are so understandably afraid; Christ has overcome the world!'

But let us remind ourselves that it is Christ who has overcome the world and all its terrifying power. It is not we who have overcome it: we are not the victors. Even though we are Christians, we still bear the stamp of the world on our brows. We grieve, we are afraid, we weep and lament and are troubled, we are shut out of the churches and destroyed. We are also scattered, 'every man to his own,' and on the evil day we forsake Christ. Christ in His victory is utterly alone. We all have a share in the world, in its poverty, its need and its guilt. But Christ is even stronger than this guilt, as the disciples realised when they once denied Him; so be of good cheer, all you who recognise guilt in yourselves. We need not look to ourselves; we can trust in Him and say confidently, 'Even where our own hearts condemn us, the prince of this world is overcome and the accuser silenced.'

'In the world ye shall have tribulation.' Yes, we are troubled and each one of us knows quite well what is causing his own particular anxiety, and where the world weighs most heavily upon him. This became clear to me the other week when we were reading these words in a large hospital ward. All the patients were thinking of their own particular troubles, and their worlds revolved round a crushed finger, or a broken leg, or an inflamed appendix, or a kidney operation; or then they were worried about the children at home, or about losing their jobs, or the sorry state of the world in general. How heavily the sorrows of the world lie on each one of us! But let yourselves be comforted by what we are told here and put your trust in Christ, who bears the whole weight of the world: 'In the world ye shall have tribulation; but be of good cheer; I have overcome the world.'

The Parable of the Woman in Labour

Verily, verily, I say unto you, that ye shall weep and lament, but the world shall rejoice: and ye shall be sorrowful, but your sorrow shall be turned into joy. A woman when she is in travail hath sorrow, because her hour is come: but as soon as she is delivered of the child, she remembereth no more the anguish, for joy that a man is born into the world. And ye now therefore have sorrow: but I will see you again, and your heart shall rejoice, and your joy no man taketh from you. And in that day ye shall ask me nothing. Verily, verily, I say unto you, Whatsoever ye shall ask the Father in my name, he will give it you. Hitherto have ye asked nothing in my name: ask, and ye shall receive, that your joy may be full.

[XVI. 20–24]

'But the world shall rejoice.' Jesus states outright the significant fact that it is possible for the world to rejoice. There are Christians who try to deny the world its right to rejoice. But fortunately few people agree with them, for really it is just as Christ says, the world can rejoice. The Creator did not make the world so poor as to leave no place for joy. Just as the Creator gave the blackbird its song of jubilation when spring comes at last, just as He created the joyous baying of every hound that follows the scent through the fields, so He has endowed every human creature with the gift of joy. He has not only given sighing and weeping; He has allowed time for joy and laughter too.

And the joys of this world are remarkably strong and attractive, so that it is difficult for a normal man to resist their lure. The world knows how tempting the joys that it can offer are. That is why all the great rulers in the history of the world never offered their people bread alone. They knew that bread is not enough and that a nation that has only bread is just as weak as a plant that has only water and manure but no sunshine. Therefore they have always added pleasure, spectacle and recreation to their promises of bread. For man does not merely want to live, he wants to enjoy himself.

But joy, like the whole of creation, is no longer what it should be. Something is gnawing at the pleasures of this world like a worm, and we can never trust them completely. The world itself is well aware of this, as the wisdom of its proverbs shows, for many of them state categorically that we should never expect too much of life and that there is 'no rose without a thorn.' The heathen poets and sages of ancient times knew that too when they complained that the dregs at the bottom of every cup of joy are bitter. That probably also explains our custom of never draining a glass to the last drop. It is as if we were afraid to find what comes at the bottom of every cup of joy in this world – that is, emptiness. The dread underlying every pleasure in this world is that that pleasure will come to an end. At the bottom of every cup of joy lurks death. The world is transitory, and so is pleasure. No less a man than Friedrich Nietzsche, the fanatically materialist philosopher, recognised that when he said, 'But all pleasure lacks eternity.' It wants just what it does not have – permanence.

In contrast to this, Christ states that His community shall have no joy in this world: 'Ye shall be sorrowful.' That strikes us as strange at first, and we want to resist. And as if seeing our objection to this, Christ introduces His words in that solemn way in which He sometimes speaks when He expects opposition: 'Verily, verily, I say unto you, That ye shall weep and lament, but the world shall rejoice: and ye shall be sorrowful.' It is indeed not readily understandable that it is the Christian community that is to 'weep and lament and be sorrowful.' Even today there are plenty of voices, within the Christian community itself, which protest against such a suggestion. It is a trick of the trade to train shop-assistants to keep a perpetual smile on their faces. Similarly there are Christians who, no doubt in good faith and with the best of intentions, put on a permanent smile of propaganda for Christ's sake, and always present a jovial front to the world, as if the Christian life were one long round of happiness. This kind of person rejects sorrow on principle, and denies that it has a place in Christian life.

But God's words on this subject are more human and more natural. Abraham weeps for Sarah; David mourns his friend Jonathan; and Job gives free rein to his misery. The Book of Lamentations is not so called by chance. Jesus weeps for the towns by the lake, and at the grave of Lazarus. And after the death of the first Christian martyr, in the Acts of the Apostles, before the joy of Pentecost has faded, we read, 'And devout men carried Stephen to his burial, and made great lamentation over him.' There is no sign here of any compulsory smile among the Christian community. It rejoices with the joyful and weeps with those who weep. Sorrow has its rightful place in the community.

Christian sorrow can bear prophetic witness before the world far more effectively than a forced smile. Today, as at all times, the community has occasion enough to refrain from joining in, when many others are laughing; and to keep its hands firmly in its trousers pockets, when others are clapping their hands for joy. If there is any one place where sorrow at the way of the world and these destructive times ought to be felt, then it is right here in the Church. Yes, sorrow over a corrupt world becomes the Christian community much more than extravagant rejoicing. The righteous lamentation of the Old Testament is not out of place nowadays, as long as the Lord of the community will hang a millstone round the neck of anyone who harms the soul or body of a child. Who but the community is capable of seeing the full extent of the destruction of these times? The world is blind to it: it cannot see what darkness is because it has not seen the Light. But you Christians have seen the great Light and therefore you can never again feel at ease in the darkness. You have seen eternal life, therefore there will be a difference between your mourning at the graveside, and that of people who do not know what death is. You have seen the one pearl of great price, therefore you can no longer be satisfied with the feeble gleam of the pearls of the world. You have tasted bread from Heaven, therefore you can no longer eat your fill of the sweetmeats of this world; you can only hunger and thirst and fast! Can you, who have seen the new Heaven and the new earth in the Word of God, ever again be infatuated with the old Heaven and the old earth? That is the reason why Christ assigns sorrow its rightful place in His community.

The Lord gave His Church yet another, deeper, reason. It has seen the Redeemer and so it is conscious of its guilt. That is the true sorrow of the community: sorrow over itself and at its own guilt. The world only recognises its guilt when painful consequences make it obvious: the community, however, has knowledge of the guilt that cries out for forgiveness. So we simply cannot go on gaily and recklessly sinning. It robs us of the smile on our lips, the sparkle in our eyes and the joy in our hearts. So many of the things from which the man of the world seems to derive harmless and unspoiled pleasure crush the Christian to the ground, because he has seen Christ. Because Christ knows about this sorrow, called 'godly sorrow' by Paul, He gives it the place it deserves in the community in this solemn and almost ceremonious way: 'Verily, verily, I say unto you, That ye shall weep and lament, but the world shall rejoice: and ye shall be sorrowful.'

Now, what we have just established about the pleasures of this world proves to be reversed where the 'godly sorrow' of Christians is concerned: in the end 'godly sorrow' becomes joyful. If we grasp this cup of sorrow rather than push it aside; if we keep it firmly in our hands in spite of our fear and trembling; and if we drain it to the last drop, we shall find, as we often did as children when we drank sugared water, that at the bottom it is indescribably sweet. The dregs of this cup are sweet because at the bottom lies forgiveness. If we drink the cup of remorse and repentance, we are rewarded with the sweetness of forgiveness and eternal life: 'But your sorrow shall be turned into joy.'

That is the unparalleled transformation that a Christian can know in spite of sorrow and the Cross. In this world there is a change from light, often very bright, dazzling light, to darkness: in the Kingdom of God, however, there is a change from darkness, often deep darkness, to light. In this world there is a progression from life, often vigorous, sparkling life, to death: in the Kingdom of God, however, there is a progression from death, often painful, slow death, into life. In this world joy becomes sorrow: in the Kingdom of God, however, suffering becomes glory and sorrow joy. Joy has the last word because God has the last word. That is the great transformation that God promises with the words: 'But your sorrow shall be turned into joy.'

We can be excused for being distrustful of this transformation. We should like to know more about it; we should like to know what is meant by a change from sorrow to joy. How does this change come about? What kind of power effects this unique progression? Is it governed by a kind of spiritual law, according to which joy follows sorrow after a prescribed time, like the return swing of a pendulum, just as night is succeeded by day, spring comes after winter, and sunshine after rain? Or is it that things always take a turn for the better in the end anyway, as a man said to me the other day?

However, that would be very uncertain and we could not be entirely happy about it. Who can guarantee that the saying, 'Sunshine follows the rain,' will always come true? Might not things just as easily get worse instead of better? If we are to be really confident in the promise of the great reversal, we must have a guarantee. We cannot put our faith in mere chance. But Christ Himself is our guarantee; we have it on His authority that the sorrow of the community will definitely be turned into joy. He Himself is the great example of the transformation of sorrow into joy. Not for nothing does the angel, on the night of His birth, call out the words, 'Behold, I bring you good tidings of great joy, which shall be to all people.' This is the only way in which sorrow becomes joy.

This reversal does not come of its own accord. It is willed and planned: it is Christ who accomplishes it. This joy is dearly bought: it has to be fought and struggled and suffered for. It is stained with blood, 'Your sorrow shall be turned into joy,' because Christ died on the Cross and rose up on the third day. We know when and where the change was brought about; sorrow was turned into joy between Good Friday and Easter Sunday. Because Jesus drained to the dregs the cup brimming over with the sin and death of this world, the cup of 'godly sorrow' is life and joy for everyone who believes. To this very day a cup stands on the table in the midst of the community, a cup of salvation, life and joy.

Although only He can, and must, endure the anguish of the Cross, it nevertheless casts a shadow over the disciples too. It is part of the humility of Jesus that, while bearing the Cross alone, He can still share a kind of fellow-suffering with His disciples. When their Shepherd has been defeated, the flock will be scattered. They will 'weep and lament,' when they see evil triumph over Him. Who would not feel the same? Their sorrow would be too great to bear if it did not pass in 'a little while.' Their share in His suffering will pass like a woman's labour: 'A woman when she is in travail hath sorrow, because her hour is come: but as soon as she is delivered of the child, she remembereth no more the anguish, for joy that a man is born into the world. And ye now therefore have sorrow: but I will see you again, and your hearts shall rejoice, and your joy no man taketh from you.'

Jesus's words remind us of that remarkable phenomenon, confirmed by more than one mother, that a woman can recall the pain of having a tooth out or some other operation, but not the pains of childbirth, which are almost unbearable. But a little time after the birth, the mother can no longer imagine the pain clearly. In His loving kindness, the Creator has taken care that the pain should fade from the memory at the joy in the child. So, like the pains of labour, the pains of those who bear the Cross after Christ are of a special kind. They reflect something of the promise that His yoke is soft and His burden light. All this helps to illuminate the mystery of martyrdom. The suffering of the martyr is comparable to the pains of the woman in labour; it is made bearable by the knowledge of what is to be achieved. Perhaps there would be no martyrs in the Christian Church if this were not so. This brings to mind those exceedingly comforting words of Jesus about the tribulations preceding the Last Judgment, which, He says, no one could endure 'except those days should be shortened.' 'But as soon as she is delivered of the child, she remembereth no more the anguish, for joy that a man is born into the world.'

The weeping and lamenting of the disciples for their crucified Master is not entirely the pure suffering of martyrdom. There is an undercurrent of guilt in their lamentation. They know that Christ on the Cross is suffering for them and their sin. For 'a little while' everything seems to have come to an end. There is neither hope nor forgiveness left; only the crushing weight of their guilt hangs over them. We see Peter weeping when the cock crows; we hear the desolate words of the two disciples on the road to Emmaus. This is the kind of weeping and lamenting which springs from unforgiven sin that weighs heavily on the conscience. They have lost sight of Jesus and do not know where to take their guilt. Are we not familiar with such 'weeping and lamenting' too? Have we not also experienced days and even weeks, when we have been without forgiveness, and without hope and joy, when we have dragged ourselves through the weary days and nights with troubled thoughts and guilty consciences? I am sure that there is at least one person here today, perhaps only one – in which case I am preaching today for one person – who feels like running outside to some quiet place and weeping his heart out with grief at having lost the comforting sight of Jesus. The good news that in 'a little while' there will be a joyful reunion is intended particularly for him and people like him: 'And ye now therefore have sorrow: but I will see you again, and your hearts shall rejoice, and your joy no man taketh from you.'

But what if there are other people listening (and I am sure there are many of them), to whom this joyful message means nothing, and who are perhaps even bored by it? Perhaps there are people here who have nothing in their hearts but that indifference or apathy, which inhibits both joy and sorrow; people who are in that neutral state, where one can no longer laugh with the world because one has seen through the attraction of its pleasures, and yet where one cannot share the 'godly sorrow' of the community, which brings life and joy, because one is sitting between two stools, so to speak? If you are one of these people, then your need is very great. But Jesus surely has your need in mind when He gives the friendly advice: 'Ask.' And once again He urges us in that solemn way: 'Verily, verily, I say unto you, Whatsoever ye shall ask the Father in my name, he will give it you. Hitherto have ye asked nothing in my name.' I wonder how many of us have literally never asked anything of God in Christ's name? Let us remind God, by calling for help in the name of Jesus, that Christ has turned our sorrow into joy. This prayer in the name of Jesus has every prospect of being heard: 'Ask, and ye shall receive, that your joy may be full.'

What is fullness of joy? It is what we should all like. What has finally brought us together here this morning is the longing for a joy that is perfect. Perfect joy is fundamental and lasting; neither time nor circumstances can take it away. It does not come from the world: it is sent from Heaven and is established in the spirit. This is 'joy in the Holy Ghost,' and if we ask the Father in the name of the Son, we shall have a share in it. Because it comes from Heaven this joy is dependent on nothing in the world. If any of you here today can see no prospect of joy in your lives, be assured that there is still a possibility of joy for you, perfect joy, which no man can give you and no man can take away.

Perfect joy gives strength. Every day we can read a number of holiday advertisements with the slogan, 'Strength through joy.'[1] Strength through joy indeed, for joy brings strength. But it all depends on the kind of joy and the kind of strength. Strength is perfect when it can overcome the world and death and hell. It is no coincidence that perfect joy is often seen on the face of a dying man. I well remember some words from a man on his

[1] This was written before the Second World War: the reference is to the German National Socialist 'Kraft durch Freude' movement.

death-bed, which I shall not forget for a long time. He said, 'People often speak lightly of "passing away," and of our "eternal home," but when it really comes to dying, then everything is rather different. But the Gospel is always good tidings.' So it is with perfect joy: it is still good tidings in the face of death. 'Ask, and ye shall receive, that your joy may be full,' even until your last breath and beyond it into eternity.

Jesus's High-Priestly Prayer for Himself

These words spake Jesus, and lifted up his eyes to heaven, and said, Father, the hour is come; glorify thy Son, that thy Son may glorify thee: as thou hast given him power over all flesh, that he should give eternal life to as many as thou hast given him. And this is life eternal, that they might know thee the only true God, and Jesus Christ, whom thou hast sent. I have glorified thee on the earth: I have finished the work which thou gavest me to do. And now, O Father, glorify thou me with thine own self with the glory which I had with thee before the world was.

[XVII. 1–5]

When Christ prays to the Father to glorify Him here, let it be clearly understood in our hearts and minds at the very outset, and, please God, confirmed by the Holy Ghost, that Christ has finished the work that the Father gave Him to do. Let us rid ourselves of the discouraging notion that God has done nothing either for man or for the world. Also let us stop being provoked into that foolishly pompous and presumptuous attitude that God's work on earth depends on us as individuals, and that His cause would be lost if we were to fail Him. That is the case with the kings of this world: they are dependent on their subjects and are lost if every man does not remain at his post. But this does not apply to God. Without consulting us or enlisting our aid, He has let His work on earth be completed all alone by His Son. He has needed no help. He is not frail and dependent on us: far from it, we believe in a God who can achieve His ends by Himself. Indeed, people who have thought it necessary to run to His aid, or even to save His cause, have always come to grief in the attempt.

Whether we like it or not, the fact remains: 'I have finished the work which thou gavest me to do.'

What is the nature of the work the Father gave Him and which He now says He has finished? Christ says it is that He has glorified the Father: 'I have glorified thee on earth.' What is this unusual word that runs like a golden thread through this great chapter? What does He mean by 'glorify'? How has He 'glorified' the Father? What does this word suggest to us? To begin with, Christ has quite simply glorified His Father by coming from Infinity, where He had been eternally, into the finite world of time, and becoming a man who can say, 'He that hath seen me hath seen the Father.' The Son has glorified the Father by making the eternally Invisible visible, so to speak, here on earth. He has revealed God, little by little, until the final revelation at His very last breath. Every time that He breaks bread He looks up to Heaven to give the Father glory and thanks before men. And He makes the glory of God visible, where it has been terribly distorted out of all recognition, and where it would not even have been remotely possible to recognise this poor earth as God's. He has shown the splendour of His Father's glory in the blind and lame, in lepers, in the rich and the poor, and even in the dead. The world is corrupt, groping in darkness and ignorance, and choked with indifference or hatred towards God and His cause, and the name of God is abused daily. In a world like this, Christ does not take the name of God in vain, but uses it for the honour of God; He calls upon Him, and prays, and teaches us to pray, 'Hallowed be thy name.' He glorifies God by establishing the commandments of His Father in Heaven, wherever He passes in this sordid world, and by respecting the will of God even to the point of dying on the Cross. Having become a man and knowing that He will die on the Cross, He can now stand before the Father and say, 'I have glorified thee on earth: I have finished the work which thou gavest me to do.'

By finishing His work of glorification in this poor world, Christ has become its 'bright morning star,' and the 'Light of the world.' If we follow this Light, we shall no longer walk in darkness; and if we stand in it, we shall no longer stand in darkness but shall become children of Light. But it is He who is the Light of the world, not we: He and no other has glorified the Father. If you are looking for someone else who has done this, then do so by all means, if you want to give yourself trouble for nothing. Any number of people are looking for a man in whom they can see the glory of God. In their disillusioned search for such a man, you often hear them complaining bitterly that they have never met anyone who keeps the commandments of God, and who is a true Christian and a proof of God's existence. How right they are. However far you travel you will still fail to find the man who will not disappoint you. For you see, it is not we who have glorified the Father: it took Christ to do that. What even the best of us can do for the glory of God is comparatively but a drop in the ocean. Only be thankful if you do not bring disgrace on Him. Are we not all like children with sticky fingers who leave marks on everything they touch? And do we really think we can glorify God? Christ came into the world with the very definite mission of glorifying the Father here. He has done this: the Father in Heaven is glorified on earth once and for all. If you are looking for proof of God's existence, then look to Christ and not to men. 'Cursed be the man that trusteth in man, and maketh flesh his arm, and whose heart departeth from the Lord.' And do not be dazzled by the illusory light of world events: God's glory is not to be found there. The God of history is ever a God of blood and tears. And do not look to the lights of our churches and chapels: the candles that we claim to light to the glory of God all smoke, more or less. And do not look to the carefully and ostentatiously dimmed lights of our studies and centres of learning, where the attempt to glorify God has long since been abandoned. Look instead to Him whose unique mission it was to glorify the Father here on earth. Look to Him alone. In this case narrow-mindedness is a virtue. Light comes to us through the Son: the Light of His countenance shines brightly into our hearts, as the Apostle Paul says: 'For God, who commanded the light to shine out of darkness, hath shined in our hearts, to give the light of the knowledge of the glory of God in the face of Jesus Christ' (II Cor. IV. 6).

We are told very much the same thing in today's text. Because Christ has glorified the Father on earth, what we call knowledge of God has come to us. 'And this is life eternal, that they might *know* thee . . . and Jesus Christ, whom thou hast sent.' We can know God here and now. I use the word 'now' intentionally. The darkness that the world has always known has lately been gathering force, and it is becoming clear that man is no match for this dark power on earth. For instance, if anyone thinks that it is his business to keep God's light shining in the world, and that he is responsible for spreading the knowledge of God and Christ, let him make sure that he is not deluding himself. Whether you are parents, whose consciences are troubled because you can see your children plunging deeper into this darkness, and can do nothing about it; or whether you know that as Christians it is your duty to bring as many people as possible to the knowledge of God; or whether you have the interests of the missions of the Church at heart and have to admit that the darkness is creeping up steadily and irresistibly – whatever your particular concern may be, cast it on the shoulders of the Son, who has completed the work of glorifying the Father on earth, so that men may come to the knowledge of Christ. If we who work for God had to rely on ourselves, we would be simply overwhelmed by the odds against us. No, do not look to us clergymen and lay-preachers, look to God and entrust His affairs to Him and Him alone. Christ has done the work of the Father so effectively that it will be able to stand up against all opposition. Admittedly the storm that is raging in the world today is capable of extinguishing all sorts of lights, even in churches and chapels. May God have pity on us! But no storm will ever put out the Light that Christ brought into the world: 'And this is life eternal, that they might know thee the only true God, and Jesus Christ, whom thou hast sent.'

The Father has been glorified: Light has come into the world for ever. But what if you cannot comprehend that? What if the darkness that has now broken over the nations shrouds your mind too, and you begin to grow depressed? What if the Light shines, but you are empty, and dark, and cold inside? But you must not look inside yourself, where it may well be dark, and cold, and empty. Look away from yourself to the face of the eternal Mediator. In Him the Father is glorified on earth. Or suppose it really were true, as a scientist recently stated, that 'the capacity for faith is rapidly diminishing in the present generation'? What if this capacity for faith should shrink to almost nothing? Has God founded His cause on earth on our capacity for faith, or on the work that Christ accomplished for us? Capacity for faith or no, the fact remains that the Son has glorified the Father on earth and has added, 'And this is life eternal, that they might know thee the only true God, and Jesus Christ, whom thou hast sent.'

But what if you do not *want* to understand? Perhaps there are times when you would like to see the Light of glory, and would like to be drawn into it and then suddenly you change your mind? Perhaps the natural laziness of the flesh is stronger than all your good impulses, and the apathy of your heart weighs down your life like lead, so that time and again you love certain sins more than God? Perhaps you have been praying night and morning for years, 'Create in me, O God, a pure heart and give me a new, resolute spirit,' but alas, anything new in you seems so little and hardly worth the trouble of asking? So little, in fact, that at best your resolutions are mere shaming tokens of a new way of life? Is that not enough to make you despair? It certainly would be if you had to look to yourself and your own heart. But who said you must look to yourself? In spite of yourself and in spite of your heart, Christ has glorified the Father on earth. It is for the very reason that our hearts are in such a sorry state that He undertook His work on earth without asking our help: He knew that He and His Father would have been 'left in the lurch,' if He had wanted to build on our hearts. We can come to true knowledge of God and understand that He is the Father and that Christ is Christ, because the Son has vicarious pity on this very weakness of ours.

Christ has glorified the Father in our weakness by bringing us eternal life: 'As thou hast given him power over all flesh, that he should give eternal life to as many as thou hast given him. And this is life eternal, that they might know thee the only true God, and Jesus Christ, whom thou hast sent.' We have lately been thinking a great deal again about the meaning of 'life.' How very insecure and vulnerable this thing called 'life' has become. It seems to be hanging by such a slight thread. We are beginning to be more conscious of the words: 'In the midst of life we are in death.' And now we whose lives are so uncertain are offered not a life of ten years, or a hundred years, or even a thousand years, but life eternal. Obviously we cannot grasp this. We are as unsuited to bear eternal life as our hands are to holding glowing coals, for we are flesh. Flesh perishes like mown grass and the flowers of the field. Our capacity to live is proportionately as bad as our capacity for faith. I can understand only too well the people who cannot grasp that we who are flesh are to have eternal life. The man who is troubled by the frailty of all flesh, is often a man of greater faith than the one who is only too ready to talk complacently about eternal life, as if it were a foregone conclusion. But thank God that, when He promises us eternal life, Christ does not consider our capacity to live, but rather the fact that the Father has given Him 'power over all flesh.' We, who are flesh, are not to bear eternal life in our hands: Christ bears it in His hands, which came to earth expressly to bring it to us. The Father has made Him the bringer of what no flesh could bear. He has been given power over all flesh. So let the funeral bells ring out, let death take its toll, let the crematoriums do their work, and let the worms eat what they can, our eternal life is in good hands: 'As thou hast given him power over all flesh, that he should give eternal life to as many as thou hast given him.'

We must bear in mind that Christ is talking as a man of flesh and blood. This is on the eve of His suffering on the Cross; His Passion is not yet behind Him. Very soon He will be humiliated, dishonoured and defiled by men. In that hour of His complete eclipse even the sun will lose its light, and it will become evident that man, even the pious man, is not only incapable of glorifying God, but that he can even go to the very opposite extreme and crucify the Son. But through this very hour Christ is able to perfect the work of His Father; He glorifies the Father in Heaven to the point where we hear Him cry out, 'Father, into thy hands I commend my spirit.' Three days after this last, steep part of the way to the Cross, the whole world is to learn how the Father glorifies the Son and gives Him a name that is above all names. On Easter Sunday the disciples see their Master victorious in His splendour and glory. The mystery of Easter reveals how the Father has given the Son power over all flesh, and how everyone who knows the Son shall have eternal life: 'These words spake Jesus, and lifted up his eyes to heaven, and said, Father, the hour is come; glorify thy Son, that thy Son also may glorify thee.'

After the Son has presented Himself to the Father, like a servant who has done his day's work, and has said, 'I have glorified thee on the earth: I have finished the work,' He requests, 'And now, O Father, glorify thou me with thine own self with the glory which I had with thee before the world was.' It has been said that this is the only prayer that Christ makes on His own behalf. On further consideration, however, we see that this is not true. In actual fact Christ is not praying for Himself here at all. It is not for His own sake that He asks the Father to glorify Him, but out of consideration for us and this poor earth. He knows very well that, as a man here on earth, He has finished the work of the Father. The job that His Father gave Him to do between Christmas and Good Friday is nearly done now. Even so Christ does not intend to rest yet, thank God. Christ knows that 'the whole creation groaneth and travaileth in pain.' This groaning is not to last for ever. He knows about that last great day when God will 'turn again the captivity of Zion.' He will not always be alone as 'the first-fruits of them that slept'; there will come a day when every grave will open and the sea will give up its dead. What is happening now is merely a foretaste of the perfection of the new Heaven and the new earth. Until this perfect day there is still a great deal for Christ to do. So when He prays to be glorified by the Father, at the end of His days on earth, it means that He is placing Himself at the Father's disposal for the work that awaits Him in Eternity. He will soon carry on the Father's work from Heaven, as the eternal High Priest, and will not rest until He appears in His glory and all the holy angels with Him.

In his account of the Transfiguration of Christ, Matthew tells us that the three disciples, who went up the mountain with their Master, fell on their faces and covered their eyes, because they did not dare to look upon the splendour of God. We have a similar case here, where we are witnesses of an intimate conversation between the Father and the Son. Christ's words go high above our heads and yet they concern us. It is for our sakes that the Son stands like a priest before the Father. Therefore He does not prevent human beings from being present as witnesses, and catching the sacred words, as if from afar, with their inadequate earthly senses. These words come to us from a very great height. We Swiss are used to looking up at mountains, and some of us have even had the opportunity of climbing some very high ones. There is no scaling these heights, however. The mountains we are looking at here tower above all others. They are the truly eternal mountains from whence our help comes. In all our darkness and distress we must never cease to look up to this high and distant Light, nor to surrender ourselves to it. By striving after the glory of God our generation will be restored to eternal life.

Jesus's High-Priestly Prayer of Gratitude

I have manifested thy name unto the men which thou gavest me out of the world: thine they were, and thou gavest them me; and they have kept thy word. Now they have known that all things whatsoever thou hast given me are of thee. For I have given unto them the words which thou gavest me; and they have received them, and have known surely that I came out from thee, and they have believed that thou didst send me.

[XVII. 6–8]

'Men which thou gavest me out of the world: thine they were, and thou gavest them me.' Thus does the Master speak of His disciples. So that is how it came about that two men, whom Jesus met at their work by the Sea of Galilee, left their nets and all that they had and followed Him; and two more, who were with their father, mending nets, did the same thing when He called them! So that is what happened when He met Matthew, sitting at the receipt of custom, and invited him, 'Follow me,' so that he left his job and became a disciple! So it was the Father who gave these men to the Son! In every new disciple He saw a new gift, until their number was complete. So it was not Christ, who won them by His fiery speeches, or His miracles or the power of His personality! No, while Jesus was calling His disciples on earth, they were chosen for Him in Heaven, each one allotted to Him by God: 'Men which thou gavest me out of the world: thine they were, and thou gavest them me.' This is truly an astonishing assertion.

The Lord sees His disciples as gifts for which He is beholden to the Father. We, on the other hand, so often play the part of busybodies, fondly imagining that we have to bustle around and win people for God. We are always so proud of our own cleverness and achievements. And yet the Psalm tells us: 'Children are an heritage of the Lord: and the fruit of the womb is his reward.' If this is said of our own children, how much more does it apply to children of God! If you yourself are fortunate enough to be a child of God, or if you are a mother or father whose children are children of God, then it is not to your credit but thanks to God's mysterious gift of grace. If this were not so, who would seriously dare to become a father or a mother? Who would be a teacher or a clergyman if we could not have faith in the words of Jesus: 'Thine they were, and thou gavest them me'?

This doctrine of election by divine grace – for that is what we are considering, of course – is quite particularly welcome news today, in view of the rising generation. Thank God that the final decision about our sons and daughters is not made on earth. We have to accept the fact that there is a vexatious, as well as a pleasant, side to good tidings for us men. So we must not be surprised to find some indignant, if not actually angry, people among us here this morning. We have just finished a 'century of education,' an age when education was all. I know a village in the canton of Berne, whose secondary school stands on a high hill, like a church, with a clock-tower, while the church looks like an ivy-grown ruin, hidden away in a corner. This is characteristic of the spirit of yesterday. I can remember innumerable conversations, during my visits to various homes in town and country. People were not interested in the Gospel and salvation through Christ, but if the conversation turned to education, it livened up immediately. People can easily be drawn out by any mention of education. Knowledge, culture, education: these were our pride, the most brilliant jewels in the crown which we men of the nineteenth and twentieth centuries placed on our own heads. Education was the answer to everything. Heinrich Pestalozzi, quite against his own will, I am sure, became the idol of this education-mad generation. And what was the outcome? We were able to mould human beings into what pleased us, a picture in our own image; and what we made pleased the Devil too. But we can never make human beings into what would please God. That is and will remain a gift. We have come to the limit of our ability to influence and shape men. A child of God can only be born of that one Spirit, which is not ours. We cannot become children of God through a system but only through a miracle. That is why the most important word in the Scriptures is not 'education' but 'salvation,' and that is why Christ is not the Educator and Teacher, but the Saviour of the human race. For a long time the Church has pandered to this spirit of the age. We thought that we could give people some sort of Christian education, and we tried to do it too. What came of it? A Western world with a smattering of Christianity! But what few Christian standards we managed to instil into the people collapsed like a house of cards at the first trembling of the earth. Our Christian education failed: Salvation, however, will never fail. The men whom the Father gave to the Son will always be His. It is with the people who have been saved to be children of God through the mystery of grace that Christ builds His community.

But if the decision has already been made by the Father, is there anything left for Christ to do for men? Indeed there is. He tells us here quite clearly that He does two things. Firstly He says, 'I have manifested thy name unto the men,' and secondly, 'I have given unto them the words which thou gavest me.'

Christ manifests the name of God to those people given to Him by the Father. It is true that the name of God was already known to the civilised world; but that name had lost all meaning, and become empty and hollow. But now that Christ has come, His words and actions have given new weight, value, and respect to the name of the Father. When Christ came into the world, people began to fear the name of God once more and to depend on Him again. The man who looks to Christ, and through Him knows the name of God, knows that when he calls upon God it will not be in vain; and he knows too that it is no empty thing to begin and end his work in this world, in the name of God. O for a generation that would go about its day's work in the name of God again! A short time ago, when I had to wait some time between trains at Schwyz, I took the opportunity of going to look at the national archives, and to see all the old federal covenants. With increasing awe and nostalgia I read at the beginning of one document after another, '*In nomine Domini, Amen*'! 'In the name of God, Amen.' If this is not a mere empty formula, then contracts great and small, including marriage contracts, are indestructible, and we can take courage again, knowing that our family and national lives have a firm foundation. Formulae such as these are endowed with power and life, as soon as Christ manifests the name of the Father to men. When we begin to call God 'our Father' again, through Christ, then we shall once more understand what it means to be baptised in this name, and the certificate of baptism will cease to be a meaningless piece of paper. Then baptism will once again become the living seal of those who belong to God. We often see a notice saying 'Sold' on a house still in the process of being built. By analogy, each one of us who is baptised bears a notice saying 'Sold.' The bargaining has been done. As a baptised person you have been sold to God and are now His property. That is the meaning of the words: 'I have manifested thy name unto men.'

Then the second thing that Christ does for those whom the Father has given Him: 'I have given unto them the words which thou gavest me.' Unfortunately, we know only too well how little influence the words of God have on men today, because they have become despised and neglected. But because 'the Word was made flesh and dwelt among us' they have become current and effective again. For instance, the centurion of Capernaum said, 'Speak the word only, and my servant shall be healed': and Peter decided, 'At thy word I will let down the net'; and the people who saw Jesus call into the grave, 'Lazarus, come forth,' stopped scorning and despising the Word of God. That is how Christ gave to men the words that He received from the Father.

That is what Christ did. But now, what is there for the disciples to do? If they have already been chosen by the Father, is there anything more that they can do? Most certainly: three things in fact. The Master says that 'they have received them, and have known surely that I came out from thee, and they have believed that thou didst send me.'

'They have received them.' That is the first thing that the disciples do. They receive the words which the Father has given them through Christ. They take them in and give them shelter. They belong by grace to those of whom we read: 'As many as received him, to them gave he power to become the sons of God.' They open the door to the words which are seeking to dwell in them. The miracle of receptiveness to God's Word has taken place in the disciples. The Word has not merely fallen on their ears, aroused a little interest, and then been forgotten: it has found its way into their hearts, their minds, their feelings and their wills, and has taken possession of their whole being. And where God's living Word is accepted like this, the effects soon become apparent. There is always light within you and light to guide your footsteps in safety. When it is accepted, God's Word becomes caustic and eats away everything that is unhealthy and corrupt, so that Christ can say to the disciples, 'Ye are clean through the word which I have spoken unto you' (ch. xv). Furthermore it becomes nourishment which daily refreshes, and builds us up and preserves us from spiritual starvation. And it becomes a vaccine that gives us resistance to the corrupting powers of hell and the grave. So when it is received by the disciples, the Word of God is not only like a fire and a hammer that can split rocks; it is also like a seed that germinates new life; and like milk and bread that give strength for the journey to eternal life.

'They have received them,' and then Jesus adds, 'and have known.' Received and known. The sequence is significant. We always try to do it the other way round; first of all we want to know, and only then are we willing to receive. But the Word of God will remain a mystery to you, as long as your willingness to receive is conditional upon your knowing. Therefore accept it, as a child would accept an apple or as you would accept a parcel from the postman, perhaps wondering who has sent it but nevertheless accepting it. That is how you should accept the Word of God: without first being able to know and understand, you should simply receive it. The Bible will remain a mystery to you, as long as you will not sacrifice reason and self-will, and are not unconditionally prepared to receive. But if you receive like a child, then you will begin to understand. If you accept 'blindfold,' so to speak, the darkness will change to light, and then God will begin to talk to you, and everything will become clearer and clearer. If you receive the Word, you will be able to see 'His glory, the glory as of the only begotten of the Father, full of grace and truth.' Then it will seem as if scales have fallen from your eyes and it will dawn upon you who Christ is. The identity of Christ was disputed in those days no less than today. Some said that He was of men, others that He was of the Devil, and others that He was of God. If you accept Him like a child, you will know that Christ, together with all that He says and does, is truly of God.

And now the third thing that the chosen disciples can do: they can receive, they can know – *and* they can believe. Notice the progression. Belief is greater than knowledge, because belief is not dependent on seeing.

So, to sum up, each party has its appointed role. The Father in Heaven has given the disciples to the Lord; Christ has manifested God's name to the disciples and given them God's Word; and in their turn the disciples have received, known and believed.

And now let us consider the position in which Jesus finds Himself here with regard to His disciples. In all there are eleven disciples, one of the twelve having been taken from Him again already. From a human point of view we might well ask, 'Is that all? Is that the result of His tremendous efforts?' Any other man would answer sadly, 'Yes, that is all I have left.' But what about Christ? In this prayer we hear Him thank the Father for having given Him the eleven and for letting Him keep them. Any other man would, quite understandably, be worried, and would call for an effort to increase the number of disciples, and to improve the results of his life's work. But not Christ: He shows an utter lack of anxiety. Because it is the Father who has given Him these eleven, He sees the continuance of His work in this world ensured, in spite of this small number. He speaks with such an air of calm, as if to say, 'Only eleven, you ask? Yes; why not? In Noah's time there was only one, and in the time of Abraham too; but the Father has given me as many as eleven!' Christ's situation puts us in mind of Elijah. When a man endowed with the authority of the Father appears, He will draw unto himself a hitherto invisible reserve of 'seven thousand men, who have not bowed the knee to the image of Baal.' A similar thing will happen here, for we read: 'And the same day there were added unto them about three thousand souls.' This is the reason why the High Priest is so full of gratitude.

And one final thought. A woman I visited the other day told me sadly that, a few years ago, she had laid out a little garden and planted various flowers in it. And lately, while she was digging it over, it had struck her that most of the rarer plants had disappeared, while the common types had survived. She commented rather gloomily that it was almost a reflexion of our world and times: the finer type of person is being forced out of existence, while the more common sorts are thriving. For my part, I should like to ask whether the question of rare or common types, where people are concerned, is ultimately of importance? Surely the essential point is that God is the gardener who has planted them all, and that no plant that He has sown will be uprooted? They are 'like a tree planted by the rivers of water, that bringeth forth his fruit in his season; his leaf also shall not wither.' That is why the eyes of the High Priest are filled with gratitude to the Father as He looks upon these men 'which thou gavest me out of the world.' In the fullness of His gratitude and adoration He proclaims, 'Thine they were, and thou gavest them me; and they have kept thy word. Now they have known that all things whatsoever thou hast given me are of thee. For I have given unto them the words which thou gavest me; and they have received them, and have known surely that I came out from thee, and they have believed that thou didst send me.'

Jesus's High-Priestly Prayer of Intercession

I pray for them: I pray not for the world, but for them which thou hast given me; for they are thine. And all mine are thine, and thine are mine; and I am glorified in them. And now I am no more in the world, but these are in the world, and I come to thee. Holy Father, keep through thine own name those whom thou hast given me, that they may be one, as we are. While I was with them in the world, I kept them in thy name: those that thou gavest me I have kept, and none of them is lost, but the son of perdition; that the scripture might be fulfilled. And now come I to thee; and these things I speak in the world, that they might have my joy fulfilled in themselves. I have given them thy word; and the world hath hated them, because they are not of the world, even as I am not of the world. I pray not that thou shouldest take them out of the world, but that thou shouldest keep them from the evil.

[XVII. 9–15]

Jesus is praying for His disciples, those whom the Father has given Him. Everyone will understand and agree with this. But not everyone can understand why He finds it necessary to add to this prayer of intercession, for those nearest Him, the words, 'I pray not for the world.' We cannot help feeling that it was not Jesus who said this. We remember John the Baptist's universal witness of Christ: 'The Lamb of God, which taketh away the sin of the world,' and those other familiar words, 'God so loved the world'; we think of Jesus's own testimony: 'Be of good cheer; I have overcome the world,' and yet here He says, 'I pray for them: I pray not for the world.' Is this the same Jesus who, Matthew tells us, 'was moved with compassion toward the multitude'; who loves the whole world, and even the birds in the sky and the lilies of the field; who takes pity on the blind by the wayside; who sends His servants out to the poor and crippled in the highways and byways; whose compassion embraces the publicans at their seat of custom, the devout behind their fences of piety and the rich behind their fences of gold? Yes, it is the same Jesus; it is that Saviour of the world, who found the woman of Samaria by the well, who says here, 'I pray for them: I pray not for the world, but for them which thou hast given me.'

We may find it a source of annoyance that Christ should favour anyone as He does here. It may go against the grain that He should place the disciples first and the world after them. This looks like an order of precedence. He prays in the first place for His disciples, and only then for the world, just as elsewhere He bids us first of all seek His Kingdom and His righteousness, adding that everything else we need will then be given us. The Lord knows perfectly well why He sets up this order of precedence, however much it may offend us. As we have seen, He is full of gratitude when He looks on these eleven men who are left to Him. They are to Christ what a handful of seed is to the farmer whose harvest has been destroyed by frost and hail. He can sow his field once more with this handful, and on it he lays his hopes of a new harvest in due course. In the eleven disciples Christ sees the seed for that great field which is the world, and that is why He concentrates His intercession first and foremost on them. What would the world be without this seed? It would remain desolate and barren, and would become a wilderness of weeds. Far from failing the world, when Christ prays for the disciples first, He does so in the world's own interest. They are the living seed, they are 'the salt of the earth,' they are the 'light of the world.' To them He has given His Word, the authority to bind and redeem; to them He has entrusted the key which locks the gates of hell and opens the portals of Heaven. That is why the Lord does not pray in the first place for the world, but for His disciples. This is a parallel to the occasion in Bethany when Christ justified Mary to Martha with the words: 'Martha, Martha, thou art careful and troubled about many things: but one thing is needful: and Mary hath chosen that good part, which shall not be taken away from her.' The condition of this world naturally causes us a great deal of care and anxiety. But when the world threatens to engulf Christianity, like an avalanche burying the flowers of the meadow, then Christ intervenes. He halts the avalanche because the field comes first; He will sow it and will not let His seed be buried. 'I pray for them: I pray not for the world, but for them which thou hast given me.'

Unless we are mistaken, today is one of those times of urgency in the Kingdom of God which call most particularly for prayer and intercession, for the one thing that is needful. The world is pushing itself forward everywhere. On every front it is clamouring for first place, and it screams out its demands daily through loudspeakers. Who is there to contradict or resist? Christ can refuse this unconditional claim. He tells the world that there are more pressing needs than its own. The burning problem of the day is that the Church should be kept alive. (Yes, I said the Church!) The Church itself is not to be confused with those usages so dear to us, which we have inherited from the past, and to which our feeble hearts cling so fondly. Beautiful and precious ritual ornamentation, and so on, can, perhaps with no harm to the Church whatsoever, be done away with overnight. The Church, however, must be preserved for the nations and for our own people. We do not pray for the preservation of our own lives, or even the religious pattern of our lives, but for the Church itself, the substance, the seed, the salt, the light. What is of the utmost urgency is that the preaching of the Gospel to the nations should continue, that the Church should be and remain accessible to the people, and that the 'eleven' should remain alive. 'I pray for them: I pray not for the world, but for them which thou hast given me.'

But is this prayer of our Lord's not unrealistic? Certainly! Happy the man who has this unworldly attitude! There is a kind of knowledge of the world that does not help the world; and conversely there is an unworldliness which helps it incomparably more than any so-called realistic approach. Strength to preserve the State and the world is not to be found where the loudest claims are made but, quite simply, where the living Church is. Therefore anyone who surrenders even one hair's breadth of the tiny bit of space that the Church still has, in the lives of the nations today, is a traitor, a traitor to the world as well as to the Church. It is the prospect of the more widespread preaching of God's Word that gives life to our nation and to all others; and any further limitation of the Word would amount to suicide. If it is true that man does not live by bread alone, but by every word that comes from the mouth of God, then we can have some idea of the weight carried by Christ's intercession, 'I pray not for the world, but for them which thou hast given me.' Even the small part of the world that is most dear to us, even our motherland, takes second place in the order of precedence, and woe betide the community that ever forgets this.

And now let us go one step further. The disciples are undoubtedly the men who have the greatest need of Christ's intercession. In fact, they need praying for more than the world does. Within limitations the world can live in its own way without the intercession of the High Priest, but the community cannot do so for one single day. It would die. It is a branch that is incapable of life without the Vine; it is a sheep that needs the Shepherd's daily care. It is the unique privilege of the Church of Christ that it needs Him who prays for it here, and would be lost without Him. What a blessed lack of self-sufficiency is betrayed by the Lord's prayer of intercession!

Christ points out here two reasons why the disciples need Him so much: 'Holy Father, keep through thine own name those whom thou hast given me.' He Himself has kept them so far, and He asks God to keep them from now on, so that they will not be left behind like orphans. The disciples are the bearers of God's name. It has been stamped and imprinted on them, as it were. Christ has glorified the Father in them, and therefore they are the enemy's main target. If he can corrupt, strike, kill or capture one of them, then the enemy of Christ has gained more than if he ruined a hundred others. In the battle of the Kingdom of God against darkness the disciples are, so to speak, major military objectives.

Strong evidence that the Tempter has singled out the disciples for his main attack, and that therefore they particularly need Christ's intercession, is evinced above all by the fact that they can never agree amongst themselves. In a certain sense, the world is much quicker and more ready to unite than the Church. That is not surprising, because it is at the Church that the Tempter has directed his aim, and not for nothing is he called '*diabolos*,' which can be translated as 'the one who throws into confusion.' It is he who constantly throws the members of the Church into confusion trying repeatedly by his mischievous attacks to prevent Christians from coming together in one place in unity and concord. So we have the rift and the painful discord in the Church of this world. It is because of this that the Church especially urgently needs Christ's plea of intercession, 'Holy Father, keep through thine own name those whom thou hast given me, that they may be one, as we are.' When we consider the fury of the Tempter's onslaught, we are no longer surprised at the schisms in the Church; on the contrary, we are amazed that a community does in fact still exist with any unity in faith at all. It is not our work or merit that there is still a group of men and women in every nation, who cling tenaciously to unity in faith; it is the work of our eternal High Priest. Because He prays for the preservation of unity, we are not yet completely thrown into confusion. His intercession is stronger than the Devil's attempts at destruction, and therefore the Church is given life by the prayers of the High Priest.

And now the second reason why Christ's own come first in His prayer of intercession. Through the fact that the disciples are bearers of God's Word, and that in them the name of the Father is glorified, Christians have been given a character of their own. There is something about Christians which is lacking in other people, something of a foreign air, a kind of aura of eternity. Of course, the disciples do not emphasise this foreign quality, it is simply there. The Christian has a place in the world and performs his daily task as well as any other man, it is to be hoped; but there is something about him that will not let him simply join in everything just like other people. He has scruples and says so, whereas other people are quite unburdened by conscience. You can tell by his every action that he is a Christian, just as they said of Peter, 'thy speech betrayeth thee.' The girl told him straight to his face that he was one of Jesus's followers, however much he protested. So you can see that the Christian belongs to another place; he is a child of two homes and a citizen of two worlds. Naturally this difference has its consequences. The Christian is never very popular with the world. People always fight a little shy of him. They are always somewhat distrustful of his presence. Even if he says nothing, they know and feel what he is thinking, so they are never quite at their ease with him. Even in his native land he is looked upon as a man who has dual citizenship. It is this foreign air that causes the Christian to be not quite welcome or popular. Indeed, Jesus says outright, 'I have given them thy word; and the world hath hated them.' If we accept the Word of God and allow Christ to glorify the name of the Father in us, we need not seek unpopularity, for the hatred of the world is bound to reach us sooner or later. Because Christ sympathises with this plight of the disciples', He prays for them in particular, 'Keep through thine own name those whom thou hast given me.' And because our eternal High Priest never ceases to pray that the Father may keep them in His name and His Word, there has always been a community of people foreign to the world. These strangers would long ago have been wiped out, or else assimilated into the world, if Christ were not so constant in His intercession. This praying High Priest is the hidden, eternal core of resistance of the Christian community in this world. Christ even tells His own not to be resentful and down-cast about their estrangement; after all they have gained something. So He prays at the same time, 'that they might have my joy fulfilled in themselves.' This puts us in mind of what He says about fasting, which should not be a matter for sadness, but 'when thou fastest, anoint thine head, and wash thy face.'

Christians could spare themselves the distress of estrangement by identifying themselves with the world, as we have just seen. Fortunately this danger is constantly being averted by Christ. But they could also make things easier for themselves in the opposite way, namely by withdrawing from the world, shutting themselves off in their own little circle, and fleeing from the temporal world to some little island, so that they really would be coming together, but in a false sense. This has been a great temptation for the Christian community throughout the ages. We are always coming across people whose hearts are deeply filled with the desire to be able to live together, once and for all, with people of like mind, as one flock under one Shepherd. Every living Christian knows this nostalgia. But we must not yield to it; we must remain in the world and not withdraw from it. Christ remains true to the world. Admittedly the world does not love Him, nevertheless that does not prevent Him from loving it. It hates Him but He remains faithful to it. 'They are not of the world, even as I am not of the world,' is immediately followed by 'I pray not that thou shouldest take them out of the world, but that thou shouldest keep them from the evil.' There is a kind of worldliness that is unfaithful to God; but similarly there is a certain piety that is unfaithful to the world, which Christ does not allow us to indulge in. Peter understood what the High Priest meant. He introduces his first Epistle with the words: 'To the elect . . . strangers,' who are 'scattered.' These scattered strangers are the Christians. Some day the time will come when the strangers will no longer be scattered. That time will see the fulfilment of the words, 'And he shall send his angels . . . and they shall gather together his elect from the four winds, from one end of heaven to the other.'

Jesus's High-Priestly Prayer for Sanctification

They are not of the world, even as I am not of the world. Sanctify them through thy truth: thy word is truth. As thou hast sent me into the world, even so have I also sent them into the world. And for their sakes I sanctify myself, that they also might be sanctified through the truth.

[xvii. 16–19]

The foundations of the Church of Christ are laid bare here before us and we can look into the innermost mystery of evangelical discipleship. The man who has eyes to see will draw great comfort and confidence from these words, and he has every reason for gratitude. The eternal High Priest is praying that His disciples may be sanctified. What does He mean when He prays to the Father, 'Sanctify them through thy truth'? And what do His words predict for His disciples when He prays, 'I sanctify myself, that they also might be sanctified through the truth'?

Sanctification is one of the fundamental principles of Christianity. Therefore it is of very great importance that we should understand the meaning of it. If we are not clear about this, we shall never in all our lives know what the Church means. So bear with me for a moment while I work it out a little; it is very well worth while. Fortunately we do not have to elucidate and explain for ourselves. Here again all we have to do is to follow the Bible, which explains everything we need to know. In the case of His disciples, Christ takes it for granted that they know from the Bible what sanctification is, and they are certainly not hearing this word for the first time. In our reading of the Old Testament – and what a blessing it is! – we meet at every turn people who have experienced the sanctification that Christ is asking for, on behalf of His disciples; 'Sanctify them through thy truth.' In the Old Testament we often see how God sanctifies people; He arrests them and gives them a place, serving Him, in the plan that He has for this poor world. Sanctification is not only being called up for God's service, but being impressed for it. The saints of the Old Testament are those men who, like Abraham, were taken away from their friends, their town and their country, and commandeered for God's cause. In his first Epistle, Peter talks of 'holy women' too. By this he means that long succession of women from Eve, Sarah, the harlot Rahab, Ruth, and Hannah down to Elizabeth and Mary at the threshold of the New Testament; women who were taken into service for a special mission by the Father of all men. The man who is in God's service, a kind of reservist if you will is sanctified and therefore holy.

The Bible does not only speak of holy men in this special sense: the conception is occasionally extended to places and things. We hear of a holy place, as opposed to an ordinary dwelling; we hear of the Holy Scriptures, as opposed to ordinary literature. The Holy Land is not just ordinary territory; there is a distinction between the Holy Supper and ordinary eating and drinking. Hence the opposite of 'holy' is 'ordinary.' The Holy Scripture of the Old Testament, as the disciples well know, does not just speak of individuals made holy by God; it tells boldly of how God gathers a whole nation round these individuals, singles it out from all the other nations, calls it into service in His plan of salvation, and contrasts it with the so-called 'nations.' The chosen race is Israel, to whom God speaks from Sinai; 'Ye shall be a peculiar treasure unto me above all people: for all the earth is mine. And ye shall be unto me a kingdom of priests, and an holy nation.'

So Israel is not holy because it is better and more noble than ordinary nations, but because God has chosen it and taken it into His service. Only God, who alone is holy, can sanctify. Yet now we are confronted by the astonishing fact that here is a man who says, 'I sanctify myself.' Who is this who can sanctify Himself? Could Abraham or Elijah, David or Daniel do it? Nobody has ever been allowed to say such a thing until now. If anyone had said it, it would have been blasphemy. The One who says it now is the first and last to do so. And He is allowed to say it because He has a unique share in the mystery of God's holiness. For here is someone who is 'greater than . . . Abraham.' It is the Son who is able to say the exceptional words, 'I sanctify myself.' How does He go about sanctifying Himself? Christ performs the service that only He can and must perform. He does so in voluntary obedience, in accordance with the counsel and will of the Father. He serves as Mediator between Heaven and earth. He sanctifies Himself by placing Himself completely at His Father's service and saying, 'Not my will, but thine, be done.' His path of duty leads through the Cross and the grave to Resurrection, and up to the right hand of the Father, from whence He shall come again. This absolute, voluntary filial obedience is the secret of Christ's self-sanctification. That is what He means when He stands alone before the Father here and vows to Him, 'I sanctify myself.'

And now Christ goes on to do an extraordinary thing. He prays to the Father that the disciples may benefit by His sanctification of Himself on the Cross, and that through His service God may sanctify the disciples too. He asks the Father to overlook the past, present, and future shortcomings of these His disciples. He asks Him to sanctify them in spite of the fact that they are poor men, filled with original sin and driven out of Paradise. 'Father, take this man Thomas into your service, in spite of his tendency to cowardice and doubt. Take this man Peter into your service and sustain him, even when he swears, "I know not the man." Sanctify them, not for their sakes but – for mine! "For their sakes I sanctify myself, that they also might be sanctified through the truth." '

'For their sakes'! That is the all-important thing here: 'I sanctify myself for their sakes.' Their holiness is not self-acquired; it is given to them, and what a gift it is! This means no less than that they are accepted into the circle of Abraham, Isaac and Jacob.

James, John and Peter are to be sanctified, just as Jacob, Elijah, and Moses once were. As fathers of the New Testament they are to sit at table in the Kingdom of God with the fathers of the Old Testament, set above the twelve tribes of Israel. This is their gift of sanctification. This being so, we need have no hesitation about calling them Saint Peter, Saint Thomas, Saint John and Saint Paul. We can do so happily and readily, for now we know that their holiness has been given to them. If I were a painter, even as a Protestant, I should be quite happy to paint haloes round the heads of these men of the Old and New Testaments, knowing that the light of their haloes does not spring from the brightness of their own virtue, but from somewhere quite different. There on the Cross we can see the light which is reflected in the haloes round the disciples' heads. In the blood of Jesus Christ is sanctification. Therein lies the glory that adorns us, even to the radiance around our heads.

That then is the group of men, who have been taken into Christ's service and will remain His through thick and thin, and in the face of hell and the grave, in spite of their own sins and shortcomings. These are the men He has pressed into His service. They are now '*douloi*,' as the Apostle Paul likes to call himself, slaves and bondmen of Jesus Christ. He intends to use them as His messengers: 'As thou hast sent me into the world, even so have I also sent them into the world.' He needs men like these in His vineyard, not because they are able-bodied but because He has sanctified Himself 'for their sakes.' The Church is founded on men like these, and so the gates of hell cannot overcome it. And now we also understand what was meant when we talked at the beginning about the foundations of the Church and the innermost mystery of evangelical discipleship.

Christ's sanctification of Himself does not stop short at the disciples. Because He dies for the eleven and sanctifies Himself 'for their sakes,' far more than these eleven men are affected. By sanctifying Himself for their sakes, He sanctifies Himself for every person who will let the disciples call him into the Kingdom of the Son. The disciples, the apostles, and the prophets are, after all, only the first row of the bricks which are built up on Christ, their cornerstone. But Christ does not rest satisfied with only one row of bricks; He goes on adding more layers to the foundations and will not rest until the building is finished. 'Living bricks' are added daily to the original apostles and prophets. In the early days of Christianity, when people knew that sanctification can only be received as a gift and when it was quite clear on which tree this sweetest of all fruits grew, members of all the Christian communities began to call each other 'Saint' quite naturally, and with no guilty feeling of presumption. They greeted one another by that name in the streets, and at their meetings, and addressed their letters to the Saints of Jerusalem, the Saints of Rome, the Saints of Asia or the Saints of Corinth! And therefore this form of address is applicable to all those who let themselves be converted by the words of the apostles and the prophets; it applies just as much today to all of you who can say with conviction, 'This is my only support that, body and soul, in life and in death, I am not my own but belong to my beloved Saviour, Jesus Christ.' If only we could grasp the fact this morning that this 'for their sakes' finally includes us too! Then we would realise that 'for your sakes' is the same as that which we shall hear next week at Communion, where Christ addresses us with the words '... given for you ... shed for you.' 'I sanctify myself, that they also might be sanctified through the truth.'

'Through the truth'! It is noteworthy that the truth is mentioned twice here. I wonder why? It is probably because sanctification is always encircled by falsehood. This falsehood has its origin in a very deep need. In the Christian Church a considerable number of people are always to be found who are consumed all their lives by an unquenchable, nostalgic longing for sanctification. They would like to be holy, and so they torment themselves and work themselves to death in the struggle for sanctification. This group existed in the time of Jesus too. These were the people He had in mind when He called, 'Come unto me, all ye that labour and are heavy laden, and I will give you rest.' He was inviting all those who were weary and broken by the desperate attempt to sanctify themselves to come to Him and to accept as a gift from His hands the sanctification that He had won 'for their sakes.' The man who accepts this invitation will find that His 'yoke is easy' and His 'burden is light.' The man who does not accept it will have to continue his forlorn efforts to sanctify himself; but he will never succeed. The moment will come when he realises that no man can sanctify himself, and he will have reached that dangerous point when the temptation to lie and the first step to falsehood are very near. He will feel a need to shine before men, and to pretend that he has succeeded in sanctifying himself after all. He will want to exalt himself, and so he will lapse into false piety and hypocrisy. A man resorts to false piety when he is weary and heavy laden, yet cannot summon up the courage to admit openly that he has confessed his sins and eaten of the bread of repentance. He pretends to the world that he has mastered sin instead of owning that he is a hardened sinner. Yes, the Lord of the Church knows only too well why He asks the Father to 'sanctify them through thy truth,' and He has good reason for adding, 'For their sakes I sanctify myself, that they also might be sanctified through the truth.'

Furthermore the Bible says, 'Thy word is truth.' It is not mere chance that these words are to be read here. Is it not a fact, and does not the history of the Church often show us, that all efforts to achieve holiness by oneself are in danger of bringing the Holy Spirit into conflict with the Word? Where the call to self-sanctification rings out, the Word is always scorned and despised. Despise the Word then! Set the desire for sanctification against the Word! But then take care that all you are achieving is not gross self-deception. 'Thy word is truth,' says Christ. And that is an end of it.

And now the last point. In the Church of Christ you can always meet a great many others, perhaps even superior in number, who boast that they have never felt the need for sanctification. The question of holiness has not yet caused them any sleepless nights nor given them any grey hairs; they can boast that they do not belong to that group of weary and heavy-laden people who feel themselves compelled in fear and trembling to create their own salvation. To them I say, 'Take care! That is a very dangerous boast.' I should like to warn the man who can brag that he has never bothered very much about his salvation in all his life, that there is another besides God who can arrest and lay claim to us, who would also like to have us in his service, and who also has a word and a doctrine. Innumerable loudspeakers and microphones, transmitters and receivers are at his disposal. Today more than ever it is true that a man who is not claimed by Christ will fall into the clutches of the other. Either we let ourselves be sanctified through Christ, or we become tools and subjects of the Devil. That well-meaning neutrality towards God, that easy spectatorship that was formerly so widespread, has completely gone astray. The easy-going indifference of the people who do not care much about their sanctification is a broad harvest-field where the powers of darkness reap as many serfs and slaves as there are dead leaves in autumn. No sanctimonious hypocrisy is to be found there, but only a cynical lie in the face of the whole world.

Christ, as our High Priest, petitions the Father for His community and asks Him, 'Sanctify them through thy truth.' The Lord's high intercession is our assurance, but at the same time it contains the urgent warning to every man: 'It is time to think of salvation!'

Jesus's High-Priestly Prayer for Perfect Unity

Neither pray I for these alone, but for them also which shall believe on me through their word; that they all may be one; as thou, Father, art in me, and I in thee, that they also may be one in us: that the world may believe that thou hast sent me. And the glory which thou gavest me I have given them; that they may be one, even as we are one: I in them, and thou in me, that they may be made perfect in one; and that the world may know that thou hast sent me, and hast loved them, as thou hast loved me. Father, I will that they also, whom thou hast given me, be with me where I am; that they may behold my glory, which thou hast given me: for thou lovedst me before the foundation of the world. O righteous Father, the world hath not known thee: but I have known thee, and these have known that thou hast sent me. And I have declared unto them thy name, and will declare it: that the love wherewith thou hast loved me may be in them, and I in them.

[XVII. 20–26]

'Neither pray I for these alone, but for them also which shall believe on me through their word.' This means that the Lord is praying to the Father here for all those who have come to the Church of Christ in the well-nigh two thousand years that have elapsed since His death; God alone knows their names and their number. But it also means that Christ is pleading for all those who will believe in Him, and will come to the Church in the future through the spreading of His Word. In other words, whenever a missionary and apostle sets foot on some distant, foreign shore, Christ has preceded him. This apostle might well be living in Basle, and the foreign shore might be any doorstep in this town. An apostle never gets there first: Christ has always been there already, for as High Priest He has prayed for all those 'which shall believe on me through their [the disciples'] word.' Therefore we are not only allowed, but commanded, to apply these splendid words to ourselves this morning. It is my duty to address you outright as people who are included in Christ's prayer for His Church, and to remind you that Christ had you in mind when He prayed for all those who would believe in Him. From the day when we recognise that this intercession actually took place and begin to reckon seriously with it, we look at people quite differently. Every person we meet might, after all, be one of those for whom the Lord has prayed here, for you cannot tell at first sight whether someone belongs to the chosen of Christ or not. They are chosen before even they themselves realise it, for Christ is praying here for everyone who will believe in Him, through the disciples' word, throughout all future ages. This consideration for the future should not surprise us. Long ago God asked Abraham if he could number the countless stars in the sky, and told him that his seed would be as numerous as the stars in the heavens and the grains of sand upon the sea-shore. Christ can number them, for He is Lord over Heaven and earth. Christ is greater than Abraham. And so He prays for all those who will believe in Him through the words of His disciples. Thus does the Lord pray for His Church.

What precisely is it that the Lord is praying for on behalf of His Church? What is the exact content of His prayer? We might very well ask, 'What else can He ask in addition to everything that He has already prayed for on their behalf?' As we have heard, He asked the Father to keep them through His own name; then He went on to pray the Father to sanctify them through His truth; and now His intercession for His own goes to such lengths that, if He were not the Son, we should feel inclined to say that it had gone a bit too far. Now He prays that all those who will believe in Him may be one with Him and the Father, as He is one with the Father. We hardly dare to say it – Christ is now praying that we might be given a share in the unity of the Son and the Father!

Let us envisage what this means for a moment. Every man has his family and dependants. A man who gets married sometimes has dependants whom he wants to go on looking after. He may have brothers or sisters, or an aged mother, or an invalid father, whom he would like to bring into the marriage. Perhaps he is a widower and brings with him into his new partnership a number of children from his first marriage. And now here is Christ talking of dependants, whom He has gathered unto Himself and will continue to gather until the Day of Judgment. He does not want to leave this following of His outside; He would like to take them into Heaven with Him, and let them share in His glory. And, let us not deceive ourselves, these dependants whom He wants to bring home to His Father are not particularly presentable. The angels in Heaven will open their eyes in surprise when He brings in all these people whom He has picked up on the highways of this world, and called from behind the hedges. But that is exactly what He wants to do. He prays to the Father for permission to bring them all in, 'that they all may be one; as thou, Father, art in me, and I in thee, that they also may be one in us.'

This prayer is so far-reaching that we human beings have difficulty in understanding it in its full height, and breadth, and depth. Again and again we will not admit these words about unity in their fullness and splendour, but minimise them and regard His High Priest's prayer merely as a request that all Christians on earth should be one under Him. Certainly He is praying for that too; but His petition is more comprehensive. He is praying that all Christians on earth may be one with Heaven itself; that is, one with the Father, through the Son, in the Holy Ghost. Or then we even belittle Christ's intercession to the point of looking upon it simply as a plea for some kind of unity among men. He is not doing that. Christ is fully aware that there are many kinds of unity here on earth. A crowd of twenty thousand people can gather in unity around some silly little ball. In a twinkling the Devil can 'unite' two hundred million people in a very questionable cause. The Lord, however, is not asking the Father for just any kind of unity, or for unity at any price. What He is concerned with is a quite particular and special unity, the unity of the Church with the Father, through the Son, in the Holy Ghost.

'That they all may be one; as thou, Father, art in me, and I in thee, that they also may be one in us.' Christ has good reason for stressing this 'in us' and this 'as thou art in me, and I in thee.' He does not want to leave the world in any doubt whatsoever that it is the Father who wants their salvation, and that it is the Father who sends Him out into the highways and behind the hedges, there to seek the lost. He wants to avoid giving the false impression that the Father is not in agreement with Him, or that the Father thinks that the Son has been a bit too liberal in His work of salvation after all. On the contrary, the world is to be given to understand expressly that complete harmony prevails between Father and Son. It is the Father who has sent the Son as Saviour, 'That they all may be one; as thou, Father, art in me, and I in thee, that they also may be one in us: that the world may believe that thou hast sent me.'

How is this to come about? On the one hand we have men, and on the other God, in His eternal majesty and splendour! There is such a gulf between the two, and yet they are to come together as one! Did not God say to Moses, 'Put off thy shoes from off thy feet, for the place whereon thou standest is holy ground'? And did not Moses have to forbid the ordinary people to enter the holy place where he was to receive the Word of God, because 'the stranger that cometh nigh shall be put to death'? And now here is Jesus breaking down this barrier and saying, 'Let them all come in to the Father.' What an unheard-of prayer! He reminds the Father that He, the Son, has brought about the forgiveness of men's sins that separate them from God and has fitted them for union with Him. He has made them fit to appear in Heaven, and He wants them to be right inside and not merely onlookers. And so we have a message that is only just within the bounds of our comprehension. When Christ forgives a man his sins, He is not only taking away darkness from Him but giving him light; He is giving him the eternal brilliance and splendour that He Himself has received from the Father. There is a *doxa*, a heavenly glory, in comparison with which the clearest mountain light is merely a distant reflection. And Christ says, 'I have given them' this glory. But we cannot help thinking of the final words of the Lord's prayer; 'Thine is the kingdom, the power, and the glory.' This glory, which is God's alone, is now to be given to the Son as well, and through Him we are to have a share in it. Everything that He has received from the Father He will give to us. This almost incomprehensible message makes us think of 'the cloven tongues as of fire' that appeared over the disciples when they were filled with the Holy Ghost at Pentecost. We think of the new linen given to all those who come to the marriage feast of the Lamb. We think of the countless multitude 'clothed with white robes, and palms in their hands,' who have 'washed their robes, and made them white in the blood of the Lamb.' We think of the promise that the righteous shall 'shine forth as the sun in the kingdom of their Father.' Christ means all this when He prays, 'And the glory which thou gavest me I have given them; that they may be one, even as we are one: I in them, and thou in me, that they may be made perfect in one; and that the world may know that thou hast sent me, and hast loved them, as thou hast loved me.'

Jesus's self-denial is so far-reaching that He even prays the Father to love them 'as thou hast loved me.' He is prepared to share the love that the Father gives Him with all those who depend on Him. He wants to bring His disciples to the high place which the Father has given Him since His Ascension. He wants to share with them His appointed place at God's right hand; 'Father, I will that they also whom thou hast given me be with me where I am; that they may behold my glory.' How strange the words, 'Father, I will,' sound on Jesus's lips. It is the only time that the Son says, 'I will,' to the Father. Yet in making this demand He is seeking nothing for Himself. All He desires for Himself is to redeem His own and it is for their sakes that He says, 'I will.' They are to see His glory. His glory is to shine round about them. They are to awake after His likeness. They are to see Him face to face, and feast their eyes on His glory. The Beatitudes are to be fulfilled in them.

And Christ, the High Priest, prays for this for all who will come to believe in Him. This is a privilege that all those who believe in Him will enjoy, unlike all the others who might have had the opportunity to believe but did not want to; a privilege not accorded to all those who could also come to Christ but will not, nor to those who know the name of Christ but are ashamed of Him. He will be ashamed of them too. We may think that God is being arbitrary and biased in granting this privilege, but surely it is in full accordance with eternal justice that the Father should give precedence to those who have let themselves be saved in this world, rather than to the others who were offered the new dress and scorned it, who spurned the gift of sanctification and trod His mercy underfoot instead of grasping it with both hands? Surely that is the reason why the Son appeals to God's justice: 'O righteous Father, the world hath not known thee: but I have known thee, and these have known that thou hast sent me. And I have declared unto them thy name, and will declare it; that the love wherewith thou hast loved me may be in them, and I in them'?

The unity of the Church of Christ, whose members we are allowed to be, has its roots in the unity of the Father, the Son and the Holy Ghost. It is founded entirely on Christ and His work. It depends wholly on Christ and Heaven, and is in no way related to the earth. Christ is the Vine; the man who believes in Him is a shoot, dependent on that Vine. Christ is the Head: he who believes in Him is a limb, dependent on that Head; and is taken into, or, as the ancients said, 'embodied' in, the eternal unity of the Father with the Son. It is Christ alone who can, and does, and will effect this unity of His Church. He has brought it about by taking His dependants in to the Father with Him, in His eternal pity, instead of shaking them off and leaving them behind, for which we could certainly not have blamed Him. So now His dependants have a place there for ever, and no power on earth and no cunning of hell can ever destroy the unity of the Church since Christ, the High Priest, prayed, 'That they all may be one; as thou, Father, art in me, and I in thee.'

We believe in the unity of the Church. We believe 'in the Holy Ghost; the Holy Catholic Church; the Communion of Saints.' When we say that we 'believe,' we mean that when we speak of the unity of the Church and testify that we belong to this unity, we are considering Christ and His work as Redeemer, and not thinking about ourselves. There are Christians who have been troubled all their lives because there is so very little unity to be seen. They have been searching for it everywhere from their childhood, and have occasionally thought that they have found it, only to be disappointed. Are we not all familiar with this anxiety? Is it not a source of great distress to all of us that, when we look at men, even at Christians, the only signs of unity that we can see in the Church of Christ are shaming, and unsatisfactory, and so inadequate that we are often in danger of doubting the unity of the Church, and of despairing instead of believing?

We suffer from this want of unity. We are suffering because there are many churches in the world instead of one Church, and because there is a Protestant Church and a Roman Catholic Church as well. The Protestant Church is so very split and disrupted as a result of its refusing, quite rightly, to allow any kind of compulsion in matters of faith; and on the other hand the Roman Catholic Church can maintain its unity only with great difficulty, and by the un-Christian means of coercion. This frailty of the Church of Christ, which appears on the Roman Catholic side as unholy constraint, and on the Protestant side as equally unholy disunity, is part of the intermediate state in which we are still living. We are waiting for the completion of God's work and so we are always in Advent, in expectation of perfection. The fact that death is still with us can never alter the truth of the Resurrection of Christ; and just as little can the fact that there are still many churches instead of one Church alter the truth of the unity that Christ Himself has won for the Church in His High Priest's prayer. Therefore we believe in the unity of the Church, even if we cannot see it yet. Anyone who does not believe in the unity of the Church because there are still many churches, is like the madman who does not believe in the Resurrection of Christ because there is still death. We believe in a holy catholic Church, and we cling fast to this belief while we wait for the day when we shall see our faith realised and 'there shall be one fold, and one shepherd.'

The Arrest and Trial of Jesus

When Jesus had spoken these words, he went forth with his disciples over the brook Cedron, where was a garden, into the which he entered, and his disciples. And Judas also, which betrayed him, knew the place: for Jesus ofttimes resorted thither with his disciples. Judas then, having received a band of men and officers from the chief priests and Pharisees, cometh thither with lanterns and torches and weapons. Jesus therefore, knowing all things that should come upon him, went forth, and said unto them, Whom seek ye? They answered him, Jesus of Nazareth. Jesus saith unto them, I am he. And Judas also, which betrayed him, stood with them. As soon then as he had said unto them, I am he, they went backward, and fell to the ground. Then asked he them again, Whom seek ye? And they said, Jesus of Nazareth. Jesus answered, I have told you that I am he: if therefore ye seek me, let these go their way: that the saying might be fulfilled, which he spake, Of them which thou gavest me have I lost none. Then Simon Peter having a sword drew it, and smote the high priest's servant, and cut off his right ear. The servant's name was Malchus. Then said Jesus unto Peter, Put up thy sword into the sheath; the cup which my Father hath given me, shall I not drink it?

Then the band and the captain and officers of the Jews took Jesus, and bound him, and led him away to Annas first; for he was father in law to Caiaphas, which was the high priest that same year. Now Caiaphas was he, which gave counsel to the Jews, that it was expedient that one man should die for the people.

The high priest then asked Jesus of his disciples, and of his doctrine. Jesus answered him, I spake openly to the world; I ever taught in the synagogue, and in the temple, whither the Jews always resort; and in secret have I said nothing. Why askest thou me? ask them which heard me, what I have said unto them: behold, they know what I said. And when he had thus spoken, one of the officers which stood by struck Jesus with the palm of his hand, saying, Answerest thou the high priest so? Jesus answered him, If I have spoken evil, bear witness of the evil: but if well, why smitest thou me? Now Annas had sent him bound unto Caiaphas the high priest.

[XVIII. 1–14, 19–24]

The account of the arrest of Jesus is of real significance for the Church today, which, if not actually persecuted and suppressed, is at least obstructed and restricted in its expansion. The community is beginning to perceive again what the captivity of the Church of Christ entails. The possibility of such captivity should not surprise us any longer, in the light of today's text, which reminds us that captivity is a fundamental part of Christianity. As early as the Old Testament we read of the long bondage of the people of God, first of all under the Egyptians and later the Babylonians. There is a strain of captivity running throughout the Psalms; we think of the captives of Zion 'that sow in tears' and 'reap in joy,' and of the song of those 'who passing through the valley of Baca make it a well.' And now that Christ Himself, the Head of Christianity, stands captive before the whole world, the members should not be surprised perhaps to find themselves arrested one day. Because the Church is in captivity today, we Christians have very strong reason to sit up and take notice when we are told of the captivity of Jesus.

The Evangelist John has preserved a short passage which relates clearly how the Lord of Christianity behaves in captivity. We are told that when Jesus was standing before the well-known religious leader and former High Priest, Annas, that night, the latter's servant struck Him for not conducting Himself in a fitting manner. In those days it was customary for prisoners to weep when they were being interrogated, or even to whine, in order to soften the hearts of the judges. And if they did not do this, it was in their own interests at least to behave in a humble and submissive manner. But this Jesus of Nazareth, far from behaving like a prisoner, talks like a nobleman and equal, like a free man among free men. Although old Annas questions Him about His teaching and His disciples, Jesus is aware that Annas is well informed and knows all about Him. In Jesus's eyes, therefore, the whole interrogation by Annas is only a manoeuvre, to save face, and give a show of justice. The judgment was made at least as long ago as the raising of Lazarus. The old church leader's questions are thus fundamentally deceitful. Jesus lets him feel this by giving him the dignified answer, 'I spoke openly in the synagogue and in the Temple. What else do you have to ask? Ask those who heard me. They should know.'

These are not the words of a prisoner. For you can have your hands bound and yet be free. You can stand accused before your judge and yet be superior to him, because right is on your side and wrong on his. That is the case with Jesus and Annas. It cannot be stressed often enough that the passion of Jesus in no way implies that He bows before the power of men. On His way to the Cross, what He does bow down to is the throne of His almighty Father, and to Him He submits readily. We can truly understand the Cross and the humility of Christ only if we see there filial obedience and humility before the Highest. It can never be interpreted as obeisance to power or bending to injustice, and certainly not as uncomplaining acceptance of baseness or meek acquiescence in evil. Anyone who regards the Cross of Christ as a submission to tyranny, and who teaches this to other people, preaches a false doctrine, and has neither seen nor heard what the accounts of the Passion have to tell us. By going to the Cross, the Lord lets neither God's nor men's justice be humbled or broken, but exalts them all the more, for all time and for all nations, for ever.

The manner in which Jesus reacts to the rebuke of the servant of the court is instructive in another respect too. In the Sermon on the Mount, Jesus teaches that if we have been struck on one cheek we should 'turn . . . the other also.' It is interesting that here, where it is a case of injustice, Christ does not turn the other cheek. Instead of doing so, He protests against the man's unjust action; 'If I have spoken evil, bear witness of the evil; but if well, why smitest thou me?' Christ is at their mercy. They have tied His hands because He is prepared to do the will of the Father, which will lead Him to the Cross. But it is to be made quite clear that, although power may well be on their side, right is certainly not. There is a kind of Christianity that tries to be more Christian than Christ. It is offended because Christ stands up to His tormentor. But the type of Christianity which will be meek at any price, and confuses weakness of character and cowardice with gentleness, cannot identify itself with the Christ who here protests against this slap in the face. In a recently-published book by the Swiss author, Jeremias Gotthelf, we find a passage which is pertinent at this juncture: 'There is a time for everything. Gentleness and patience are all very well, but there are times when these qualities seem to conceal a smug egotism, which is loth to be disturbed in its cosy niche. There are times when we have to assert ourselves and protect ourselves with every weapon at our disposal because all that we hold most sacred is in danger.'

We can follow Christ by being silent in patience; and in certain circumstances we can also follow Him by speaking out in patience. The way to the Cross is not always silent; there can be times when a Christian must speak out. Christians who bear the Cross of Christ are bound to raise their voices in protest from time to time as their Master does here before the High Priest Annas, standing with bound hands – yet free. And a community that confesses Him remains free even if its hands are tied, its feet chained and its mouth gagged, or if it is suffering privation. There is freedom in captivity just as there is strength in humility, joy in misery and life in death. Believing in the freedom of the captive means believing in Jesus Christ. And not to believe in this kind of freedom, to countenance tyranny and acknowledge its victories of might, is to deny Him who stands here before Annas. The German poet, Friedrich Schiller, writes, 'Man is free, even though born in chains.' This is hardly true: man is not free. But Christ, fettered and insulted before Annas though He is, is free. He is free because in His absolute filial obedience He even submits to death on the Cross. And if you believe in Christ and let yourself be drawn into His filial obedience; if you let Him give you some of that strength which upheld Him on His way to the Cross, then you too will be free. When you are made free by the Son, you are free indeed. Therefore it is not man but the Christian who is free, 'even though born in chains.' The Christian is free, even if he is not only born in chains, but has to live and die in chains. The Christian is free because he believes in Christ standing bound, but free, before Annas.

The manner of Jesus's arrest in itself testifies to the freedom of the captive. Properly speaking Jesus is not arrested: He gives Himself up. It is He who takes the initiative throughout the whole episode. The very place of His arrest is significant. There in Gethsemane He has bowed in obedience to the Father, and has made the hard decision to drink the cup. This readiness has made Him immune to any harm that men can do to Him. And we recognise this freedom which results from His obedience to the Father in the fact that it is He who not only determines the place of His arrest but also the time, by sending Judas away from the supper. He goes to Gethsemane intentionally, knowing that Judas will assume that He is there and will be able to find Him: 'And Judas also, which betrayed him, knew the place; for Jesus ofttimes resorted thither with his disciples.'

They lie in wait for Him with their torches and weapons at the entrance to the garden. However they do not have to seek him out, for He walks majestically into the light of their lanterns and addresses them first, like a master with his servants. We notice that He asks them twice, 'Whom seek ye?' And twice He gives them the answer, 'I am he.' In fact this significant phrase, 'I am he, is mentioned three times: 'I am the man you are looking for.' Anyone who has the Greek text before him must be struck by the fact that these are exactly the words used time and again by Jesus throughout the fourth gospel in speaking of the mystery of His person: '*Ego eimi*.' 'I am.' 'I am the Light of the world. . . . I am the Bread of life. . . . I am the Way. . . . I am the Truth. . . . I am the Life. . . . I am the good Shepherd. . . . I am the true

Vine,' and finally, 'You call me Master and Lord and so I am.'

This 'I am' is like a triumphant cry of victory in the face of His captors. They may arrest Him, but He is the Light of the world. They may defile Him and desecrate His name; they may spit at Him and pour scorn on Him, but one thing they cannot alter and that is that He is the bright Light that shines for ever in the world. They may strip His clothes from Him, and make Him so poor and needy that He calls out, fainting, 'I thirst'; but in spite of all this, they cannot prevent His remaining the Bread of life and His calling out to the whole world, 'Take, eat,' and 'Drink ye all of it.' They can kill the Shepherd and scatter the flock now, but this very act of theirs ensures that He will become the one good Shepherd who gives His life for the sheep. They can take His life, but they cannot alter the fact that by dying He saves the lives of all those who believe in Him.

This majestic 'I am' is said first of all to those who intend to destroy Him. He says it to the soldiers, but His words are also directed at Judas, and Judas feels their impact. But He says it for His disciples too; He means it to be heard by all the angels; indeed He says it in such a way that every devil who is about to rejoice at His arrest must hear it, and so that Heaven and the earth and hell will ring with the words 'I am.' It is little wonder that here, where He comes to meet His captors with those words, we read that the soldiers and Judas 'went backward and fell to the ground'. This detail, recorded by John with so many details of the Passion of Christ, has been called 'legendary'; but if we have noted the recurrence of this 'I am' throughout this whole gospel, then we should hardly be surprised by the effect of His words. Just like His protest before Annas, His action here indicates who is the stronger. And the stronger is not the one who succeeds by force, but the One who is the Son of the Almighty, even if He is defeated for the moment. Anyone who has God on his side can be comforted in defeat with the knowledge that God likes to gain victory through defeat.

Then He asks for the second time, 'Whom seek ye?' This time it is in order to protect His disciples. He does not want them to be arrested as well and so He gives Himself up. He is protecting His sheep, as a good shepherd should. He dismisses His disciples by saying, 'If ye seek me, let these go their way.' He knows that they are not ready to bear captivity, for the strength to be free, though captive, has not yet been given them. The time is still to come when, as fettered Apostles, they will be witnesses of freedom. But that hour is not now. Just as one sends away a child when something unpleasant is likely to happen, so He sends away His own: 'If ye seek me, let these go their way.'

Peter, however, does not want to be treated like a child, and will not let himself be spared and sent away: on the contrary, he wants to protect his threatened Master. Because he tries obstinately to thwart the will of the Father with his sword, he is rebuked with the words: 'Put up thy sword into the sheath: the cup which my Father hath given me, shall I not drink it?' Peter tries to do more than he should. This is a very real danger for us Christians. We not only suffer because we do nothing or too little: there is always a risk that we will try to do more than we should and can. Let Peter be a warning to us. By trying to do more, he achieves less in the end than he ought. Peter does not want to be a sheep and behaves instead like the shepherd, with the result that he becomes a lost sheep that gives his shepherd extra trouble. Peter wants to play a part, and so he does; but the part that he gets is not one that he would have chosen.

Peter Denies his Master

And Simon Peter followed Jesus, and so did another disciple: that disciple was known unto the high priest, and went in with Jesus into the palace of the high priest. But Peter stood at the door without. Then went out that other disciple, which was known unto the high priest, and spake unto her that kept the door, and brought in Peter. Then saith the damsel that kept the door unto Peter, Art not thou also one of this man's disciples? He saith, I am not. And the servants and officers stood there, who had made a fire of coals; for it was cold: and they warmed themselves: and Peter stood with them, and warmed himself.

And Simon Peter stood and warmed himself. They said therefore unto him, Art not thou also one of his disciples? He denied it, and said, I am not. One of the servants of the high priest, being his kinsman whose ear Peter cut off, saith, Did not I see thee in the garden with him? Peter then denied again: and immediately the cock crew.

[XVIII. 15–18, 25–27]

'Though I should die with thee, yet will I not deny thee.' Peter, the Rock, once made this solemn pledge to his Master. The first proof of the fact that Peter really is prepared to die for his Master is his behaviour when Jesus is arrested. He draws his sword and thus risks dying by the sword. His willingness to die is shown a second time when he cannot bear to leave Jesus after He has been arrested. Peter imprudently follows his Master right into the heart of the rambling palace of the High Priest, as John takes pains to point out. He passes through the great gates, and follows his Lord all the way so as not to lose sight of Him, and, as Luke tells us, Jesus can see him too. And once in the inner courtyard, Peter does not hide behind pillars and shrubs; instead he rashly mixes with the people, joins in their conversation, and sits down by the bright light of a watch-fire.

By despising death like this, Peter has the prospect of the noblest fame that man can win in the whole wide world; that is, the fame of having remained faithful to the end. Peter has the chance to join the glorious ranks of those whom we rightly praise for having remained true 'to the last drop of their blood.' Loyalty to one's master is the greatest and most inspiring of the qualities sung by man. We think of King Saul's armour-bearer who, even when the battle was lost, held out with his master to the very last on Mount Gilboa. We think of the portrayal of loyalty in the *Nibelungenlied*, which there appears all the brighter against the dark background of betrayal. We remember the Lion Memorial in Lucerne, witness to our own country's esteem for the men who gave their lives for an ill-fated monarch, over one hundred and fifty years ago in Paris.

And it is this sort of fame among men that seems to await Peter here. No doubt it will one day be said of him, 'Peter remained faithful to his Master, even in the court of judgment.' But we must not forget that the prisoner, standing before His judges, says to them, 'My kingdom is not of this world.' Therefore, since it is not a king of this world who is involved, there is no question of earthly loyalty either, and that is why Peter's fate is not what we have come to expect in a case like this. That virtue so highly esteemed by every king of this world, and which every ruler has longed for when his star was setting, is exactly what this particular King rejects. Peter stumbles and falls horribly in the court of the High Priest, and Christ lets it happen. Peter does not die for Jesus: he denies Him. There is no call for a lion memorial here!

That is to say, Peter does die but he does not die as a servant does for his master in this world. He does not meet a hero's death there in the courtyard of the High Priest; he meets the death of discipleship. The death of discipleship is an extraordinary and incomprehensible thing. Having set out as a hero, Peter denies his Master before two women. He does so the first time in front of a woman who, the fourth gospel tells us, is the door-keeper; the second time is in the forecourt; and according to Matthew he denies his Master with curses and oaths. The cock crows. And now Peter is like a child, who really wanted to do his duty but lost himself in a game, only to be awakened suddenly to harsh reality again. The realisation of what he has done strikes him like a thunderbolt, and so we see this man, who set out like a hero, behaving like a child: Peter weeps. As a man one is ashamed to hear this. A man like Peter – and Peter is indeed a man – 'wept bitterly.' That is the death of discipleship. That is what happens to a man who has sworn loyalty to the one and only King. He meets death too, but a very special kind of death. His will – and Peter certainly has a will – must die; his reason, his honour, his earthly loyalty, everything that is best must die. Everything that Peter has is taken from him, and all that is left is a weeping wretch, lying outside the walls, consumed with disgust and shame. Death in the service of the King whose kingdom is not of this world is as radical as this. This is the death of discipleship.

But Peter is no isolated exception. He is in the company of all the Apostles and Prophets. How valiantly Moses sets out! How manfully and heroically he fights against the Egyptians! But then we see him tending the sheep for forty years in the wilderness. That is another example of the death of discipleship. And what a man, and a hero, Paul is, to start with! And then we see him lying broken on the sand between Jerusalem and Damascus, the very counterpart of Peter. There is no call for memorials for valour in the history of the Apostles and the Prophets. And yet they set up a memorial for themselves; but it is a memorial to their hour of weakness. Why do they do this? After all, they would have had it in their power to omit the all-too-dark shadows from their narratives. They do not do so. And they have good reason, for the memorials to their hours of weakness are at the same time memorials to the grace of God. In this way they have set up a memorial to Him who remained all alone at the end, forsaken by all His followers. Only the One who was true to the last drop of His blood is commemorated, and that is their

Master. There is only One who does not fail; there is only One who never disappoints, and that is the Lord. For Him there is no merciful death. The death of discipleship begins when a man can confess, 'Not I for Him, but He for me.' In the Church of Christ there is therefore only one memorial, and that is the Cross of our Redeemer.

Far from being a loss, the death of discipleship is a gain. It is a gift from Him who died for all of us; He lets His own share in His death, so that they can testify, 'We always bear the death of the Lord Jesus in our own bodies.' Even the tears which Peter sheds beside that wall are a gift. Where the Church is truly Christian it has never been without this gift. In his beautiful little book, *Columban und Gallus*,[1] Professor Blanke mentions that Tutilo, a ninth-century monk of St Gall, a giant of a man and very like Peter in character, was given 'the gift of tears,' a gift which we hear about as early as the third century among the monks in Egypt. He tells us that the Roman Missal stills contains three prayers for the 'gift of tears,' one of which runs: 'Almighty and merciful Lord, who didst make a stream of living water spring from the rock for thy thirsting people, draw from our hard hearts tears of penitence, so that we can weep for our sins and, through Thy mercy, obtain forgiveness for them.' It is this same 'gift of tears' that is given to Peter beside the High Priest's wall. The greatest thing that the rulers of this world can give is a hero's death. But Christ, the Lord of the Church, gives more; He gives the gift of tears for our sins; He gives the death of discipleship. If Peter had been allowed to persist in his stubbornness, it would have been his greatest loss. He would then have taken his place in this world's halls of fame. Fortunately Christ prevents that. Peter does not succeed in grasping the fading laurels of this world. Christ has greater things in mind for him. He is not to become a hero; he is to remain a disciple. And as a disciple who has been drawn into Jesus's death, Peter is, so to speak, not a private individual any more. If he were, he would no longer be of any interest to us. But Peter becomes part of the

[1] F. Blanke, *Columban und Gallus*, Zürich 1940.

Divine purpose, as a kind of official representative of the Kingdom of God; 'Thou art Peter, and upon this rock I will build my church.' And similarly God will build his Church on John, James, Paul and all the other Apostles and Prophets. But how strangely God goes about building His Church. Every man He intends to use has first to be broken. Peter and Paul become children; they all become children of God and experience the gift of penitent weeping before they become the foundations of the Church by their witness. 'Except a corn of wheat fall into the ground and die, it abideth alone: but if it die, it bringeth forth much fruit.'

From this point of view, the story of Peter's denial of Christ – in itself one of the saddest in the whole of the Scriptures – is transformed into good news for us through God's will. We are told here, 'See what frail material Jesus can use to build His Church!' The pillar has first of all to be shattered on the desert sands on the way to Damascus; the rock has to crumble into sand; but a grain of sand in God's hand becomes the rock on which the Lord builds His Church. The Lord of the Church can afford to build upon sand. A builder of this world would be ill-advised to do so. In this context I should like to quote the words of Pandita Ramabai, an Indian Christian attached to our foreign mission: 'Praise and thanks be unto you, O God, who break the power of selfishness and use for this purpose those who are despised by the world. A wisp of straw in your hand is as strong as a flash of lightning.'[1]

The collapse of Peter and Paul, and of all these men of the Bible, is full of promise, because they are overshadowed by the Cross. Failures and bankrupts like these are the most promising building-material for the Builder of the Church. Bricks and stones which are rejected by the builders of this world can become His corner-stones. It pleases Jesus to build His Church in this way, with discarded and cast-off material. Christ uses what is despised in the eyes of the world, and the object of pity and contempt. But He is at work. He is building today, at a time when the Church in every nation is lying weeping outside the walls like Peter. He is build-

[1] Nicol Macnicol, *Pandita Ramabai*, London 1926.

ing His Church in defiance of the pride which rears high on every side at the present time. He is building in such a way as to humble our pride as men and women, as fathers and mothers, as cultured and educated people; He even humbles our pride in our missions, and wherever else it was to be found in the Church of yesterday. We have been an arrogant, puffed-up generation. All this arrogance has become fused to form one towering fortress of human pride, and this stronghold of the Prince of this world is now apparent everywhere in the shape of national pride and racial discrimination. The world is drunk. It is reeling with its new, national, and racial self-consciousness. As opposed to this fortress, the Christian Church is a small, broken Peter. An hour of penitent weeping is beginning for the Church. The sinister onslaught of the powers from below has given rise to much disloyalty, weakness, failure and bitter weeping in the churches of the nations. But right in the middle of this hour of remorse the Lord calls to His Church, 'Feed my lambs. . . . Feed my sheep. . . . Thou art Peter, and upon this rock I will build my church; and the gates of hell shall not prevail against it.'

Jesus before Pilate

Then led they Jesus from Caiaphas unto the hall of judgment: and it was early; and they themselves went not into the judgment hall, lest they should be defiled; but that they might eat the passover. Pilate then went out unto them, and said, What accusation bring ye against this man? They answered and said unto him, If he were not a malefactor, we would not have delivered him up unto thee. Then said Pilate unto them, Take ye him, and judge him according to your law. The Jews therefore said unto him, It is not lawful for us to put any man to death: that the saying of Jesus might be fulfilled, which he spake, signifying what death he should die. Then Pilate entered into the judgment hall again, and called Jesus, and said unto him, Art thou the King of the Jews? Jesus anwered him, Sayest thou this thing of thyself, or did others tell it thee of me? Pilate answered, Am I a Jew? Thine own nation and the chief priests have delivered thee unto me: what hast thou done? Jesus answered, My kingdom is not of this world: if my kingdom were of this world, then would my servants fight, that I should not be delivered to the Jews: but now is my kingdom not from hence. Pilate therefore said unto him, Art thou a king then? Jesus answered, Thou sayest that I am a king. To this end was I born, and for this cause came I into the world, that I should bear witness unto the truth. Every one that is of the truth heareth my voice. Pilate saith unto him, What is truth? And when he had said this, he went out again unto the Jews, and saith unto them, I find in him no fault at all.

[XVIII. 28–38]

'Art thou a king then?' Anyone who cannot understand Pilate's astonishment has not grasped what is in question here. Early one morning a stranger is brought to the chief Roman magistrate, more or less by the way, as the waves wash up a piece of wood on the shore. His accusers say he is a malefactor, but the stranger does not look like one. Eventually it transpires that this man claims to be the King of the Jews. On asking what crimes he has committed, the Governor receives the strange answer from the unknown man, that his kingdom is not of this world, and that he has no soldiers to protect him from the Jews. 'If my kingdom were of this world, then would my servants fight, that I should not be delivered to the Jews: but now is my kingdom not from hence.' And strangely enough this king does not even appear to regret his apparent powerlessness. He speaks as if all this were quite natural and not at all surprising, as if complete defencelessness were a normal attribute of his kingship.

Pilate cannot help being surprised at this stranger's claim to be a king, considering His whole outward appearance. That is why he asks, 'So you are a king after all?' After all? In spite of the fact that you wear no crown and carry no sceptre? In spite of the fact that you call no land your own and rule no nation; possess no throne and no king's castle, and have no army which can command obedience to your royal will? After all, in spite of the fact that absolutely everything contradicts it, you are a king?

Yes, a King. But 'my kingdom is not of this world.' These words show that this man who claims to be a king obviously makes a distinction between two kinds of kingdom: His own Kingdom, which is not of this world, and the kingdoms of this world. He states that the difference between the two is that in the kingdoms of this world kings have soldiers to fight for them, whereas He in His Kingdom has none. But this is just the point that Pilate cannot grasp. His understanding is limited to the kingdoms of this world, which spend their time in preparing for war, and in winning or losing wars. Pilate can understand the kingdom that carries war to North Africa, and to the Rhine, and to the Volga and perhaps even to our own frontiers. Pilate can understand the world of the armaments industry, which thrives on war, though it may be far from the battle. Pilate can understand the world of the press, which is prepared to open its hungry columns to all the terrors of war, and which, recently, has been depicting for its credulous public a hell of poison gas with its accompanying horrors, and following this up with the strange injunction that the public can, and must, protect itself against such a hell. That is Pilate's world. The other world, however, passes his understanding and, let us be honest, it passes ours too. Let us not pretend that naturally we do not belong to the other side like Pilate. It is presumptuous of us to creep over to the side of the unknown King who here stands before Pilate.

'Art thou a king then?' This same question has lately given Christians a good deal to think about. It has worried and tormented us. In the last few months we have all been looking anxiously for the King. In our extremity we have called out to Him, in the hope that He might appear from somewhere after all in these dark times. We have been asking, 'Is Satan entirely free to work without restraint or opposition? Will no one stand up to him? When Christ says that His Kingdom is not of this world, does it imply that His Kingdom is entirely meaningless, and without influence in the course of events? Is this King before Pilate only to rule over future generations and regions not of this earth, while we are to go on depending on bomb-proof shelters?' Pilate's question constantly gnaws at the mind of many a Christian today.

'Art thou a king then?' Yes, certainly He is. The Stranger does not leave Pilate's question unanswered; 'Thou sayest that I am a king. To this end was I born, and for this cause came I into the world.' He did not stay in His heavenly Kingdom. He was born and came into the world as a man. That is the great mystery of His Kingdom. That mystery is what we are concerned with every time we assemble here, and open the Book and preach. That is why there is a Church, and that is why there are pulpits: because the King was 'born and came into the world.'

'And it came to pass in those days, that there went out a decree from Caesar Augustus, that all the world should be taxed. (And this taxing was first made when Cyrenius was governor of Syria.) And all went to be taxed, every one into his own city. And

Joseph also went up from Galilee, out of the city of Nazareth, into Judaea, unto the city of David, which is called Bethlehem, (because he was of the house and lineage of David,) to be taxed with Mary his espoused wife, being great with child. And so it was, that, while they were there, the days were accomplished that she should be delivered. And she brought forth her firstborn son, and wrapped him in swaddling clothes, and laid him in a manger; because there was no room for them in the inn.'

There it is. He was born and came into the world. His Kingdom, which is not of this world, came into this world. It left home, so to speak, and settled in the strange surroundings of this world and time. And now this Kingdom is standing in the flesh before Pilate, for the unknown man is the Kingdom in Himself. Pilate can see, and hear and touch it, if he wants to.

And at His birth this King with His Kingdom within Him is 'wrapped in swaddling clothes, and laid in a manger.' Because His Kingdom is not of this world, it is bound to suffer here. Before long it 'suffered under Pontius Pilate.' Soon the King wears a crown, but not of gold and precious stones. Soon He is raised up; but no king of this world would like to be raised up as this King, at the command of Pilate, will be raised up – that is, upon the Cross.

In the face of the Cross, Pilate's question presents itself again: 'Art thou a king then?' Even now? Just look at the inscription over His head in Latin, Greek and Hebrew. 'Thou sayest that I am a king.'

But the King dies, and is buried. Pilate has the tomb closed up and sealed. And once again the question obtrudes itself, 'Art thou a king then?' Even now? Here is the answer: 'In the end of the Sabbath, as it began to dawn toward the first day of the week, came Mary Magdalene and the other Mary to see the sepulchre. And, behold, there was a great earthquake: for the angel of the Lord descended from heaven, and came and rolled back the stone from the door, and sat upon it. His countenance was like lightning, and his raiment white as snow.'

Pilate's question is answered in the mystery of the early hours of Easter Sunday. Christ is King in spite of His death on the Cross. Since then there has been no other possible answer to the question than, 'Christ is King all the same.' Nothing can alter this, not even a poison-gas hell, nor anything else, however dreadful, for there never was anything more dreadful than His death on the Cross.

Every aspect of Christ's life in this world contains this incongruity. Instead of being born in a palace, He is born in a stable; nevertheless He is King. As a baby He lies in a manger; nevertheless, He is the 'Creator of all things,' and shepherds kneel before Him, and the Magi worship Him. He has neither sceptre nor throne; nevertheless the spirits have to obey Him, and He rules the wind and the waves. He has neither property nor wealth; nevertheless He can feed five thousand men. He has no soldiers; nevertheless no king ever had such an army as His, which has penetrated to the ends of the earth, singing its Christian battle-song. He has no throne, and nevertheless all power in Heaven and earth is vested in Him. 'He hath no form nor comeliness. He is despised and rejected of men'; nevertheless the fourth gospel gives an eye-witness report: 'And we beheld his glory, the glory as of the only begotten of the Father, full of grace and truth.'

Since that first Easter the mystery of His Kingship has become clear. Easter has transformed Pilate's doubting question into a cry of victory. Christ is the absolute King, who makes His unconditional claim to each one who confesses Him. He is the only King who can legitimately claim us in body, and soul and spirit.

But wherever and whenever His claim is not recognised, Christ sets Himself up as the absolute 'anti-King,' in opposition to all kingdoms that resist Him. That is the fundamental reason why there are wars in this world. The nations reject the absolute King, therefore they must have Him as the absolute anti-King, and break themselves against Him. He is the symbol that can be reversed, so that many come to grief. War is not the result of fate, but of guilt. And the greatest guilt of the nations is that they reject the

King who stood before Pilate. War is the sign of our revolt against Him, the sign of our rebellion.

With this in mind, let us take a closer look at the few verses of the Bible which we read at the beginning. As we study these words more carefully, Christ increases in brightness and stature. He is the only King here. His persecutors think that they are taking Him to the judge; but they themselves are being led and judged. They think they have bound Him, yet He is the only free man among them. They hover round Him like a cloud of dust raised by the wheels of a king's chariot. Christ is the King.

Even Pilate is part of the cloud of dust. He finds Jesus a source of discomfort, and would like to be rid of Him. He would like to hand Him back to the Jews, and let them stone Him according to their custom. But he is forced to execute Him on the cross according to Roman Law. We can feel John's amazement as he remarks at this point in his account, 'That the saying of Jesus might be fulfilled, which he spake, signifying what death he should die.' It is Christ, and not the Jews or Pilate, who has predicted 'what death he should die.' The decision is not made by the Jews, far less by Pilate, but by the One who has not for one moment let the reins fall from His hands. All their actions are directed to the end 'that the saying of Jesus might be fulfilled.' Without knowing it, they are acting at the will of the King who stands bound before Pilate.

Pilate may think that he is making history, but the initiative is not his. We have given this chapter the customary title: 'Jesus before Pilate.' That is not accurate. Pilate – and indeed not only Pilate, but all of us with him – is standing before Jesus, the King. Pilate is the pupil, Jesus the Teacher. Pilate asks the questions, Jesus gives the answers. Jesus stands there in dignity, Pilate runs to and fro like a servant. See how compliantly Pilate bows to every side, and how obligingly he runs around for the One who confronts him as King, and who gives him the answer, 'Thou sayest that I am a king. To this end was I born, and for this cause came I into the world, that I should bear witness unto the truth. Every one that is of the truth heareth my voice.'

'Every one that is of the truth.' A Roman governor knows something of what is commonly called truth; probably more than the average European of today. For instance, no twentieth-century man needs to tell a first-century Roman that lying is an odious thing, and that telling the truth is a virtue, for that is something that the Roman, like us, learned in the nursery. But one thing that Pilate did not learn in the nursery is that, one day, a man would stand before him and say, 'I was born and came into the world to witness to the truth. "Every one that is of the truth heareth my voice." ' He is hearing that for the first time today. Pilate is also aware of the fact that there is a concept that the scholars of the world call Truth, and he knows that we must always strive to come nearer to it if we want, as far as possible, to be decent people. But that Truth could be a person, standing inside the gates of his own house one morning, uncomfortably near and demanding an unavoidable decision, that is new to Pilate – and not only to Pilate. That is the great embarrassment of Pilate throughout the ages, and that is the universal difficulty.

What does it mean to be 'of the truth'? Old Nicodemus asked the same sort of question and Christ, cutting short any further discussion, answered, 'Verily, verily, I say unto thee, Except a man be born again, he cannot see the kingdom of God.' We feel like calling out to Pilate, 'Pilate, reach out! Truth is standing in front of you in the flesh. Accept it!' But Pilate does not reach out. He turns away from this man standing less than an arm's length away from him, and in so doing, he turns his back on Truth and therefore has to ask, 'What is truth?'

Christ, who is the Truth, does not answer. Pilate is incapable of hearing any more answers, for he has made the decision against the Truth.

Pilate himself gives part of the answer. He turns his back on the Truth, and crucifies it. Pilate is showing the truth about himself, and about the kingdoms of this world, and about our human nature. That is what we are like. We have to ask, 'What is truth?' because we turn away from it and crucify it. That is the sad truth about us men.

But fortunately it is not the whole truth. The whole truth is that Christ, who is the Truth, lets Himself be crucified by the world, but then rises on the third day. For Christ is King nevertheless. That is the whole truth. 'Every one that is of the truth heareth my voice.'

Jesus or Barabbas

But ye have a custom, that I should release unto you one at the passover: will ye therefore that I release unto you the King of the Jews? Then cried they all again, saying, Not this man, but Barabbas. Now Barabbas was a robber.

Then Pilate therefore took Jesus, and scourged him. And the soldiers platted a crown of thorns, and put it on his head, and they put on him a purple robe, and said, Hail, King of the Jews! and they smote him with their hands. Pilate therefore went forth again, and saith unto them, Behold, I bring him forth to you, that ye may know that I find no fault in him. Then came Jesus forth, wearing the crown of thorns, and the purple robe. And Pilate saith unto them, Behold the man! When the chief priests therefore and officers saw him, they cried out, saying, Crucify him, Crucify him. Pilate saith unto them, Take ye him, and crucify him: for I find no fault in him. The Jews anwered him, We have a law, and by our law he ought to die, because he made himself the Son of God. When Pilate therefore heard that saying, he was the more afraid; and went again into the judgment hall, and saith unto Jesus, Whence art thou? But Jesus gave him no answer. Then saith Pilate unto him, Speakest thou not unto me? knowest thou not that I have power to crucify thee, and have power to release thee? Jesus answered, Thou couldest have no power at all against me, except it were given thee from above: therefore he that delivered me unto thee hath the greater sin. And from thenceforth Pilate sought to release him: but the Jews cried out, saying, If thou let this man go, thou art not Caesar's friend: whosoever maketh himself a king speaketh against Caesar. When Pilate therefore heard that saying, he brought Jesus forth, and sat down in the judgment seat in a place that is called the Pavement, but in the Hebrew, Gabbatha. And it was the preparation of the passover, and about the sixth hour: and he saith unto the Jews, Behold your King! But they cried out, Away with him, away with him, crucify him. Pilate saith unto them, Shall I crucify your King? The chief priests answered, We have no king but Caesar.

[XVIII. 39–40; XIX. 1–15]

'Ye have a custom that I should release unto you one at the passover: will ye therefore that I release unto you the King of the Jews?' This question of Pilate's is not new to those of you who are being confirmed today. In all your preparation-classes this question has been present in one form or another. Which of these two men that Pilate offers to the Jews do you want: do you want Jesus, or do you want Barabbas? You will have noticed that, whichever way you are inclined, you have to make a choice. A railway-carriage rolls smoothly along the track once it has been set on the rails, but you know that your path of life is not like this. In this life a man has to choose between one course and another, and decide between various possibilities. Which of these two is your choice?

And now the wonderful, and at the same time serious, day of your confirmation has come, and it seems as if God, in giving us this text for today, wanted to make it quite clear to you once more which two you have to choose between in life and what they are like. There stands Jesus, and beside Him Pilate places Barabbas. But is there any choice here? Is it not obvious that we will choose Jesus? I trust that each one of you has already made this decision. And I hope that you yourselves will never believe any of your companions capable of being attracted by the career of Barabbas, for 'Barabbas was a robber,' accused of murder and sentenced to death. Jesus or Barabbas: which of these two is your choice?

But on the first Good Friday morning why does Israel reject Jesus and choose Barabbas? A whole nation rejects Jesus and prefers a murderer! Is this not disturbing? We would have expected it of the ordinary people least of all. We tend to say, 'Well, yes, the authorities perhaps, but the people would be all right; they would never choose a murderer.' And yet here they are choosing the murderer after all, though admittedly, as John points out, under considerable influence from higher up. We could understand a small group rejecting Jesus and crucifying Him. But how sinister that a whole nation should lend itself in broad daylight to the murderous designs of this group! And among these people there are parents and grandparents of the children Jesus once blessed; brothers, and sisters, and uncles, and aunts of those numberless people who have benefited by Jesus's kindness. Some of this Good Friday crowd are the very people who only a week ago welcomed Jesus with joyous cries of 'Hosanna!' after the raising of Lazarus. And now their cries have changed to, 'Crucify him!' They are shouting at the tops of their voices, 'To the cross with Him!' This startling change gives us a great deal to think about.

There is one fact that can perhaps take us a stage further in understanding this strange event. The Evangelist Matthew has recorded that Barabbas is not an ordinary, but a particular kind of murderer, an '*episemos*,' as the Greek calls him, a notable, well-known murderer. Barabbas has been arrested in a riot in which people were killed. Barabbas is a political murderer, who belongs to a movement which has been plotting to throw the Roman rulers out of the country, with all the means at its disposal, but his plan has failed. Men like this are not usually called murderers if they are successful: the people call them heroes and saviours of their country. If they succeed in carrying out their plans, they are crowned with laurels, and their names are recorded in poetry. Barabbas is a popular murderer. He is a confident man who promises the people freedom if they will only help themselves, and he goes to any lengths to gain his ends from below. Barabbas is a man of force. Barabbas is flesh of our flesh and spirit of our spirit. Barabbas has our natural, human sympathy and our hearts go out to him. The name Barabbas means 'son of his father' – favourite, beloved. He is the idol of the people in every age, the universal favourite.

Beside Barabbas stands another Son of His Father; but this is the Son of quite a different Father. This Son is also a favourite;

not a favourite of the world but of Heaven. This Man also came to help the people, not from below but from above. It is hard to grasp how far down Jesus had to come to help us. Which of these two are you going to choose now: the one from below, or the One from above? Look at Jesus standing here on this first Good Friday morning! Does He make any effort to help Himself? Not a word of defence or of appeal to the crowd passes His lips. He need only stretch out His bound hands a little to the excited crowd to silence it immediately. One small plea for freedom on His part would calm the people. But one word would be too many. Jesus is what He is not by the grace of the people, but by the grace of God. Jesus does not beg His freedom of the people and certainly not of Pilate. He has asked the Father in Heaven, 'Father, if it be possible, let this cup pass from me: nevertheless not as I will, but as thou wilt,' and now He is going the way that His Father leads. He takes His life and His death from no other hand but His Father's. He is free to do this even though He is bound. Perhaps you have seen pictures of this scene, where Jesus is represented as an imposing, almost supernaturally tall figure, towering up to Heaven. Yes, this captive, condemned to death, towers free above all the people. He says nothing. He is taking the way of sacrifice. The way He is going does not suit us human beings at all: every drop of our blood rebels against it. His way of obedience is the way to the Cross. Which do you want: revolt or sacrifice, self-assertion or obedience, brutish resistance or patient endurance? Which of these two is your choice, Jesus or Barabbas?

After seeing these two side by side, is it not obvious why these people reject Jesus and choose Barabbas? After all, it is not only these people who have done this; today more or less all the nations in the world have done the same thing. The whole world today bears the mark of Barabbas and sails under his flag. These young men and women before us have been brought up in the spirit of Barabbas at school, and to a very great extent at home. There are parents and godparents who, when they realise who Christ is, would like to call out to these young people in the words of

Pilate's wife, 'Have nothing to do with that just man!' Just a little piety, just enough morality to be good, suits us very well. But choosing Christ? Good heavens, no! That could harm you. Being a convinced Christian might be a disadvantage in getting on in this Barabbas-world! Quite so. That is why this question does not only apply to those who are being confirmed today: it applies to parents and godparents, to this community this town and this country. The question is there for every nation in the world: 'Which of these two is your choice, Jesus or Barabbas?'

This is an agonising choice if ever there was one. Could it not be made easier? We should like to avoid having to choose, and declare ourselves neutral. But neutrality implies acceptance of both. In other words, we should like Barabbas as a firm foundation, and Jesus as outer decoration. We are just emerging from an age when people really did choose both Jesus and Barabbas. We kept up this wicked fraud for many years. But I believe that now I can see signs of the passing of this era. If I am not mistaken, there is a pronounced tendency today to face up to the fact that we must choose either Jesus or Barabbas. You who have come to be confirmed today have the hard good fortune to live in an age where you have to make up your minds. I call it hard because it confronts us inevitably, nevertheless it is our good fortune that the decision has to be made. It is a unique and splendid thing to decide for Jesus.

Lastly you may wonder if it is not asking too much of these young people to lay on them the whole responsibility of such a decision. Is it fair? If it really were the case that they are facing Jesus, quite alone, then it would be too much. But it is not quite like that. After all, it is Jesus Himself for whom they are allowed to decide. And what does that mean? On that first Good Friday morning, when Jesus was standing before Pilate and the latter asked Him, 'Art thou a king?' Jesus answered, 'Thou sayest that I am.' So it is the King for whom they are allowed to decide, the supreme King. Not for one moment before Pilate did He renounce His claim to be the King. He is Pilate's King too. It is not as if Jesus and Barabbas stood here as equals: Jesus is Barabbas's

King as well. He is King over all. And this King sought you long before you sought Him. He held out His hand to you long before you even raised yours. Jesus the King made His decision for you long before you could decide for Him. Jesus, in whose name you are baptised, is powerful, the most powerful of all. He is no longer standing bound before Pilate in Jerusalem today. Jesus, the King, is sitting at the right hand of God, the Father Almighty. Today Jesus the King is at work in every corner of the world, gathering His subjects. He has drawn all of you into His Kingdom, and that is why you come into His presence with your hands folded in prayer rather than raised in salute. Everything depends on Him in the end. The responsibility rests on His shoulders and not on yours. We have asked this question repeatedly: which of these two is you choice? And now comes the unique and wonderful answer: one of these two wants you: Jesus wants you. It is for you that He stood before Pilate, for you that He died on the Cross and for you that He rose from the dead. Therefore be comforted and say, 'This is my only support in life and in death, that, body and soul, in life and in death, I am not my own but belong to my beloved Saviour, Jesus Christ.'

The Crucifixion of Jesus

Then delivered he him therefore unto them to be crucified. And they took Jesus, and led him away. And he bearing his cross went forth into a place called the place of a skull, which is called in the Hebrew Golgotha: where they crucified him, and two other with him, on either side one, and Jesus in the midst. And Pilate wrote a title, and put it on the cross. And the writing was, JESUS OF NAZARETH THE KING OF THE JEWS. This title then read many of the Jews: for the place where Jesus was crucified was nigh to the city: and it was written in Hebrew, and Greek, and Latin. Then said the chief priests of the Jews to Pilate, Write not, The King of the Jews; but that he said, I am King of the Jews. Pilate answered, What I have written I have written.

Then the soldiers, when they had crucified Jesus, took his garments, and made four parts, to every soldier a part; and also his coat: now the coat was without seam, woven from the top throughout. They said therefore among themselves, Let us not rend it, but cast lots for it, whose it shall be: that the scripture might be fulfilled, which saith, They parted my raiment among them, and for my vesture they did cast lots. These things therefore the soldiers did. Now there stood by the cross of Jesus his mother, and his mother's sister, Mary the wife of Cleophas, and Mary Magdalene. When Jesus therefore saw his mother, and the disciple standing by, whom he loved, he saith unto his mother, Woman, behold thy son! Then saith he to the disciple, Behold thy mother! And from that hour that disciple took her unto his own home.

After this, Jesus knowing that all things were now accomplished, that the Scripture might be fulfilled, saith, I thirst. Now there was set a vessel full of vinegar: and they filled a sponge with vinegar, and put it upon hyssop, and put it to his mouth. When Jesus therefore had received the vinegar, he said, It is finished: and he bowed his head, and gave up the ghost.

The Jews therefore, because it was the preparation, that the bodies should not remain upon the cross on the sabbath day, (for that sabbath day was an high day,) besought Pilate that their legs might be broken, and that they might be taken away. Then came the soldiers, and brake the legs of the first, and of the other which was crucified with him. But when they came to Jesus, and saw that he was dead already, they brake not his legs: but one of the soldiers with a spear pierced his side, and forthwith came there out blood and water. And he that saw it bare record, and his record is true: and he knoweth that he saith true, that ye might believe. For these things were done, that the scripture should be fulfilled, A bone of him shall not be broken. And again another scripture saith, They shall look on him whom they pierced.

And after this Joseph of Arimathaea, being a disciple of Jesus, but secretly for fear of the Jews, besought Pilate that he might take away the body of Jesus: and Pilate gave him leave. He came therefore, and took the body of Jesus. And there came also Nicodemus, which at the first came to Jesus by night, and brought a mixture of myrrh and aloes, about an hundred pound weight. Then took they the body of Jesus, and wound it in linen clothes with the spices, as the manner of the Jews is to bury. Now in the place where he was crucified there was a garden; and in the garden a new sepulchre, wherein was never man yet laid. There laid they Jesus therefore because of the Jews' preparation day; for the sepulchre was nigh at hand. [XIX. 16–42]

This man, hanging on the Cross, the soldiers casting lots for His coat, His farewell to His mother, His cry for water and His death, the ill-treatment of His body and finally His burial, might all be details from a picture of the world we live in. In the last few years the world has degenerated into such a pitiful condition that the events of the first Good Friday, outside the gates of Jerusalem, do not even make very much impression on us nowadays. We are beginning to get accustomed to things like this. We read about them daily in our newspapers, and our hearts have become impervious to them. It seems to us that the cruel treatment of this one man on Good Friday is meted out today to thousands of people at a time. We see whole populations, towns and provinces thrown into physical and mental torment; countries and continents are divided into lots as carelessly as a few small possessions; thousands of sons are taking leave of their mothers, and having to commend them to the care of friends. Only God knows every place where people are dying of thirst and hunger, and God alone sees the corpses of all those who were once His image, and who now litter the earth, mutilated beyond recognition.

However, although this Good Friday appears to represent the world today, there is more to it than that. The secret of eternity hangs over the martyrdom at Golgotha. It is not just anyone at all who is being tortured here; this is a very special case. God's heart is certainly moved by the murder of any man, but He is fundamentally concerned in this murder at Golgotha. To a certain extent God Himself is being tortured here. It is God who lets Himself be nailed to the Cross by human hands; it is God who allows the soldiers to cast lots for Christ's coat and to share out His other clothes; it is God who takes leave of His mother and who cries out, 'I thirst.' It is God who is wound in linen and buried like a man.

God does this with a special purpose, in accordance with His plan. When He takes our human wretchedness upon Himself, His aim is not merely to share all hardships and privations with His people, like a good leader: when He bears the same things as we human beings have to bear, then they are not the same thing. God bends to our torment and distress as a man, yet He is still God; and because it is God who is suffering here, this suffering is not humanly restricted but has a far-reaching significance. That means that He who is 'all in all' suffers the pains of all and bears the wounds of all. The fact that God bends to our sufferings, and takes them upon Himself, means that our sufferings are overcome. God has proved Himself stronger than all our sufferings. That is why our eyes are drawn to this figure of pain, whose clothes are shared out, who has to take leave of His mother, who is dying of thirst, and whose dead body is pierced by a spear; and that is why we are comforted by the contemplation of His suffering. To hang a crucifix on the wall opposite a sick man's bed so that he can see it, as is often done in Roman Catholic hospitals, is not wrong in itself. What is wrong about it is that it represents the Passion of Christ indirectly, through an image, instead of presenting it directly through the gospels themselves.

It is not only our privilege, but our duty, to contemplate the Passion of Christ. That is why it occurred in full view of everybody. The publicity of the Crucifixion is all the more striking because the greatest events in the life and work of the Lord took place so privately. Naturally God has His own reasons for letting the Lord suffer publicly like this. In the first place, evil will be brought to light. The Passion of Christ sees the final unmasking of everything evil. In the end, every enemy lives by secrecy. Every enemy profits by the fact that we are ignorant of his position and his true strength, and therefore overestimate or underestimate him, and fear him too much or too little. Christ on the Cross achieves something unheard-of: He compels the evil one to come out of his cunning concealment, and forces him into open battle; so that at the Cross the enemy has to produce his very last reserves, and to reveal his full strength and cunning, his strategy and tactics. This is how Christ deprives His enemy of one of his most effective weapons, the weapon of secrecy and cunning. From now on, the whole world will know how it stands with this enemy, and how to deal with him. The enemies of Jesus certainly did not reckon with this exposure in their original plan of action. Jesus was to be disposed of with a minimum of publicity. They would not have chosen a festival, but would have preferred an ambush or the seclusion of a prison cell; in short, the enemy intended anything but what actually does happen. His execution takes the form of public crucifixion very near the capital, and that on a day when all the streets of the town are bound to be swarming with pilgrims, going to the Feast, from all the neighbouring lands. Moreover the Cross is on a hill, visible from afar, with neither tree nor bush nor ridge to give the desired concealment.

But God decrees that the Passion of Christ shall occur by the broad light of day for a second reason. You will have noticed the formality with which St John relates even what seem to be quite trivial details of the trial and execution. He mentions an inscription which causes dissension among the enemies of Jesus. The inscription is written in Hebrew, Greek, and Latin, the principal languages of the day. It is the ancient equivalent of making the trial and execution open to the press of the world. John also remarks on Jesus's clothes. The newspapers have recently been reporting a case where a murderer burnt the clothes of his victim in a wooden box, in which he had hidden them, and where the police carefully collected the charred remains of wood and cloth, and produced them in evidence. In the same way, Jesus's clothes are circumstantial evidence. We read that John is there and the mother of Jesus; there is a stick and a sponge soaked in vinegar. The old religious painters took care not to leave these small details out of their paintings. They are dumb, but eloquent, witnesses of that unique occasion. I think that a generation which suffers quiet mass exterminations must learn to appreciate this detailed evidence which John hands down to posterity.

But there is a deeper significance in all these small things. When we read that Christ dies on the Cross between two criminals, that over His head there hangs a sign with the inscription, 'The King of the Jews,' that lots are cast for His coat, that He is given vinegar and gall to drink, and that His legs are not broken, but that His side is pierced, we are told that in all these things 'the scripture is fulfilled.' Why is this of such supreme importance to all the four Evangelists? Now that Christ is hanging on the Cross, He can no longer bear witness of Himself. In fact, His appearance at this moment rather testifies against Him. He is completely unrecognisable now as the Son of God and the Redeemer of men, utterly weak, helpless and forsaken as He is. He has no control over the description of His person and His death, that will be handed down to posterity. His last possessions, His clothes are auctioned under His very eyes. Is this the Redeemer? He has to commend His nearest relative to the care of others. Is this the Saviour of all the world? Certainly He looked like a Saviour in the days when He had the power to feed five thousand men with two fishes and five loaves of bread; but not now. He has to call for water because He is tormented by thirst. He looked like a Redeemer in the days when He restored numberless people to health; but now He has to call for a cooling drink, just like a helpless patient in hospital ringing for the nurse. He is quite unrecognisable. But it is the very symbols of His degradation, completely obscuring His greatness, that point their fingers at Him from the Scripture. This is of such decisive importance to John, because it demonstrates that another plan is being worked out here as well as the designs of the heathen and the Jews. Over and above the turbulence and destruction of the earthly powers in the foreground, a hidden purpose is revealed, in which all the threads are drawn together. In the final count, the conclusive decisions about what happens here lie neither with death, nor hell, but with God. This explains why Christ says, 'Father, forgive them; for they know not what they do.' They really do not know. When Pilate writes the inscription which is handed down unchanged to posterity, it is God who guides his hand. When the soldiers cast lots for His coat, they do not realise that Someone else is throwing dice as well, and that they themselves are at this moment dice in an almighty hand. And the soldier who breaks the legs of the two men crucified with Christ, and hesitates when he comes to Christ, and the one who pierces Christ's side with his spear, are both activated and guided by God, who mysteriously controls the course of events.

This is how the eye of faith looks at the scene that was enacted on Good Friday on that hill outside Jerusalem. Faith interprets these events quite differently. In the eyes of faith the utter helplessness of the One on the Cross no longer appears as weakness in the face of the enemy, but as obedient submission to the Father, who is here fulfilling His great plan of salvation. Christ is the Lamb that lets itself be sacrificed without a word of protest. His defeat on the Cross, by death and the Devil, is seen to be childlike obedience to the supreme Command, and as such, is very victory over death and hell. Letting His Son go to the Cross is God's way of triumphing over darkness. So the unmasking of death and hell on Good Friday constitutes a revelation of Heaven. Wickedness and the grave have not only been laid bare, but overcome. Christ knows that His defeat on the Cross is God's means of gaining His victory. Hence His last words on the Cross are, 'It is finished.' Does this not strike you as remarkably impersonal? Instead of saying, 'I have finished it,' He states, '*It* is finished.' The will of God according to the Scripture has now been carried out. It has been fulfilled. 'It is finished'; victory has been won. Death and the Devil have not won the victory, and nor has Christ: the victory has been provided for Him by the Father, who has brought it about. Christ's share in the Crucifixion was to comply unresistingly with the almighty will, even to the point of coming down to earth, to hell and the realm of the dead in order to conquer them. No less than that is accomplished on the Cross.

In other words, the Cross has breached the enemy line, and has set up a position where death can no longer prevail, because its sting has been taken away, and where the Devil is disarmed and bound. The epic heroes of the heathen all had one weak spot: Siegfried had the leaf mark between his shoulder blades, and Achilles his heel. It seems as if the nations sensed that apart from God there is no one who is invulnerable. Even Death and the Devil have their fatal spot now, and that is why Christ called out, 'It is finished.'

God's plan of salvation is not yet completed, however. It is carried out in stages, so to speak. Death has not been abolished, and the Devil is still at work. The Apostle Paul teaches expressly that Death will be the last enemy to be overcome. It is not for nothing that Christ teaches us to pray: 'Deliver us from evil.' We are still living in enemy territory, but we have a refuge from the poisonous arrows of the evil one. There is now a sanctuary where the belaboured and distressed conscience, which is beginning to feel the unbearable burden of its sin, can find a peaceful retreat; and that is the Cross, where our sin can be washed away even if it is blood-red.

Only the poor sinner knows what it means that the Crucifixion of Christ has become a refuge from the persecutor. I wonder how many poor sinners there are among us? And how many more there must be who are certainly sinners, but are far from being poor sinners! All those who are not poor sinners, and who can quite easily endure their wrong-doings, will live through Good Friday without feeling the need for forgiveness of their sin. And any man who does not feel the need for forgiveness has every reason for anxiety and alarm. But the man who thirsts after healing for his own spirit will soon need to be comforted, for the guilt and waywardness of his country and generation. Particularly to those who are overwhelmed by the darkness of our century, I should like to say, 'Death and hell may be powerful but, whatever the coming years may bring, since we have known the Cross they will not be able to bring us anything new and certainly nothing that could be worse than this Crucifixion, for there Christ said, "It is finished." Therefore let us remind one another continually that, however much death may flourish and hell triumph, "It is finished." '

However, 'finished' does not mean perfected. But if God has fulfilled the Scripture as literally as He did on Good Friday, is it not reasonable to suppose that He will just as faithfully fulfil that part of His Word that is still waiting to be perfected? The King of the Jews has not ceased to be King. He will come again and will gather the nations unto Him. Our hope for our own future and for that of the entire world hangs on the King of the Jews. Countries and continents are being divided up as if they were a few trifling possessions; but our sinful covetousness will not eternally cast lots for the coats of the helpless. Through the grace of Jesus Christ we know about the new Heaven, and the new earth in which righteousness dwells. Sons will not eternally have to take leave of their mothers; there will be an end of thirsting and fainting, breaking of limbs and piercing of bodies; and the groaning of the thirsty and faint will cease, for 'there shall be no more death, neither sorrow, nor crying, neither shall there be any more pain.' And all this will come to pass as surely as it is promised us in this crucified 'King of the Jews,' and as surely as God's other promises have been fulfilled.

The Resurrection of Christ

The first day of the week cometh Mary Magdalene early, when it was yet dark, unto the sepulchre, and seeth the stone taken away from the sepulchre. Then she runneth, and cometh to Simon Peter, and to the other disciple, whom Jesus loved, and saith unto them, They have taken away the Lord out of the sepulchre, and we know not where they have laid him. Peter therefore went forth, and that other disciple, and came to the sepulchre. So they ran both together: and the other disciple did outrun Peter, and came first to the sepulchre. And he stooping down, and looking in, saw the linen clothes lying; yet went he not in. Then cometh Simon Peter following him, and went into the sepulchre, and seeth the linen clothes lie, and the napkin, that was about his head, not lying with the linen clothes, but wrapped together in a place by itself. Then went in also that other disciple, which came first to the sepulchre, and he saw, and believed. For as yet they knew not the scripture, that he must rise again from the dead. Then the disciples went away again unto their own home.

But Mary stood without at the sepulchre weeping: and as she wept, she stooped down, and looked into the sepulchre, and seeth two angels in white sitting, the one at the head, and the other at the feet, where the body of Jesus had lain. And they say unto her, Woman, why weepest thou? She saith unto them, Because they have taken away my Lord, and I know not where they have laid him. And when she had thus said, she turned herself back, and saw Jesus standing, and knew not that it was Jesus. Jesus saith unto her, Woman, why weepest thou? whom seekest thou? She, supposing him to be the gardener, saith unto him, Sir, if thou have borne him hence, tell me where thou hast laid him, and I will take him away. Jesus saith unto her, Mary. She turned herself, and saith unto him, Rabboni; which is to say, Master. Jesus saith unto her,

Touch me not; for I am not yet ascended to my Father: but go to my brethren, and say unto them, I ascend unto my Father, and your Father; and to my God, and your God. Mary Magdalene came and told the disciples that she had seen the Lord, and that he had spoken these things unto her.

[XX. 1-18]

When Mary Magdalene first sees the risen Lord and mistakes Him for the gardener, it is not her only mistake on Easter morning. A moment later she makes a more fundamental one. On recognising the figure as her Lord, she thinks at first that Jesus has returned from the dead to earthly life. She must have been reminded for a moment of Lazarus and thought that, just as he was brought back to his sisters from the dead, the Lord had been restored again to His own. Thinking this, Mary's first reaction is to fall on the ground, and embrace Christ's knees in worship, as people did during His brief stay on earth, when they wanted to express their gratitude. Obviously she has not yet grasped the true situation. She evidently thinks that her relationship with Jesus will be the same as it was when He stooped down to the level of men. But she is deceiving herself thoroughly in this. Christ is risen from the dead; but not like Lazarus. Christ has not returned to His former state like the brother of Martha and Mary, or the young man of Nain, or the daughter of Jairus. Easter is not a return to the temporal world, but a break-through into eternal life. Between Mary Magdalene and the risen Lord there now lies that mysterious barrier that divides this world from the beyond, time from eternity and God from us men. That is why Mary Magdalene is quite unexpectedly rebuffed with the words: 'Touch me not; for I am not yet ascended to my Father: but go to my brethren, and say unto them, I ascend unto my Father, and your Father; and to my God, and your God.' Not that it would have been impossible to touch the body of the risen Lord. After all, as we shall soon see, Thomas touched Him eight days later in order to dispel his doubt. With His admonition, 'Touch me not,' the Lord is merely establishing the new relationship between

Himself and men, including His disciples. Although He has not yet 'ascended unto my Father, and your Father,' He has already passed beyond the earthly state to a heavenly one. It will only be a matter of a short time before He withdraws from the atmosphere of this earth in His present condition, and they will no longer be able to see Him, for He has risen into the life that is eternal.

Mary Magdalene would no doubt join us in saying, 'Thank God that she was mistaken at first!' Thank God that the reality of Easter turned out to be so very much more splendid than she imagined in her initial surprise, as much more splendid as Heaven is than the earth! She wept because she could not find the body. Thank God that she did not find it! And thank God that she did not find a Lord who had merely returned to earthly life! It was certainly not to her disadvantage or ours that she made this mistake. Thank God that Easter does not mark the return of the risen Christ to the prison of this temporal world! Thank God that Easter signifies Christ's rising up out of the grave into eternal freedom! The Lord has now escaped from death for ever, and is going to the place where decay can never reach Him. This is what He has gained in His triumph over death. If Mary Magdalene had been right in her original assumption that the Lord had returned to live with her and us on earth again, just like Lazarus, that would have been very nice for all those most closely concerned; but then, like Lazarus, He would only have had to die again sooner or later. But now He has entered into eternal life, which is no reason for tears; it calls for jubilation and rejoicing. He is risen, really and truly risen!

Now that she has grasped the truth of the situation, Mary is told to carry the news to the disciples, His brethren, as Christ calls them here for the first time. He wants the disciples to know about it, as it concerns them primarily. For He has not broken through to eternal life for Himself, not for His own benefit and advantage: He has done it as Saviour and Redeemer. Here too He has fulfilled the office that the Father destined for Him. And what has happened here concerns not only the narrow circle of the disciples. They are to carry the news into the whole world, so that all the nations may know that He has risen up into eternal life for them. He has risen for all those who hear and want to believe: eternal life, which triumphed at Easter, is there for the benefit of all who believe in Him. On that first Easter morning, eternal life, more explicitly your eternal life and mine, stood in front of Mary Magdalene in the garden of Joseph of Arimathaea. In bearing this news to the disciples, Mary is also bringing it to us, to you, and to me, and to all who are listening this morning: Christ's Resurrection means that He has fought for us, and saved us from death and carried us through into eternal life. What is all the news of war and victory in comparison with the news of this holy battle that has had such a mysteriously victorious outcome? What are all the decisions of this world and time, however important they may be and however eagerly we may await them, in comparison with this single decisive victory won by Christ?

Besides Mary Magdalene, our Easter gospel mentions two other witnesses of the Resurrection: Peter and John. Hearing that the grave has been found empty, the two immediately run to see for themselves. John, being younger than Peter, arrives first. There, however, something, we do not know what, holds him back. But Peter, arriving a moment after him, bravely enters the grave and examines it carefully, and then John goes in too, encouraged by Peter's example. They find the linen cloths neatly laid out and the napkin, which had been wrapped round Christ's head, lying rolled up in a place by itself. Their Lord has obviously discarded these grave-clothes and we are told that, on seeing this, John 'believed.' John would hardly mention this in self-praise to the disadvantage of Peter. He knows too well that faith in Easter is exclusively a gift. To him it is given to be the first disciple to believe in the risen Christ, and thus in eternal life. This gift is bestowed on him as soon as he sees the eloquent condition of the grave, even before he has seen Jesus Himself. None of the disciples will be able to understand without faith. Even after they have seen more than just the empty grave and the grave-clothes; even after encountering the angels; indeed, even after seeing their risen Lord with their own eyes and touching Him with their hands, it is faith alone that lets them believe, just as John says later in one of his letters. Christ has risen up into eternal life and as long as man is constricted by space and time, he can only understand that in faith.

Christ has risen up into eternal life. That means eternal life for everyone who is given faith. But we cannot help asking, 'Is that all? Does Christ's Resurrection hold meaning for us only after death? Does it only mean that we shall some day be able to die in the belief in eternal life?' If that were all, it would certainly be very much more than nothing. To be able to die comforted is no small thing. And yet I should like to take up that direct question that is asked significantly at the end of the Easter gospel in the Heidelberg Catechism: 'What use is the Resurrection of Christ to us?' What good is it to us for the seventy, possibly eighty, years that we spend on earth? If the Resurrection is a break-through into eternal life after death, as the fourth gospel emphasises, has Easter in fact any reference to our everyday lives? Have we on the one hand the great and glorious message of the splendour of Christ and on the other our gloomy, daily lives completely separated from, and untouched by, Easter?

Yes, 'What use is the Resurrection to us?' It helps us not only in this respect or that: in actual fact our living and dying depend on it. To put it even more clearly: there is nothing that affects our daily lives so radically and thoroughly as faith in the Resurrection of Jesus Christ. Let us try to prove it.

To begin with, the far-reaching significance of faith in Easter can probably be shown most clearly by considering what happens when faith has been allowed to lapse. The consequences of dwindling faith are incalculable, and when a generation ceases to believe in eternal life, the material damage becomes catastrophic. The very first result is that a generation, which has stopped believing in eternal life, soon loses all faith in earthly life too. It becomes a suicidal generation without even courage enough to propagate itself. As faith in Easter dwindles, the shadow of a decline in the birth-rate looms up. Withdrawal from the eternal always implies a false return to the temporal. So, as a result of its unbelief our own generation is characterised by a godless materialism, as fundamental perhaps as any other generation has known since the days of Noah. This worldliness which is rooted in unbelief is basically to blame for the tragic fate of the once-Christian West. The European who has tried to discard faith in eternal life has become thoroughly perverse. A fall in the birthrate is only one of the many interrelated consequences of this perversity. Our private and public lives are perverse, through and through. Yes, not only our lives but also our attitude to dying, are perverse.

For the materialistic man any interest that death has is merely worldly. He can see no eternal side to death. So death is an enemy to the worldly man, without Easter, only in so far as it can disturb or restrict his full enjoyment of worldly pleasures. For him the struggle against death merely takes the form of keeping the tiresome and importunate spoil-sport at bay as long as possible. But when death inevitably does come along, the worldly man interprets it in the most practical manner possible. He can relieve most of the pain and fear of death by means of all sorts of scientific remedies which, on the whole, work quickly and painlessly. But where unavoidable suffering and unpleasantness precede death, the worldly man is adept at changing his mind and persuading himself that death is his friend after all. He then regards death as a deliverer. It is astonishing how often on the way to the cemetery you hear people say glibly, 'These people out here are well off now.' So people with this unbelieving and perverse way of thinking, die neither happy nor unhappy; they die neutral, so to speak. But strictly speaking, this is not dying at all. Not even an animal dies neutral. At best a flame dies like this when it is blown out by the night wind, or a tool that breaks under the pressure of the hand. The harm done by unbelief is so great, and the effect of lack of faith in Easter so far-reaching in our everyday lives, that we cannot even die any longer.

But how can a man who is unable to die into Eternity any more be born out of Eternity? This perverse attitude of ours shows up most clearly at the two extremities of life, in our attitude to the child and the old man. For the man without Easter, not only death, but also birth has only an earthly significance. Where birth is concerned, the main anxiety, in fact to a very large extent the only anxiety of modern parents is that the baby should be born as comfortably as possible, that it should have a fine layette, that the baby's weight should be a credit to them and increase daily, and all too often this smooth process is rounded off by the shortened form of baptism used in hospitals. One young man I came across recently knew exactly to the ounce how much blood his wife had lost during her confinement, but had no idea of the religious denomination of one of the godparents. The ambition of parents like this is that their children should get on in life and be successful, and that they should have as good a life as their parents, if not a better one. It is this completely materialistic outlook that causes parents to say such things as, 'We are only going to have one or two children, but they will have everything they want.' In hard times, the man who has knowledge only of this world and this time has a certain justification in feeling that life is not worth living for himself and his children. This man even feels guilty for having brought a child into the world, and begins to be afraid that some day his children might curse him for the day of their conception. So the reluctance to live and give life to others is an expression of that deep despair and disappointment, experienced by those who have known only a miserable, earthly life. So you see how deeply faith or the lack of faith can affect our daily lives.

The fruits of our estrangement from Easter show up equally clearly in our perverse attitude to old age. When earthly values replace eternal ones, old age is bound to suffer for it. The more a generation discards its belief in eternal life, the more it loses its love for the aged and infirm, and its understanding for the old and rejected, who are no longer fit to work and are therefore considered as hindrances in the onward rush of life. Old age which has lost the protection of the sheltering wings of Eternity must in the end become the object of charity and social care. It is one and the same eternal God who says, 'Children are a gift of the Lord,' and who likewise says, 'Even to your old age . . . and even to hoar hairs will I carry you.' And it is one and the same unbelief that today restricts the rights of the old man and the child.

Only a generation that again goes to work believing in Eternity, and working for Eternity, will once more be able to derive pleasure from the work of its hands. Only people who have faith in eternal life can see a purpose in the solemnisation and blessing of marriages in the church, in begetting and having children, and in sacrificing one's life for them by the sweat of one's brow. For Christian parents who have faith in Easter, having children amounts to worship of God, because parents who believe do not just receive their children for a time, but out of Eternity and for Eternity. It would not be worth while to undergo the troubles of having children merely to give them a short life in an evil world. But it is worth all the sacrifices of parenthood to have children, and bring them up for Eternity. When it comes to feeding and clothing children for God, no distance to work is too great, and no labour too hard or too dirty for a father, for he is working for the sake of Eternity and not merely for a short span of time. And if the understandable fear of all worldly people should be realised, and one of your children should be unfit for life in this world. that would certainly be a cross to bear. But Christian fathers and mothers who believe will bear it in patience, for after all this child too has been born for Eternity. And if one of your children should die, that would indeed be a tragedy, but you would have to bow to God's Will, knowing that you would finally be comforted for your hour of pain by faith in the eternal words: 'The Lord gave, and the Lord hath taken away; blessed be the name of the Lord.'

Young people who have grown up for Eternity rather than for their century will probably not create Heaven on earth, but they will regard their parents and old people with different eyes and will treat them better. They will not look upon the aged as troublesome ballast to be got rid of as easily as possible: the old man will enjoy the protection of Eternity, together with the child. A generation like this will be blessed in time and in the world, and its days will 'be lengthened in the land which the Lord thy God giveth thee'. In this 'land' where the faith in Easter lives again, homes will become brighter with more children, and old men will no longer be dependent on public charity. Old men will be indispensable to a generation that has faith; they may not be able to serve by the work of their hands, but their experience and wisdom will be invaluable. The once superfluous old will again take the place which is theirs in society, and that is the place of honour at the head of the table and in open council. Then they will regain the title of Elder which the Word of the Lord bestowed on them.

Now we can see what use the Resurrection of Christ is to us. That is how we benefit by that Easter morning when Mary Magdalene was privileged to meet the risen Lord. We gain both in this world and the next. The second of the three answers in the Heidelberg Catechism runs: 'We are even now awakened to a new life through the power of the risen Lord.' The burning problems of our time are either resolved by faith in Easter or not resolved at all.

The Risen Christ Appears to His Disciples

Then the same day at evening, being the first day of the week, when the doors were shut where the disciples were assembled for fear of the Jews, came Jesus and stood in the midst, and saith unto them, Peace be unto you. And when he had so said, he shewed unto them his hands and his side. Then were the disciples glad, when they saw the Lord. Then said Jesus to them again, Peace be unto you: as my Father hath sent me, even so send I you. And when he had said this, he breathed on them, and saith unto them, Receive ye the Holy Ghost: whose soever sins ye remit, they are remitted unto them; and whose soever sins ye retain, they are retained.

[xx. 19–23]

'Peace be unto you.' We hear these words twice on that first Easter Sunday, and a third time eight days later. And at the very outset we must be quite clear about the source of this blessing. It is spoken by the One who has passed beyond the grave, and so the words reach us from Eternity. Even at His birth, Eternity proclaimed, 'Glory to God in the highest, and on earth peace, good will toward men.' And hundreds of years before that the prophet said, 'And his name shall be called Wonderful, Counsellor, The mighty God, The everlasting Father, The Prince of Peace.' It is one and the same who says here, 'Peace be unto you.' So there is a peace that is eternal in the literal sense of the word. This sounds so strange when we consider the state of the world today. Have we not heard something very similar recently, from a different source: from Geneva, then from Munich, of unhappy memory, and now from Washington and Rome? And is it not the case that the louder we hear the call, the more wary we become? We are almost compelled to think that it is hell that makes use of it. 'They say peace, peace, peace and yet there is no peace.' And now here it is Heaven calling through Him who has risen into Eternity, 'Peace be unto you.'

Eternal peace does not want to remain in Heaven. It wants to be on earth with you and with me. It longs to leave the seclusion of Eternity and to break through to us poor men on earth who have no peace. This earth is its objective; it besieges the earth like a fortress, night and day. The gates of this world and the doors of time are surrounded by hosts of messengers and servants of eternal peace. And these strong men 'who execute his word' miss no opportunity of promoting peace in this world. That eternal peace longs for the earth is proved by the whole of the Old Testament, which constitutes in itself a single, uninterrupted attack on the earth in the cause of peace. The messages of Moses, the Psalms and the Prophets could all be summed up in the one phrase, 'Peace be unto you.'

But the One speaking to us on this Easter Sunday is not just any servant and messenger of Eternity. This is Jesus, who was born 'when Cyrenius was governor of Syria,' who suffered under Pontius Pilate, and was a man of flesh and blood. Now if we could prove that the One who is calling, 'Peace be unto you,' from Eternity, is one and the same Jesus of Nazareth, then we could believe that something unheard-of had happened, for we would know that the assault from Eternity had been successful. In that case, someone from Eternity, and not just anyone, but the Prince of Peace Himself, will have succeeded in setting foot in this world. The Lord of eternal peace will have landed on this hostile island, the earth.

And this is exactly what the risen Lord does first of all at Easter. He patiently proves His 'identity' to His disciples, to show them that He is the One whom they followed until He died on the Cross. He makes sure of showing them the wounds in His hands, and feet, and in His side; and eight days later, He carefully puts Thomas's doubts to rest; 'Reach hither thy finger, and behold my hands; and reach hither thy hand, and thrust it into my side.'

Now we can begin to understand why 'the disciples were glad when they saw the Lord.' Who would not have been glad? If this man of absolute peace, whose life they have followed from His birth in the stable to His death on the Cross, is now risen – and He is indeed risen, for here He is standing among them, showing them His passport, as it were – if He is risen, then the victory has been won for the cause of peace on the earth. This again may sound strange to people in times of war, but it is true, because with Christ has risen that peace which was destined for this earth from Eternity. The risen Christ's words: 'Peace be unto you,' proclaim eternal peace on the earth once and for all. And it is not only proclaimed once and for all; it is actually here once and for all, because the risen Lord is here, untouched by scorn and mockery, untouched by knocks and blows, even untouched by the attacks of the old enemy, death; He is here in splendour and in glorious majesty. And because He has proclaimed peace, inviolable peace is here once and for all, untouched by mockery, blows and even death. Peace rose up with Him from the grave. In other words, when He proclaims peace He is not merely uttering a wish, or calling out a message, or a warning or a challenge: He is offering a gift. Eternal peace is God's Easter present to this world of death. This world has now become His dwelling; not just a temporary lodging but His home. How strange to think that this earth is the dwelling of eternal peace! But however odd that may sound, eternal peace *is* here, for Christ is risen. No war, however long, can change that. No one can destroy this eternal peace now that Christ is risen from the dead. No one can go on doubting that eternal peace has been given the final victory in this world of death. The Prince of Peace is risen. No anti-aircraft fire can shoot Him down, no gas can poison Him, no tank can crush Him. He is risen from the dead through the grave and through hell; no moth nor rust, no worm nor decay can corrupt Him. 'Then were the disciples glad when they saw the Lord.' Who among us does not rejoice with them? A breath of fresh air has reached us and we can breathe again. A ray of light has filtered through into this year, 1940.

A window has been opened. Whatever this summer may bring, never let yourselves be dragged away from this heavenly window. Stay there! Breathe the air! Hold fast to the knowledge that Christ is risen and has said, 'Peace be unto you.'

Having considered the source of this proclamation of peace, we now have to look at the place where it is heard. The risen Lord announces His peace in circumstances which are anything but peaceful. It is night. A small group of men is meeting in secret. The fear of discovery is written plainly on their faces. The doors are bolted. And it is worth noting that eight days later they are still locked. But what does the risen Lord care for 'the Jews'? What does He care for locks and bolts? He brings His peace that is eternal into this unlikely place. Some day this place might well be one of the air-raid shelters which are now being built everywhere in this town. The risen peace makes its way to places like this, where a few fearful people have sought shelter, behind locked doors, in the darkness of the night. For the peace that broke out of the realm of death, on Easter morning, is powerful enough to break through locked doors on Easter evening, and into a room filled with fear and horror. That is the sort of dwelling that eternal peace chooses on this earth. The eternal Prince of Peace does not build palaces. He sets foot in humble places. But however poverty-stricken these places may appear, when the risen Lord enters them they acquire something of the splendour promised in the words: 'Behold, the tabernacle of God is with men.' In tents and in huts, in dwellings of misery and in houses of death, God builds His Kingdom of peace. 'My peace I give unto you: not as the world giveth, give I unto you. Let not your heart be troubled' (ch. XIV). 'In the world ye shall have tribulation; but be of good cheer; I have overcome the world' (ch. XVI). This peace has positive significance. It is valid, independent of circumstances and even in spite of them. This peace would be yours even if your gas-mask should fail, or your air-raid shelter should not protect you. The world cannot give this peace and therefore it cannot take it away.

But why does not everyone simply reach out for this peace

with both hands? Why is there not a general rush for this peace? The answer is suggested in our text for today. On that Easter day the risen Lord sent out His disciples with the mission, 'Whose soever sins ye remit, they are remitted unto them; and whose soever sins ye retain, they are retained.' This explains the nature of eternal peace. The risen Christ is not the Lord of any ordinary peace: the essence of His peace is the forgiveness of sin. It is that that the risen Christ offers to the disciples that Easter evening. He might equally well have said, 'Your sins are forgiven.' The peace that has come to earth and has set up its dwelling here is the forgiveness of sin. And that is the peace that is of the greatest importance for time and Eternity, gas-masks and air-raid shelters or no. Because this is the nature of the peace for which Christ died and rose again, there is no crowding or queueing, for there are many who do not want it. When we speak of peace, we imagine a shining angel and not this Cinderella, called forgiveness of sin. But however acceptable or unacceptable this peace may be, the thing that matters is whether the risen Lord's Easter-call applies to you yourself or not. Each one of us finds himself besieged. Each one of us finds his own personal fortress assailed by this peace, and if there is no surrender, if the walls do not fall down and the gates do not open, then he has rejected the greatest and most splendid thing that has ever happened for this earth; he has shut it out and his 'sins are retained.' The tabernacle of peace on this earth is modest. Eternal peace wants to settle down and make its dwelling with 'the publicans and the harlots,' who cry out to Heaven in their distress.

The Lord of peace sends His messengers out to all the nations, gifted and armed with this peace: 'As my Father hath sent me, even so send I you.' This 'as' is significant. The Father sent Him down to lowliness, suffering and the Cross. Therefore we must not be surprised or troubled because He on His part sends out the messengers of peace with the words: 'Behold, I send you forth as sheep in the midst of wolves.' They will meet with resistance. The forgiveness of sin is regarded as a foolhardy or an irritating thing, and they will meet with mockery and contempt. The world is offered eternal peace, but it wants peace at a cheaper price; it prefers marble palaces of peace to the lowly dwellings of eternal peace. Yes, there will be strife on account of this eternal peace (ch. XVI). The Prince of Peace knows this. His messengers will have to fight. And the struggle will be so hard that no man will be able to carry it on, and endure it by himself. It is interesting to see what equipment the Lord of peace gives His own for this battle: 'And when he had said this, he breathed on them, and saith unto them, Receive ye the Holy Ghost.' This puts us in mind of the vision of the prophet Ezekiel. He saw a valley full of bones; and as the Spirit of God moved over the valley, life entered into the bones and they stood up and lived. We men are full of death, and fear and resistance, and so were those first disciples. They are in no way fit to bear to the nations the living, vital peace that is entrusted to them. But as the risen Lord breathes into this miserable group of frightened men, the dead become living messengers of the Resurrection, and the faint-hearted become death-despising witnesses of eternal peace. Fear has to give way and peace enters in. Now they are equipped to pass on what they themselves have received. And so this dark room, with its bolted doors, becomes a peace headquarters for all the nations. And a handful of disciples becomes the army which the Prince of Peace sends out to every member of the human race.

But have we come back to that familiar and maligned peace of heart which has no effect on the outside world? Have we reached that refuge of the lazy man and the coward again? Wait a moment! Do not be too hasty to condemn peace of heart. You cannot ignore it. When Jeremias Gotthelf wrote: 'The shining light of our native land must begin in the home,' he was well aware that it is even more fundamental than that: the shining light of the home must begin in the heart. And yet you are right to refuse to be content with what is hidden in the hearts of men. You are right to hunger and thirst for the peace that is more than personal experience, even if it were that most perfect experience of personal salvation. You are right to strive after a peace which reaches beyond the limits of our own person, and becomes the cause of God. Blessed is the man who clings in faith to the hope for a peace which is invisible today, the hope of peace for this whole earth. You are right to believe wholeheartedly in a general peace which cannot be seen yet. Christ's words of blessing to the disciples that Easter evening, 'Peace be unto you,' contain a promise of the universal peace that embraces the whole of the groaning creation, together with all the angels and the devils. He is speaking as the 'first-fruits of them that slept.' Finally let me describe the fullness of peace which we are longing for, in the words of the prophet Isaiah: 'The wolf also shall dwell with the lamb, and the leopard shall lie down with the kid; and the calf and the young lion and the fatling together; and a little child shall lead them. And the cow and the bear shall feed; their young ones shall lie down together: and the lion shall eat straw like the ox. And the sucking child shall play on the hole of the asp, and the weaned child shall put his hand on the cockatrice' den. They shall not hurt nor destroy in all my holy mountain: for the earth shall be full of the knowledge of the Lord as the waters cover the sea.'

The Testimony of Thomas

But Thomas, one of the twelve, called Didymus, was not with them when Jesus came. The other disciples therefore said unto him, We have seen the Lord. But he said unto them, Except I shall see in his hands the print of the nails, and put my finger into the print of the nails, and thrust my hand into his side, I will not believe.

And after eight days again his disciples were within, and Thomas with them: then came Jesus, the doors being shut, and stood in the midst, and said, Peace be unto you. Then saith he to Thomas, Reach hither thy finger, and behold my hands; and reach hither thy hand, and thrust it into my side: and be not faithless, but believing. And Thomas answered and said unto him, My Lord and my God. Jesus saith unto him, Thomas, because thou hast seen me, thou hast believed: blessed are they that have not seen, and yet have believed.

And many other signs truly did Jesus in the presence of his disciples, which are not written in this book: but these are written, that ye might believe that Jesus is the Christ, the Son of God; and that believing ye might have life through his name.

[xx. 24–31]

In view of what we have just read, perhaps we ought to be more careful about what we say in future. Otherwise, what happens to Thomas here might happen to us. When Thomas was told that the Lord had risen, he said he refused to believe it unless he could see the marks of the nails with his own eyes, and feel the wounds in the Lord's side with his own hands. And now, eight days later, Thomas has to learn that, when he was speaking so carelessly, the risen Lord was listening to him and heard exactly what he said.

Eternity is as near to us as it is invisible. It can hear our every word and can see everything we do. We are surrounded and enveloped by Eternity: to use a phrase of Luther's, it is 'closer to us than our coat or our shirt.' A few years ago we lived for a time in a flat with very thin walls. We often had to interrupt one another during a conversation by pointing warningly at the walls or ceiling to show that we should talk more quietly, so that the neighbouring families could not hear what we were saying. Time also has thin walls, separating us from Eternity. And when we talk too confidently and boastfully, we ought to remind one another that Eternity is listening to us. Of course, Eternity can hear us however softly we may speak: It hears us even before our thoughts have been put into words: 'There is not a word in my tongue, but thou knowest it altogether. Thou understandest my thought afar off.' And we can be taken at our word by Eternity just as literally as Thomas is here.

The fact that Eternity takes such an interest in us personally, and that the risen Lord is so near to us, is no less beneficial than frightening. Thomas is certainly afraid when he realises how the risen Lord has taken him at his word. He is terrified; but all the same his fear is beneficial, for it is the Lord who has surprised him in his unbelief and not just any man. He shows him the marks of the nails and not His clenched fist. He shows Thomas His wounds, the symbols of His eternal compassion and love. When Thomas sees this, he realises that Eternity can love. It can love as only Eternity is capable of loving. All the splendour of eternal love meets Thomas in the person of the living Lord, and surrounds this poor unbeliever with such light that all he can do is fall to his knees and cry out, 'My Lord and my God.'

Christ is Thomas's Lord and God. The love of Eternity can lavish all the fullness of its compassion on one particular individual. The Apostle Thomas here comes face to face with the mystery of Divine choice. There are eleven disciples present. Ten of them saw the risen Lord eight days ago. Thomas was the only one who did not see Him then, because he was not there. And when the risen Christ appears to them this time, it is for Thomas's special benefit. The risen Lord goes straight to Thomas as if the other ten were not present and addresses him alone. It seems as if Heaven has opened and has taken the trouble to let down the Lord, to whom, after all, all power in Heaven and earth is given, so that He might appear to this one man and speak to him. That is the mystery of Divine choice. Out of all the millions and millions of people who live under the eyes of Eternity, God has sought out this one little man, watched him and listened to his words; a voice from Eternity has addressed him; and a hand has stretched out and chosen him from among all other men. Thomas has a twin brother, but we never hear that he was a disciple. God's choice falls upon one of a pair of twins, and in His compassion He draws him into the circle of the disciples. When God turns His attention to us men, His acts are a mystery. 'Two men shall be in the field; the one shall be taken, and the other left. Two women shall be grinding together; the one shall be taken, and the other left.' Two children are born as twins of one and the same womb; the one becomes the disciple Thomas, and of the other we hear nothing. Thomas sinks to his knees before the immensity of this mystery and cries, 'My Lord and my God.'

The singling out of Thomas is all the more surprising and difficult to understand because there is very little merit to be seen in him. What we know of his character is melancholy and defeatist. When the Lord told the disciples that Lazarus had died, Thomas immediately gave way to despondency and said, 'Let us also go, that we may die with him,' by which he meant that things were now turning out as he had feared, and that nothing made sense any more (ch. XI). And when Jesus was taking leave of His disciples and said to them, 'Whither I go ye know, and the way ye know,' this pessimistic doubter again answered gloomily, 'Lord, we know not whither thou goest: and how can we know the way?' (ch XIV). And it was probably owing to his tendency to doubt and despair that he was the only disciple missing after the Crucifixion. When the others tell him of the Resurrection of the Lord, he not only says he cannot believe it but we hear him say outright, 'I will not believe!' Doubt has taken such a hold of him that it has affected his will; yet it is on this, humanly speaking, impossible disciple that the Lord now lavishes all His compassion, so that all he can say is, 'My Lord and my God.' That is how the risen Lord draws from this personification of doubt a testimony which transcends in glory and splendour the testimony of all the other disciples, even that of Peter. Thomas, who was literally the last of the eleven, can now say, 'My Lord and my God.' The autocratic hand of the Lord can make the first last and the last first.

Does God still choose certain people in preference to others today? Or is selection by grace restricted only to Biblical times, to the times of the Prophets and the men of God in the Old Testament, and the Apostles in the New? The answer to this is yes – and no. God no longer chooses apostles and prophets: their lists are closed. Paul's addition to the number of the disciples was, as he says himself, like a late birth. God considered those twelve sufficient. But even though He no longer chooses apostles and prophets, He has not stopped choosing. The search of the loving Shepherd continues day and night, in every nation and every age. Though He is no longer seeking apostles and prophets, He is certainly looking for children of God and heirs of His Kingdom.

His searching is prompted by the same love, however: He is still seeking the lost. The risen Lord who chooses Thomas as His Apostle has not stopped saving drowning men from the slough of sin, and from the quagmire of death, and bringing them to dry land; He has not stopped saving men from the fire of consuming passions, as one might pluck a brand from the burning. What else but this choosing grace which seeks the lost has brought us together here this morning? It is this same Divine grace that spreads its wings over us today, when the Communion table is standing prepared before us, and we are invited to come as guests and as children to accept food and drink for eternal life. If God was able to choose a man of Thomas's nature as His disciple, how can one of us be too lost and too sinful to be a child and an heir? In this sense the Apostles confidently and boldly addressed all the members of the Church of Christ as 'elect.' And because we believe in this election to childhood and eternal life, because we believe that Christ wants to be our Saviour too, therefore we also dare to address Him as 'our Lord and our God,' like Thomas. After all, we ourselves are the greatest miracle of saving grace. Remembering this, no grateful child of God can do other than reassure even the most lost of his brothers that Christ has power to choose the lost. The man who can himself say, 'My Lord and my God,' is given courage to believe and hope that Christ is the Lord and God of his brother too. Indeed, if He is my Lord and my God, why should he not also be the Lord and God of my country and my people, the Lord and God of this poor, divided and lost human race?

There is an active as well as a passive side to being chosen. In other words, the consciousness of being chosen inspires a man to go out and help his brother. The man who has experienced the love of Christ finds himself driven to his lost brother. Divine compassion is the fuel that drives charity, but today there is a different kind of fuel turning the wheels of the world: hatred has displaced pity. These wheels turn in the service of enmity and destruction, with ever-increasing speed from month to month. And the wheels of destruction will not come to a standstill until the fuel begins to run dry on one side or the other. I often wonder nowadays whether the state of affairs in the world would ever have become so bad, if Christians had used their time better, and had let themselves be driven to their brothers by the fuel of Divine compassion. But of course the oil-shafts of the Church were mostly blocked up, and the petrol pipes of European Christianity were choked. The decline of Europe followed on that of the Church. For example, we hardly dared to mention Divine choice in the pulpit. John Calvin, the man with the deepest understanding of this gospel, both in its active and its passive sense, had become an object of scorn and derision. We no longer dared to preach the gospel of Divine choice because we were afraid of the rationalistic attitude which cannot, and never will, grasp the significance of this choice. We talked of the universal love of God, and had lost sight of the fact that God is the Lord. We did say rather feebly, 'My God, my God,' but we suppressed the first part of Thomas's testimony, which, do not forget, says, 'My *Lord* and my God.' He is the Lord, and as such He can choose and reject.

We made this deep and fundamental gospel into a flat, superficial, and mediocre Christianity, and as a result, everything we did and said became flat, and superficial, and mediocre. We had a mean of propriety and conventionality, which we applied to everything, even to our enthusiasms and our worship. It was on this mediocre Christianity that the old Europe foundered. Its decline was not caused by growing godlessness, but by the convenient and deceitful moderation of European Christians, for this 'respectable' mediocre Christianity had naturally been drained of that vitality and driving-force which was needed to resolve the urgent problems of human co-existence and co-operation. I am told that it is a criminal offence to pour water into the petrol tank of a motor car, because it stops the engine. But that is precisely what has happened in the Western Church. We have poured water into the fuel-tanks of the Church and have remained miserably stuck; and thus we have adulterated and watered down the Gospel. It is no wonder that this Christianity has had to remain stranded, neither chosen nor rejected. It would have been a miracle if things had not come to the present pass.

But the testimony of Thomas runs, 'My Lord and my God.' My Lord! The man who is called as a child to the Father's table, and into His house as an heir, is then called to work in the Lord's vineyard. And the Lord of the vineyard does not divide out the work methodically, giving each man an equal share: even in the apportioning of work the Lord exercises His choice. A father does not expect the same of each of his children, and so it is with the Lord. In dividing out the work the Lord takes into account the varying gifts with which He has endowed His children. One man receives ten talents, another five, or two, or one. But a great deal is expected of the one to whom much is given. The Lord is like a doctor who visits and tends all his patients with the same care, yet does not make out his account according to a set scale of charges, but according to what the patient can afford. And there is no scale of charges in Christianity. The Lord can give an enormous amount, but His demands can be very great too. He may demand one tenth, or one-half of all your goods, or even everything you have, all according to His choice. The Christian is subject to the gifts and demands of God's grace, rather than protected by a minimum tariff. It has been left to the lords of this world to show how to get the utmost out of men as volunteer paratroops, pilots and submarine commanders in the cause of destruction. Christians could learn from this how to serve their Lord with unconditional devotion in the cause of love. When the Devil begins to work miracles, how can we Christians feel at ease even for one moment in the smug seclusion of our self-chosen mediocrity? But when the community hears and believes the Gospel of Divine choice again, it will once more be ready for the adventure of brotherly love.

The Lord expects His chosen children and servants to believe without seeing: 'Thomas, because thou hast seen me, thou hast believed: blessed are they that have not seen, and yet have believed.' But we wanted to see before we would believe. That can be the death of faith. In an effort to provoke us, God has punished us and put us to shame by the example of the children of this world. They have shown us what blind, obedient faith can achieve in the service of the Devil. The children of the world have had to show us how to sacrifice one's life, not for what is visible and attainable, but for something that seems impossible and far away, for the coming generation and age. The miracles of Antichrist have happened as a punishment for us, so that we might in the end come to realise what it would mean to live and die with faith in the coming of the Kingdom of God. Blessed are those who do not see and yet believe, who serve the greatest Lord believing in what is humanly impossible and far distant.

But can we believe? Thomas could not, and, worse, he would not. But when the Lord chooses, and He does so choose; when God's grace singles us out, then we do believe, whether we want to or not. So let us pray ceaselessly for the one thing that is needful, faith in our Lord and our God.

The Meeting at the Sea of Tiberias

After these things Jesus shewed himself again to the disciples at the sea of Tiberias; and on this wise shewed he himself. There were together Simon Peter, and Thomas called Didymus, and Nathanael of Cana in Galilee, and the sons of Zebedee, and two other of his disciples. Simon Peter saith unto them, I go a fishing. They say unto him, We also go with thee. They went forth, and entered into a ship immediately; and that night they caught nothing. But when the morning was now come, Jesus stood on the shore: but the disciples knew not that it was Jesus. Then Jesus saith unto them, Children, have ye any meat? They answered him, No. And he said unto them, Cast the net on the right side of the ship, and ye shall find. They cast therefore, and now they were not able to draw it for the multitude of fishes. Therefore that disciple whom Jesus loved saith unto Peter, It is the Lord. Now when Simon Peter heard that it was the Lord, he girt his fisher's coat unto him, (for he was naked,) and did cast himself into the sea. And the other disciples came in a little ship; (for they were not far from land, but as it were two hundred cubits,) dragging the net with fishes. As soon then as they were come to land, they saw a fire of coals there, and fish laid thereon, and bread. Jesus saith unto them, Bring of the fish which ye have now caught. Simon Peter went up, and drew the net to land full of great fishes, an hundred and fifty and three: and for all there were so many, yet was not the net broken. Jesus saith unto them, Come and dine. And none of the disciples durst ask him, Who art thou? knowing that it was the Lord. Jesus then cometh, and taketh bread, and giveth them, and fish likewise. This is now the third time that Jesus shewed himself to his disciples, after that he was risen from the dead.

[XXI. 1–14]

Christ is risen and has appeared to His disciples. This message, which has been brought home to us once again in these chapters, is still valid today. The Resurrection of Christ is as much a reality now as it ever was. But the Resurrection is a reality in a world where it is not easy to see that Christ rose from the dead, for the world and in it: for this world bears the stamp of death. Death is not inactive here, especially since Christ rose from the dead. Admittedly death may be on the defensive, but it is hard at work. The portrait of death as a human figure, with a scythe, is surely more than an empty symbol. Death wields the scythe expertly, and not only in the air or on the sea or on the Russian steppes, but also here, in this town. In the very houses around us men tremble and fall, like reeds, under the blows of death. Furthermore, death is at work inside us and strikes in our very hearts. It is only a fortnight since Easter, and already a hundred voices have whispered to us mockingly, and insinuated that there was nothing in the Resurrection after all: since then we have seen a hundred pairs of hands doing things which have made us feel like closing up the Lord's open grave again. We are living in the world for which Christ rose from the dead, but the world is hostile to Easter.

In spite of, and because of, that, this is the time to stand in faith by the empty grave and the risen Christ; and in this world of death this means resisting in faith the waves of death which threaten to engulf us. Believing in the risen Christ means opposing death in faith at the grave-side, by the beds of the sick, and the dying, and on our own death-beds when it comes to that. In spite of death's destruction, in spite of all the graves which are filled each day, and in spite of mass graves and the toll of lives taken by the sea, Christ's grave is nevertheless empty, and this one empty Easter grave reveals to those who can believe in it that the risen Lord will gain the final victory. Indeed this final victory is already confirmed in the midst of all this dying. Since Christ's Easter victory, human death does not provide a dark, uniform harvest field; since the Resurrection of Christ, dying has various meanings. Since then, millions of believers who are known only to God have not passed into death, but into life and into the Resurrection of Christ. Since that first Easter Sunday the angels of the risen Christ are present at certain death-beds, ready to snatch for all eternity the prize that death is already gloating over.

If we know our Bible, we should not be surprised that the victory of Easter is far from being uncontested in this world. It is certainly painful to us and imposes a kind of spiritual fasting on our faith, but the fact itself should no longer surprise. Christ has prepared His Church adequately for battles and reverses. And it becomes abundantly clear, through the Easter gospels, that the community can be the messenger of Easter, but in a world of death. Just look at the seven men who are presented to us in today's text. What impression do they give? Do they live up to the popular conception of messengers of Easter? It is true, is it not, that the average man imagines that, once they were convinced of the Easter victory of their Master, these first witnesses of Easter were an exultant and triumphant group of men, almost beside themselves with jubilation? It would be natural to expect that, after what they have heard and seen, these men would run through the streets of Jerusalem and shout from the roof tops, 'Christ is risen and has appeared to His disciples!' But we have to thank the Evangelists, and John in particular, for showing us the first witnesses of Easter as they actually were. Their situation and state of mind make it clear that death still hangs over life like mist on a spring night. These first messengers of Easter are dejected rather than jubilant. They seem to be perplexed and lost. In the end, Peter cannot bear the depressing situation any longer and declares, 'I go a fishing.' The other six go with him. Consider what this means! These men are bearers of a message which will shatter the world, a message that is felt even in the grave – and they decide to go fishing! A period of waiting and of groping in indecision has been imposed upon them. They are messengers of Easter and they want to go fishing!

But if the first messengers of Easter undergo a period like this, why should it not be the case with us too, who after all are not disciples? In the Church of Christ there are periods of waiting, and groping and seeking, when, like Peter, Christians have to take off their messengers' cloaks and put on their light fishing-clothes. And I feel that one of those times has come now; a period of waiting and of restricted possibilities, when the spreading of the Gospel is held up, and Christians have to go 'a fishing.' So let us go fishing with clear consciences. Peter and his fellow-disciples went fishing, and yet Easter is a reality. You can go and dig your garden, and yet be a messenger of Easter. Let us go fishing then, if that is the way it is to be, and let us not make such a tragedy of it. It makes no difference to the fact that Easter is valid and that Christ has risen.

So Peter goes fishing with the disciples, and they do not even catch anything. The other three gospels tell of another occasion when the disciples fished for a whole night and caught nothing. But at that time the situation was quite different. It was not Easter then and their Master was still living as a man, in a state of lowliness. In those days it seemed quite natural that as disciples of this humble Master they should fish unsuccessfully for a whole night. But now the great change has taken place; now death has been conquered and Easter has come. And now it is difficult to understand how they can be messengers of Easter, and still fish for a whole night without success. This shows up the extreme poverty and powerlessness of the disciples, and they are mercilessly reminded of it when a man calls to them from the shore, 'Children, have ye any meat?' They do not recognise the stranger, and presume that He is asking them for food. And they have to answer, 'No.' These messengers of Easter have to admit that they themselves have nothing, and therefore cannot give Him anything. These messengers of Easter are as poor as church mice. Even so, Easter is a reality and Christ is risen from the dead. And amid the extreme poverty and powerlessness of these messengers, the risen Lord wants to reveal Himself in the fullness of His splendour.

The rich haul of fish is intentionally mentioned here because it is a revelation. Once the disciples have recognised the stranger on the shore as Christ, they are no longer amazed at their large catch. For they know from experience that He can do that sort of thing. And now that He has been given this splendid victory over death, He can do it all the more. The importance of this huge haul of fish lies in the message it conveys to the disciples at this time. To the disciples this event is a sermon, a sermon without words, as it were, but unforgettably impressive. Its meaning is: 'You can do nothing; you cannot even catch fish without me. Even now, at Easter time, you can do nothing. But because I am risen now and because all things are given me by the Father, you will do greater things through your faith in me than anything that happened while I was only a man. And you yourselves have nothing, absolutely nothing to give. But because I am now risen from the dead, and live, I can give you more than you can ask for or understand. Look at this net full of fish, a hundred and fifty-three of them. You are poor and helpless in a very rich and ostentatiously opulent world. But be comforted in your poverty: you serve a rich Master. Be comforted in your weakness and helplessness: your Master is Lord of the ocean and all its mysterious breadths and depths.' There is no bargaining with this Master. His final victory was confirmed at Easter, and He and no other will win the decisive battle of the sea.

That is the message of this Easter catch. And the implication of this message becomes even clearer and more far-reaching. We have just said that this event is a sermon without words. And yet it is not quite without words. Christ spoke the message of the miraculous haul of fish on an earlier occasion. That was when He met these men for the first time on the shores of this lake, and threw His net over them, and they let themselves be caught. He said something to them then that flashes back into their memories now, when they are meeting Him for the last time by the lake: 'Follow me, and I will make you fishers of men.' Fishers of men! Remembering these words the disciples realise that it is not a question of a hundred and fifty-three fish in this overloaded net; it is not a matter of fish at all, in fact, but of fishing for men. Their eyes are opened when they realise this. They will soon go out into the wide world and make all nations His disciples. They will be messengers of Easter in a world that is hostile to Easter. They will often groan and sweat as fishers of men; they will pass many a sleepless night, and will frequently be conscious of their poverty and helplessness. But now they have seen this laden net at Easter time, and the memory of it will be a blessing and a promise to them on their way to the nations. The net is full to bursting, and yet it does not break.

Does this promise that the risen Lord gives to His disciples at Easter, before He sends them out into the world, apply to us too? It would be natural to answer in the affirmative, if it were not for God's order of precedence, which we must respect. The promise of the full net is given to the disciples. We are not disciples, however, and so it is by no means self-evident that we are also allowed to depend on this promise. This is a question which has become especially pertinent to many of us here this morning. In the afternoons and evenings of the past week, we have been taking part in a course of Bible-study for church-workers. Our readings there have given us renewed comfort, and strength and courage for our work at the nets. Can we today, at the conclusion of our course, take the promise of the Easter haul of fish with us as a blessing on our way? Yes, we can, for the Word is given to the disciples to pass on to the community. A Church that has become poor and helpless, and sees its only strength in Him who sends it out among the people, a discouraged and humiliated Church, can find support in the promise of the full net.

We have also had with us this week members of the Basle and district branch of the Blue Cross League, who have been holding their annual spring conference here. These guests of ours are workers who have been standing at the nets for many years, fighting with the message of the Easter victory, against alcohol, the 'coachman of death,' and its allied powers. Can you, friends of the Blue Cross, who work at the nets in your own way and in your own sphere, also take with you the words that we have heard today? Be assured that you can. You can return to your homes, to your villages and valleys, strengthened by the guiding promise of the miraculous haul of fish. Take these words with you as a blessing, and let them sustain you in your work. Never forget the heavy net with the hundred and fifty-three large fish which the risen Lord showed the disciples before sending them out into the world. And the same promise applies to all who stand by the nets anywhere in faith in Easter and are fishers of men.

But although the promise of the miraculous haul of fish has been given to the Church, that by no means implies an assurance for each and every one of us. God may well leave a whole congregation or society by the wayside. Even as members of the Church or of the Blue Cross League we can be deprived of this promise. Therefore let all of us who toil at the nets in any capacity remember not only the blessing and the promise, but also the warning that is contained in Christ's great words. You may have noticed that from the moment when John says, 'It is the Lord,' the disciples' whole attention is directed towards the shore. The knowledge that 'it is the Lord' affects these seven men as a magnet attracts iron filings. This is the warning: we must not look at ourselves and our own weaknesses nor, which is even worse, at our strength. Let us look at Christ. Nor must we look at our neighbour and fellow-worker at the net. How many a worker of the Kingdom of God is ruined by petty jealousy! Nor must we be too much taken up by the sea and its horrors. This preoccupation with the fishing-ground merely discourages and inhibits the worker at the net. But above all we must not look upon the catch as our own. It is not ours: it belongs to the Lord. In fact, nothing is ours, neither the net, nor the catch, nor the Church, nor the society. And the most urgent reminder is this: only by looking at the One who stands in splendour by the shore shall we draw the net in the right direction. For when you fish for men in the service of the risen Lord, you might pull in the wrong direction. It is possible to pull the net towards yourself instead of to the Lord. How much work for the Kingdom of God is ruined by the ambition of the workers, that false love that seeks its own ends! When we pull the net towards ourselves it usually breaks. Have we not torn or helped to tear nets ourselves? So let us take care to draw the net to the Lord. Look at Peter. As soon as he recognises the Lord on the shore, he does something that no other fisherman would do: he lets go of the net, abandons the catch, jumps into the water and swims over to the Lord, thus indicating to those left in the boat the direction in which they have to pull the net.

And a second warning is given to fishers of men. Because the Lord knows that the world into which He is sending His disciples is hard and hostile to the Easter message, He considers it necessary to strengthen them before He sends them out. He has lit a fire on the shore and prepared a meal for them. Formerly it was always they who prepared meals for Him, but now it is His turn. He calls them to eat to fortify themselves before starting on their careers as fishers of men. And so, for all time, He declares His own to be in need of sustenance. We, however, often seem to need remarkably little nourishment in the service of the Lord. That is not as it should be. The more the Church realises that it is a world of death into which it is being sent and which it has to resist, the more it will need God's Word and God's Table. Fishers of men live by the fire that the Lord of glory has lit for them on the shore, and by the meal that He has prepared for them.

Finally, what happens to all the fish that refuse to be caught in the net that we cast at the Lord's command? We know from the Bible that, besides the nets that we can cast in this temporal world, there is a great, final, universal net, which is the net of judgment. Anyone who avoids the nets of grace in the world of time, will not evade the net of judgment at the end of time. It will be cast over all the nations, and none will slip through its mesh. This net of judgment and wrath will be drawn in in the end, but not by human hands. The mighty angels of the Last Judgment will draw in this last great drag-net, and pull it to the shore where the Lord stands in glory.

Christ's Commission to Peter

So when they had dined, Jesus saith to Simon Peter, Simon, son of Jonas, lovest thou me more than these? He saith unto him, Yea, Lord; thou knowest that I love thee. He saith unto him, Feed my lambs. He saith to him again the second time, Simon, son of Jonas, lovest thou me? He saith unto him, Yea, Lord; thou knowest that I love thee. He saith unto him, Feed my sheep. He saith unto him the third time, Simon, son of Jonas, lovest thou me? Peter was grieved because he said unto him the third time, Lovest thou me? And he said unto him, Lord, thou knowest all things; thou knowest that I love thee. Jesus saith unto him, Feed my sheep. Verily, verily, I say unto thee, When thou wast young, thou girdedst thyself, and walkedst whither thou wouldest: but when thou shalt be old, thou shalt stretch forth thy hands, and another shall gird thee, and carry thee whither thou wouldest not. This spake he, signifying by what death he should glorify God. And when he had spoken this, he saith unto him, Follow me.

Then Peter, turning about, seeth the disciple whom Jesus loved following; which also leaned on his breast at supper, and said, Lord, which is he that betrayeth thee? Peter seeing him saith to Jesus, Lord, and what shall this man do? Jesus saith unto him, If I will that he tarry till I come, what is that to thee? follow thou me. Then went this saying abroad among the brethren, that that disciple should not die: yet Jesus said not unto him, He shall not die; but, If I will that he tarry till I come, what is that to thee?

This is the disciple which testifieth of these things, and wrote these things: and we know that his testimony is true.

And there are also many other things which Jesus did, the which, if they should be written every one, I suppose that even the world itself could not contain the books that should be written. Amen. [XXI. 15–25]

Christ talks of His lambs and His sheep, making it clear that there is a special kind of relationship between God and the people in this world who belong to Him. The flock of Jesus Christ is the Church; and far from being a matter of course, the presence of the Church in this world is a miracle, which God has brought about through the Good Shepherd. It is He who has made people into 'sheep of his pasture,' not they themselves. We have just read that the Good Shepherd entrusts His sheep to the Apostle Peter. He does not entrust them to Peter alone, but, as is made clear in other parts of the Bible, to his fellow Apostles as well, and thus to all the many known and unknown people who at any time have been called to be keepers and shepherds in the Church of Christ, either as pastors or simply as members of the community. And therefore Jesus's commission applies through Peter and the other Apostles to all of us who, as members of the Church, are gathered here for this service on the eve of the Synod, and particularly to those of us who have accepted the position of a synod member, or minister, or church elder, or any office whatsoever. The call of the Good Shepherd applies to each one of us personally: 'Feed my lambs, feed my sheep.'

Those of us who have taken on these duties must be fully aware of what a precious office the shepherd has. It is precious because he is concerned with pasturing the precious lambs and sheep of Jesus Christ. Once, when I was a boy, I was looking after a herd of cattle for a farmer and I asked him, out of boyish curiosity, what he thought his animals were worth. His estimate was about eight hundred pounds. When I realised the value of my charge, I understood how great my responsibility was. If we new officers of the Synod were to ask the Lord the value of the flock that we are about to lead to pasture for the first time, He would answer earnestly, 'It is a precious flock.' 'The good shepherd giveth his life for the sheep.' That is the price that He paid, and that is what they are worth. And this flock is now entrusted to our care. Our duties also include the administration of large sums of money and the careful supervision of valuable property. But what are one hundred pounds or one thousand pounds or one hundred thousand pounds in comparison with one single human soul redeemed by the Good Shepherd, and brought into eternal citizenship by the sacrifice of His life? The care of more than one hundred thousand such dearly bought souls in this town is ours. Now we can understand the magnitude of our responsibility and that of the Church as a whole. Can we really bear it?

Peter and the Apostles were able to bear it. Not because they were intrinsically capable of it but because Christ commissioned them. When God gives a man a burden He also helps him to bear it. He does not test us beyond our capabilities. He does not require more of us than we are able to give. He gives us an 'easy yoke' and a 'light burden.' Peter is no demigod and no angel; he is a man like all the other Apostles. In fact Peter has been decidedly weak; he has failed his Master by denying Him. The last thing he expects is that the Lord should say to him, 'Feed my lambs, feed my sheep.' If anyone deserved this responsibility, it would be that other disciple who is also present here, 'that disciple whom Jesus loved.' When Jesus was arrested, John followed Him right into the High Priest's palace and he remained with Jesus at the Cross. Peter expects John to be given this great duty. All the others seem more fit for this office than he himself: he has shown his unworthiness all too clearly. I was once visiting a farmer and his family, when their son came in in tears because he had been found unfit for military service. There was a day in the life of Peter when he was found unfit for service in the ranks of the King. And Peter wept too. But this is another day; and now his Lord and Commander declares him fit three times: 'Feed my lambs, feed my sheep.' Peter can hardly believe his ears. But since the Lord Himself declares it, it must be so.

What is the reason for this unexpected change for the better? Has Peter been doing penance in the meantime? Has he diligently gone into training in order to do better a second time, and be accepted as fit after all? Not a bit of it! Peter has been weeping and Christ has beheld his grief; the faithful Shepherd has inexplicably sought him out and has hidden his shame behind the marks of His wounds. Christ has taken Peter into His care just like the Good Shepherd with His sheep. And now He asks His disciple three times, 'Simon, son of Jonas, lovest thou me more than these? Simon, son of Jonas, lovest thou me?' Christ is not asking for a cheap and sentimental confession of love from the disciple. The sense of the Lord's question is more this: Peter was disappointed in his Master; he did not want a crucified Lord, nor a Shepherd who would give His life for His sheep. Peter did not want himself to be a lost sheep that is found again. That is why the Lord asks him now, 'Lovest thou me?' 'Have you reconciled yourself to this Lord and Shepherd now? Will you accept me just as I am? And are you prepared to be found again and to take as a gift the fitness that you were not able to earn? Do you love me more than these? Do you love me more than the others do because you have been a greater sinner, and your need for forgiveness is therefore greater than theirs? Simon Peter, are you satisfied with my grace?' Three times Peter answers yes. That is how this Master engages His servants. The shepherds He appoints for His flock are people who have themselves become His lambs and His sheep in their need for the Shepherd and His pasture.

There are men and women among us who have spent many long hours searching their hearts as to their own worthiness to accept office in the Church. Many of you were surprised when you were asked whether you were willing to become members of the synod or elders of the church. You asked yourselves, 'Who am I to be chosen? Am I to become a shepherd while I am still a needy sheep myself?' That is perfectly normal. It is right for us to approach office with this attitude. Indeed, it would be wrong of us to consider this precious office in any other way. Woe betide the shepherd who did not enter in to the sheep by the door (ch. x); who did not enter through the forgiveness of Jesus Christ, but by way of the back door of church diplomacy, the worst kind of intrigue there is. A man like this Christ calls a 'thief and a robber.' He is a thief and a robber because he takes what does not belong to him; and he is a murderer as well, because his sheep will die of hunger. For only the shepherd who has longed for it himself can lead the sheep to the pasture. The man who has this office bestowed upon him through forgiveness need not be troubled. Even if every neighbour's tongue were to criticise him as unfit and even if his own heart were to waver, if the Good Shepherd has pronounced him fit, then all is well. Then he has been chosen by God Himself, who knows His sheep. This year we have been elected by the unaccustomed method of a secret ballot. This is not good and none of us is altogether happy about it. But if we have gone through the testing fire of His choice through grace, the most secret of all ballots, then all is well, and God can make good our misguided efforts to interpret the clear signs of this age.

At this point we must consider what Christ actually means when He says to His Church through Peter, 'Feed my sheep.' This is a metaphor and as such needs interpretation. But interpretations can vary, therefore it is important to decide exactly what Christ means by His words. What is the meaning of 'feed'? How does one feed the flock entrusted to one, and what is the right pasture to give it? To put the question in concrete form: 'What is expected of us as elders and shepherds?' In gratitude for Christ's goodness to us as our Shepherd, each one of us would like to be a dutiful Synod member and elder. What is the right way to feed the sheep? Fortunately Christ explained exactly how he expects His sheep to be fed: 'Whose soever sins ye remit, they are remitted unto them; and whose soever sins ye retain, they are retained.' The pasture which Christ Himself gives and prescribes for His sheep is the Gospel of the forgiveness of sin. The flock of Jesus Christ lives by forgiveness. Where this pasture is withheld, the flock falters and dies. To give the community of Christ any other kind of nourishment is to give it either stones or, just as bad, sweetmeats instead of bread.

First and foremost then our duty as elders of the church and members of the synod is to ensure that the communities in this town have the opportunity to hear the Gospel of Jesus Christ, who forgives us our sins. It is by preaching and Bible study, by instruction and the care of souls, by Baptism and Communion, that the flock of God in this town is to be nourished for eternal life. You will have noticed that Christ mentions the lambs of His flock first. By that He means the children. So let your care and attention be directed particularly towards the rising generation, from the little child at Sunday school, to the confirmation candidate and the youth who has just left school. In the near future the Church is going to find itself faced with an immense task in the education and leading of the young. But what influence has an elder on the spreading of the Word within the community? Is that not almost exclusively the business of the clergy? That is true. But it is you church officers who have, practically speaking, the first and last word in choosing your ministers. The day will come when you will have to give account before the great Shepherd of whether, as a result of your choice, your communities were starved or spoiled or properly pastured. But nowadays a situation is developing in which the synod's main task is to ensure that the written and spoken Word remains free among our people, and that it can be spread without let or hindrance.

But Christ has 'other sheep' besides the community, 'which are not of this fold.' He wants to gather these in too, so that there will be 'one fold, and one shepherd.' You who are appointed shepherds of the community have therefore to make sure that you are constantly looking beyond your own fold. The command of Christ does not stop short at the confines of individual church communities and established churches, but reaches 'to the ends of the earth.' Therefore it is your duty to ensure that the Church remains ecumenical, and does not dwindle into the narrow existence of merely material Christianity. The councils of elders must devote more time to the affairs of the Church at large, and to foreign missions, than has sometimes been the practice.

In this connexion we must consider the case of Israel, one of the sheep outside the fold. We have certainly had a 'Society of the Friends of Israel' among us for many years. But this once flourishing society of 'Friends of Israel' has become strangely inactive at a time when it is important for shepherds to keep a special watch at this post. Perhaps this is an indication that each individual synod member, elder, and indeed every member of the community, is called to become a 'friend of Israel.' This would be particularly desirable in view of the mounting wave of dogmatic anti-Semitism the world over. At a time when extermination threatens the people of Israel, we must hold out to them Christ's promise of unity in the one flock under the one Shepherd.

Where Christianity flourishes these acts of faith give rise of their own accord to acts of love, and these latter are expressed in works of charity and in the manifold tasks of the home mission. I shall refrain from listing here all the branches of Christian deaconry, but from the many I should like to single out two which seem particularly urgent. The first is the service of the Samaritan to the 'stranger that is within thy gates,' help for the refugee and the homeless. This includes constantly bringing their plight to the notice of the people and the authorities, a service which is not particularly popular when to be outspoken means to be martyred by public opinion. An equally unpopular labour of love of quite another kind, which has recently been knocking for assistance more and more urgently on the door of the Church, is the care of the victims of drunkenness. Close co-operation between the Church and the Blue Cross should stand high on the agenda of any Church synod which is conscious of its responsibility. In short, it is our concern that the Gospel of Christ, the Saviour of the world, should be carried out in acts of faith and love to all the lost, here and to the ends of the earth: 'Feed my lambs, feed my sheep.'

Christ gives Peter to understand that he will not be able to carry out his task as shepherd unhindered. He will suffer, indeed he will have to die, in the service of the great Shepherd, for Christ expressly sends forth His messengers 'as sheep in the midst of wolves.' It would have been very strange if even a single one of you Synod members and elders had imagined that there was any human recognition or public honour to be gained by taking on office in the Church. If any of you had been so unsuspecting and foolish, you would have found that your idea was quite wrong. On the contrary, the man who desires such an office in these times would do better to prepare himself for trouble, shame and suffering. At a recent conference the Synod members and elders of our neighbouring canton considered what they would do if their ministers should be prevented from carrying out their duties. This question is not unrealistic today. In any case it would be a good thing for each one of us to ponder in the quiet of his own heart, 'What shall I do if some day my country should suffer the fate of Holland or Norway or Czechoslovakia?' Christ Himself always considered such questions beforehand with His disciples, so that the dread hour should not take His flock unawares. Thus here He warns Peter, and through him all future shepherds including ourselves, 'When thou wast young, thou girdedst thyself, and walkedst whither thou wouldest: but when thou shalt be old, thou shalt stretch forth thy hands, and another shall gird thee, and carry thee whither thou wouldest not. This spake he, signifying by what death he should glorify God.' How many of us will remain at our posts, as shepherds of the community, when the hour of persecution strikes for the flock? We cannot tell. All we can do is to rely on Christ's promise to Peter that he will be given the strength to 'glorify God by his death,' because the Good Shepherd will gird and lead His troubled disciple. We, this evening, should be particularly comforted by this prospect of strength and guidance.

In conclusion, there is a further reminder: 'Then Peter, turning about, seeth the disciple whom Jesus loved following; which also leaned on his breast at supper, and said, Lord, which is he that betrayeth thee? Peter seeing him saith to Jesus, Lord, and what shall this man do? Jesus saith unto him, If I will that he tarry till I come, what is that to thee? follow thou me. Then went this saying abroad among the brethren, that that disciple should not die: yet Jesus said not unto him, He shall not die; but, If I will that he tarry till I come, what is that to thee? This is the disciple which testifieth of these things, and wrote these things: and we know that his testimony is true.' How strange! No sooner is Peter unexpectedly pardoned and chosen as shepherd by his Lord than his old character obtrudes itself again, and he interrupts his Master instead of obeying Him, trying to rule rather than serve. Admittedly government is always necessary in the Church; but it exists only so that we may serve the Lord of the Church obediently, and not prescribe to Him what He must do. People often tend to forget this. On being told that he will be a martyr, Peter asks what will happen to John. He wants to know if John is also going to suffer and die, or if he is going to be allowed to live to a ripe old age and die a natural death. Thus Peter is suggesting equal treatment for all to his Master, so to speak. Christ rejects this unwarranted interference with obvious annoyance. If it so pleases Christ to lead one of His disciples in one way and another in a completely different way, what right has Peter to complain? The ways in which Christ leads His own are manifold and do not follow a set pattern. If it were to please the Lord to let John live until the Day of Judgment, what business would that be of Peter's? Thus the Lord of the Church rejects any false levelling out, any superficial uniformity or unity of the Church.

Of course that does not mean that there should be no unity of the Church. There is unity between Peter and John: they both believe in Jesus as their only stay in life and in death. They are at one in this faith in the crucified and risen Lord. Many roads may lead to Rome, but they know that there is only one Way that leads from Heaven to earth and from earth to Heaven, and that is Jesus Christ. Our text for today confronts us with a question that we are all deeply concerned with now, and that is the question of the unity of the Church. So our attention is drawn once again to the festering wound of our Church, and of the Church as a whole. If only we were convinced that in fundamentals we are all at one, like Peter and John! How generous we could then be in making allowances, and how happy we could be about the diversity of personal interpretations of faith! But unfortunately the situation is quite different. Admittedly we are agreed about many matters of secondary importance, and it cannot be denied that we all have much in common and therefore a certain cohesion. But it is in the very things that matter most that we are not as united as Peter and John. It is this unity in fundamentals that we need so desperately, and we must not conceal this need if we are to be honest. But what are we to do then? Are we to bridge the gulf by cunning, or put it to one side by force? Force is wrong. It may be the way of Rome to effect and maintain unity in the Church by means of force, but it is not the way of Jesus Christ. As Protestant Christians we must bear the disunity of the Church: we must not condone it, nor reconcile ourselves to it; we must mourn for the Church as we would for a father or mother. So the present imperfect form of the Church imposes a long fast upon us. But fasting we have faith in the unity of the Church until that day when we shall see one flock under the one Shepherd.